Contents

List of illustrations

Acknowledgements

I want to acknowledge the consistent support and encouragement I have enjoyed from my colleagues at Birkbeck, University of London. No one could wish to be part of a more interested and interesting group of scholars, individually and collectively. I am particularly indebted to Professor Julian Swann. I am also grateful to the British Academy for the award of a Postdoctoral Fellowship.

I thank the anonymous readers at Manchester University Press for their incisive comments. I have benefitted greatly from conversations with David Andress, Stephen Brogan, Máire Cross, Filippo de Vivo, William Doyle, Sarah Grant, Eva Johanna Holmberg, Philip Mansel, Munro Price, Laura Stewart and Jonathan Smyth. To those who commented on portions of the manuscript – Sara Ayres, Stephen Brogan, Mark Bryant, Jeroen Duindam, Marisa Linton – my great appreciation for your time and energy. Any remaining errors are of course entirely my own.

I wish to thank colleagues and friends at the Society for the Study of French History, the Institute of Historical Research European History 1500–1800 and Society, Culture and Belief seminars as well as the members of the Society for the Study of Court History for perspicacious comments and piquant conversation. I thank my friends inside and outside academia for their enthusiastic support, with special thanks to Dominique Fleur for hospitality and conversation in Paris.

I record my gratitude to the staff at the National Archives at Kew, the Archives Nationales in Paris, the Bibliothèque Nationale de France (BNF) – in particular the staff of the département des Arts du Spectacle at the Richelieu – the Bibliothèque Mazarine (BM), and the welcoming staff at archives and libraries in Reims and Le Havre. I thank the BNF and Waddesdon Manor for permission to use the images found here. My special thanks to the friendly and helpful staff of the Rare Books room at the British Library.

My beloved children's lives have run in parallel with the development of this book: both accompanied me in utero to archives, libraries and conferences, and have sat, crawled, walked, run and cycled by my side since. Without them, I would have much less joy and fresh air in my life. My deep and abiding gratitude and love to Marcus, without whose unwavering support in all forms none of this would be possible.

This book is dedicated to the memory of my father, who would have been proud.

This project was supported by the Isobel Thornley bequest.

Abbreviations

AMR	Archives Municipales de Reims
AN	Archives Nationales (Paris)
BM	Bibliothèque Mazarine
BMR	Bibliothèque Municipale de Reims
BMV	Bibliothèque Municipale de Versailles
BNF	Bibliothèque Nationale de France
Ms Fr	Manuscrits Français
NASPF	National Archives (Kew) State Papers Foreign

Introduction: ceremony in history

Introduction

In 1774, Louis XV died and was succeeded by Louis XVI as king of France. These bald facts were framed by a series of grand royal ceremonies, which are the subject of this book. The deathbed and funeral of Louis XV, the first *lit de justice* of the new reign, and the coronation of Louis XVI in June 1775 provide the structure for an inquiry which places ceremony in social and political context and assesses its meaning for French people in the last years of the *ancien régime*. This book is centrally concerned with possible meanings of ceremony and with the idea that ceremony reflected current understandings of the importance of kingship in the polity. It portrays royal ceremonies as key moments that brought the kaleidoscopic wider political and social context into focus, fleetingly but in striking and meaningful ways, revealing the shifting patterns of the workings of society.

This was a fertile and febrile period culturally. Philosophy had conquered society. When Jean Le Rond d'Alembert became permanent secretary of the Académie Française in 1772, it became 'a sort of clubhouse for [the *philosophes*]'.[1] Voltaire was the acknowledged grand old man of the movement and wielded his influence accordingly. In 1774, the avowedly philosophical long-serving royal administrator Anne-Robert Turgot entered the royal ministry after a career as a royal administrator. The preposterous Cagliostro spellbound the nobility with tales of his immortal wanderings. A new style of French opera was born when the composer Gluck, through the offices of his patron, Marie Antoinette, the Austrian queen of France, introduced his innovative operatic style to Paris in 1774 with the rapturously received *Iphigenie en Aulide*.[2] Enlightenment was now part of the required cultured veneer of the élite, combining a craze for all things 'natural' with amateur enthusiasm for experimental science. A cultish devotion to Rousseau, for his novels not his political theory, was widespread. Though Jean-Jacques now earned his living as a music copyist, he remained in touch with the influential, organising readings of his *Confessions* in private salons, sharing botany notes with Lamoignon de Malesherbes and accepting invitations to noble châteaux.[3] Rousseau's sudden death at Ermenonville in 1778 was followed swiftly by the erection of a classical mausoleum which attracted many visitors, including Marie Antoinette, Gustav III of Sweden, and Maximilien de Robespierre. Views of the tomb were incorporated into linen fabrics for use in costume or furnishings.[4] Non-secular forms of piety were also reinvigorated as individuals re-evaluated their religious beliefs, using the tools of the *philosophes* to argue for renewed faith.[5]

The early 1770s were also a time of great political tension. A confrontation between the Paris parlement and the government had been ended by an audaciously authoritative move when the parlement was effectively abolished and replaced with a more compliant body from April 1771. Contemporaries saw this as a test of French government: these events would reveal its true nature and they feared the truth would be unsavoury. As Diderot wrote, it was 'a crisis which will end in slavery or liberty: if it is slavery, it will be slavery like that which exists in Morocco or Constantinople'.[6] Public opposition extended even to the king's cousins, the princes of the blood, who publicly implored the monarch not to replace the parlements, and so were forbidden the court for a period of years. The new parlements remained in place at the time of Louis XV's death. They were far from popular and lobbying to recall the old parlement, which had begun almost as soon as it was abolished, only intensified with the accession of the young king.

Where did the king stand in all this? Two daunting and weighty terms, absolutism and desacralisation, have dominated our understanding of the monarchy in the second half of the eighteenth century. Recognising that both terms have been increasingly challenged and disaggregated by historians, we must then ask: what is left? How do historians now understand the monarchy in the 1770s? How can it be described? How can it be classified? This book offers a partial answer to these questions: an answer framed by the royal ceremonies that took place in a single eventful year.

Looking closely at the short span from May 1774 to June 1775, when one king died and another came to power in France, ceremony is the *fil conducteur* guiding us to new perspectives on this brief period which was particularly rich in public ceremonies and political events, affording excellent examples of the centrality of ceremony to current affairs. It was a moment of transition, one of great optimism. As a long and unpopular reign ended and a new one began, all eyes turned to the ceremonial enactments where sumptuous decoration and impressive ritual choreography proclaimed the grandeur of monarchy while well-known political differences provided a frisson of uncertainty. Looking at the death and burial of Louis XV, at the coronation of Louis XVI and the first great political ceremony of his reign, the *lit de justice* of November 1774 recalling the parlement, yields new insights into the meanings of these ceremonies and, importantly, into attitudes to the monarchy at the beginning of Louis XVI's reign. The most widely-shared stance towards the monarchy and its ceremonies at this moment in its history was one of interest. Whether favourable or not, commentators did not choose to ignore these great public set-pieces and the élite could not afford to shun them. Other people created their own complementary ceremonial forms in response: mistreating ministerial effigies and organising healing ceremonies at the coronation. These ceremonies varied in size, place and participation, and several were not organised directly from Versailles: they were initiatives taken by people responding to the great events of their times. Not all of the ceremonies discussed, therefore, were sumptuous, but they were all significant. Their significance lay in their meaning for the organisers, the participants and the spectators, demonstrating a general feeling of the importance of ritual in marking events in the period, even where a particular ceremonial form had not been in use for many years. Their significance is revealed by looking at the larger context of these rites and seeking deeper meanings or longer historical roots of themes such as the burial of kings 'without ceremonies' (*sans cérémonies*), the personal religious practice of Louis XV, the political wrangling around the first *lit de justice* of Louis XVI's reign or the use of the ceremony of the royal touch for scrofula at the coronation of Louis XVI. In all of these cases, the convening and conduct of a ceremony reveals a previously unsuspected layer of meaning. The novelty of this approach to ceremony will be discussed below.

It would be a mistake to think of monarchy at this juncture, or perhaps any other, as a neatly definable phenomenon beyond, at the very simplest level, a government whose most prominent feature was a king. By the last decades of the eighteenth century, the French monarchy was an unwieldy amalgam of theories, traditions and practices, none of which was ever discarded, continually in the process of definition by numerous scribes, functionaries, thinkers, artists and, by their very actions, kings, resembling most that philosophical elephant which 'looks' like a snake, or a fan, or a tree trunk, depending on which part is most closely observed. The best working definition of the Bourbon monarchy is that advanced by Joël Félix: the institution rested on the king's claim to absolute power *and* functioned through collaboration.[7] Theory and practice were not incompatible but neither did they align with perfect symmetry.

Though the power of the king was represented as ubiquitous,[8] and indeed the king's name and image circulated on official documents, coins and medals, kings were most emphatically publicly present in ceremonial forms. A wide survey of events and commentary related to a particular ceremony, public reactions, participation and parallel ceremonies can unveil something more, and perhaps unexpected, about what may seem, at first glance, to be an exclusive event. As Munro Price points out, '[m]ore than any other reign in European history, that of Louis XVI has been distorted by contemporaries and historians writing with hindsight'.[9] This is particularly true of the events of the first year of Louis XVI's reign, as the death of Louis XV, his burial, the recall of the parlement of Paris and the coronation of Louis XVI have all been treated as historical clichés. Where the persistence of some ceremonial forms in 1791–92 created public unease about the king's status within the new order, here the celebration of and participation in public ceremonies is a strong indicator of acceptance of and adherence to the monarchy at the beginning of the reign.[10] If nothing else, the monarchy was the status quo and the status quo was, as yet, unchallenged.

The school of thought which sees ceremony as only a constraint – something individuals were obliged to perform or were inhibited by – has dominated this area of research for some time. Rather than treating ceremony as a discrete category of behaviour, separate from the rest of life, this work will show how individuals came to participate in ceremonies as a result of their personal wishes and beliefs as well as because of social dictats.[11] Rethinking the court society is part of the revisionist programme centred on absolutism.[12] This is a problem very specific to the study of ceremony in France because of the powerful image of the court of Louis XIV and its association with ceremoniousness. Given the long cultivation of strong associations between the court, absolutism and the rise of the modern state in France, re-evaluating the court is a vital part of the construction of a new view of absolute power, particularly in the eighteenth century, and one to which a study of ceremony will make a valuable contribution.

On ceremony and absolutism

Historians of the state since the early 1980s, working after the strong revisionist arguments made by William Beik, Roger Mettam and others, have been freed from the obligation to provide definitions, and redefinitions, of 'absolutism' in every new work. Those first assays served to decouple the practice of the state from the theory of absolutism; the 'absolute monarchy' was refined and expanded to become a rather fluid, somewhat fuzzy term. Historians have moved away from concrete notions of states as machines and come to understand absolutism as something more intangible: a brief phase in the governance of France experienced under Louis XIV; as aspiration ('pouvoir absolu'); or the rallying cry of a certain sort of political thinker.[13] The idea of an absolutely powerful king incrementally increasing his command over the land and people of France is no longer tenable. Historians of the state have little to say about marvellous or sacred aspects of kingship given their more practical focus, though their investigations have yielded new characterisations of the state specific to the period. No longer do we face the redoubtable monolith of 'absolute monarchy' dominating the seventeenth and eighteenth centuries. This has particular implications for the study of royal ceremony in France since the influential neo-ceremonialist historians, led and inspired by Ralph Giesey, proposed that royal ceremonies reflected developments in the public law of the absolute monarchy. As historians' understanding of the nature of the French state evolves, this linkage also requires revisiting and revision: if the nature of the monarchical state is not simply absolute, surely this must be reflected in the ceremonial of the monarchy? It is clear that many royal rituals involved a significant dynastic element, in line with the priority, almost sacrosanctity, accorded to shared royal blood, beginning in 1576 with Henri III's Ordonnance of Blois and consolidated under Louis XIV. Dynasticism provided a reassuringly solid reference point in the troubled political times which coincided with the contraction of the royal blood line in France under the last Valois and first Bourbons.[14] As Fanny Cosandey has demonstrated, these rules of precedence were not merely the emanation of the king's will: given their basis in the order of succession governed by Salic Law, the king was as much subject to them as everyone else. Cosandey draws an instructive parallel between such ritual rules and the law of the land. In both spheres, the king might be called upon exceptionally to make a ruling, based on fundamental laws which he could not alter. On matters of precedence or distinction, his decision was clearly labelled as not creating a new precedent (*sans conséquence*).[15] Given Guy Rowlands' contention that in the early eighteenth century, France operated as a dynastic state, it makes sense to ask what happened to this formation later in the eighteenth century, as the Bourbon dynasty expanded and dissent took on political, rather than military, forms.[16]

This effort to take a fresh look at ceremony is allied to a wariness of the functionalist impulse to make ceremony say something, mean something, beyond what it did for contemporaries. Ceremony is not always an enactment of something else. Often the ceremonial form is just that, a form which must be correctly observed in order for some status or occurrence to be recognised to the standards of the society.[17] This work is also sceptical of intentionalist readings of royal rituals, tending as they do to imbue organisers of ceremonies with a high level of self-consciousness as regards the meaning and control of performative acts, while at the same time inferring a shared skill of interpretation between the actors and the audience.[18] This book seeks a meaning for ceremony beyond propaganda.[19] Intentionalism and functionalism, which have operated as the two dominant interpretitive strands of royal ritual, both link ritual to power – the power to persuade or the more subtle and complex assertion and enactment of new legal forms of royal power. Such power operates in a unidirectional fashion, projected from actor to audience. There is always an underlying assumption of passivity or, more pessimistically, subjection. Acknowledging the element of projection, since royal ceremony is, after all, organised and performed by someone, this work seeks to move beyond it and to ask who we should name as interested parties to royal ceremonies and what meanings they brought to and took from such events. If, following William Beik, we can now understand 'the absolutism of Louis XIV as social collaboration',[20] then the ceremonies enacted in that political context must be understood as social collaboration in turn.

Approaches to the historiography of ceremony

The great public events which brought the king into contact with his people during the eighteenth century have been seen as ahistorical re-enactments of little relevance to the wider public, something akin to the band playing on as the Titanic slowly sank. Closer examination shows that this is not so, and that the ceremonial aspect of the French monarchy remained vibrant, important to many different sectors of society, in the decades before the revolution.

How was ceremony seen in the eighteenth century? The broader question will be addressed in the body of the book; at this point, I wish to elucidate how ceremonial professionals worked in order to improve our own assumptions. It is supremely important to reject any notion of ceremony as static. Grand masters and masters of ceremonies, intendants of the *menus plaisirs*, those who organised grand ceremonials were certainly concerned to produce a correct performance. This was entirely ruled by precedent: the last performance determined the outline of the current project. There was no incontestable template and each iteration of a ceremony was informed and formed by contemporary circumstances. Funerals, in particular, were susceptible to change due to personal wishes. In a slightly different context, Giora Sternberg has rightly asked: was there a script at all?[21] Even the grandest sorts of ceremonies, such as those examined here, were organised on the basis of precedent, rather than in line with any immemorial text handed down over the generations. The coronation might be cited as an exception, given the existence of the *Ordo*, though this was an order of religious service that did not encompass the sheer range of ritual moments performed in the course of the coronation. The idea of ceremony as an attempted performance, a reiteration, of an ancient form is misleading, and has had particular consequences for how historians have viewed ceremonies: '[c]eremony more often than not is pictured either as shrewd manipulation, or as an impregnable fortress of ingrained symbols and signs'.[22] This book argues that ceremony was contemporary and responsive to current needs and interests. At the same time, and while the mindset of the 1770s undoubtedly offered new frameworks of interpretation and new glosses on the ceremonies, what was not possible at that time was to change the basic structures of existing ceremonies. Contemporaries might invent or co-opt little-known rituals such as the rose festival of Salency, but they would not have allowed major alterations in something as well documented as a coronation – such as a move to Paris.[23]

Though the history of the court in this period has attracted serious study in recent decades,[24] royal ceremony remains relatively untouched.[25] Studies of ceremonies have tended to focus on individual events or types of events, tracing them over long periods of time, detecting and interpreting changes in forms of observance. While these works are impressive and informative, their very concentrated nature has meant that they are perceived as of specialist interest. I propose a different methodology, one more in line with the anthropological approach to history exemplified in the work of Peter Burke and perhaps begun in Marc Bloch's seminal work on the royal touch for scrofula.[26] Burke has defined such an approach as a deliberately qualitative one which seeks to interpret the 'social interaction in a given society in terms of that society's own norms and categories',[27] the kind of 'thick description' made famous by Clifford Geertz.[28] Seeing 'man suspended in webs of significance he himself has spun', analysis then becomes an interpretative search for meaning and, by implication, a search for meaning behind behaviours rather than simple description of sets of behaviours.[29] As Geertz memorably puts it, describing a Beethoven symphony in terms of its musical structure does not convey the sublime experience of playing it or, indeed, hearing it.

Doubtless a similar point can be made about royal ceremonies. On the one hand, they are not simply tables of ranks ambulatory in gorgeous costumes, obsessively observing the length of each train as exact markers of hierarchy. On the other hand, it is not necessary to assert that contemporaries did not attempt to understand or analyse ceremonies rationally,[30] since they clearly did. They often had definite rational interests for participation in ceremonies and for anxiety in relation to participation, notions which were very relevant, for example, to parlementaires in the run-up to the funeral of Louis XV in the summer of 1774. It was also possible, and even likely, simultaneously to experience an irrational impetus to participate and an illogical impulse to find a ceremony meaningful: this 'marvellous royalty' is an aspect highlighted by Bloch in *Les Rois thaumaturges*.[31] The real and imputed rational motives of individuals have too often been emphasised to the detriment of the less obviously rational. The question of the attendance of the princes of the blood at the funeral of Louis XV, discussed in Chapter 2, is a case in point: they had a public political position to maintain though their social position stipulated performance of roles at the rites. Yet their personal relationship to the old and new monarchs was undeniably central to their approach. Ceremony can be relevant for many reasons: rational, irrational, political, social, emotional. It is one aim of this study to identify the diversity of spurs to participation in public ceremonies experienced by a wide range of individuals.

Individuals participated in ceremonies as members of groups. Ceremonial distinctions are by their nature tautological: they make worthy those who are already worthy participants; confirm the nobility of those who are already noble.[32] In eighteenth-century France, participation in royal ritual was corporate: princes of the blood, dukes and peers, members of the Paris Parlement and other bodies all attended by virtue of their group adherence and not because of their personal status.[33]

More lowly individuals presented the royal family with compliments on the same basis of membership of a recognised social unit. The fishwives of Les Halles or Reims would have been unlikely to be received with such regularity and royal indulgence without the combined clout of incorporation and tradition. In this way, ceremonies show the power of group ideology and precedent in the period. One was worthy to participate in a group and, therefore, to participate in a ceremony which publicly confirmed one's status: a significant attraction for the hierarchically-minded people of early modern Europe.

In the twentieth century, most work on royal ceremonial in France was carried out by a small group of American historians working on French history, led by Ralph E. Giesey, collectively known as 'neo-ceremonialists', or as the 'American school' in France. Giesey's 1960 work on *The Royal Funeral Ceremony in Renaissance France* is a richly documented study over the *longue durée* which did much to establish the political importance of this ceremony.[34] His rich analysis is essentially functionalist, seeing the peculiarities of the French Renaissance funeral ceremony as serving to resolve tensions between an older theory of the necessity of coronation to confirm the king's power and the newer idea of instantaneous accession, that power passed immediately on the death of the incumbent. Giesey's awareness of the chance emergence of innovation and the early modern tendency to ex-post facto rationalisation lends subtlety to the work. His pupils – Richard A. Jackson, Laurence M. Bryant and Sarah Hanley – took a similar approach to coronations, royal entry processions and the legal ceremony of the *lit de justice* respectively.

Giesey's studies, and those of his students, on the ceremonial aspect of French monarchy[35] are firmly grounded in the work of his teacher, Ernst Kantorowicz, on the king's two bodies though, as Alain Boureau among others has pointed out, applying this analysis to France is problematic.[36] Marina Valensise elucidates the point succinctly: no legal or political theory of the king's two bodies was developed in France.[37] If the theory of the king's two bodies is not a good fit with French monarchy, then the study of ceremony should look beyond reflections or developments of this theory, and its working out in public law, in ritual performances.[38] Royal ritual is messy and complex, the messages conveyed manifold, shifting over the years, in tune with particular political contexts. Boureau suggests that the neo-ceremonialists have erroneously placed ceremony at the heart of the working out of monarchical power,[39] imbuing both ceremonies and royal power with a false sense of formality and ridigity in the service of a misleading 'totalising dogma'[40] which seems very close to the notion of absolutism so convincingly dismantled by revisionist political historians.

In France itself, Marc Bloch's early interest in royal ritual did not attract a wide following among his fellow Annalistes.[41] Jean Jacquot orchestrated work on Renaissance festivals in the 1950s, though the professed intention of a contextualised and broad analysis of these events was not well reflected in the essays he collected.[42] Interest in ceremony then appeared to wane. Elias's *The Court Society* was well received on its publication in French in 1973, garnering an enthusiastic review from François Furet in *Le Nouvel Observateur*,[43] and the Eliasian vision of the court rapidly became the accepted view and point of departure for studies of the court. Emmanuel Leroy Ladurie was one of the few scholars who systematically rejected this model in his articles and books on the court,[44] opposing what he has called the 'hegemony' of Elias just as consistently as Roger Chartier, for example, defended it.[45] In an amusing historical quirk, one which bespeaks deeper reflections on the modalities of monarchy, the bicennential of the French Revolution saw an uptick of interest in ceremony with the publication in 1988–89 of works by Michèle Fogel and Alain Boureau which dealt with ceremony as a system of representation, fully acknowledging all the inherent problems of reception.[46] Thus, they took a rather different approach to the neo-ceremonialists, generally presenting a more interconnected and muddier picture of the role of ceremony in society. This difference of approach is perhaps the sole uniting factor: no new 'school' of ceremonialists has decisively emerged from France, though scholarly interest has certainly continued.[47] A new multi-faceted vision of ceremony is being assembled and with it, though more haltingly, a new vision of the court. Most recently, scholars have begun to focus on the role of emotion as both a motor and a product of all kinds of ritual and this study also looks closely at collective and individual emotions in the rituals under examination.[48]

These Anglophone and French scholars, who produced the most detailed studies of the ceremonial in France, have usually not dealt with the second half of the eighteenth century; neither has the kind of intensive study of several ceremonies and their companion events in a short period of time, which I am proposing, been undertaken.[49] In this book, ceremonial moments are described in context, in the belief that these forms had meanings specific to the date of their performance. Hence, the funeral of Louis XV or the *lit de justice* of November 1774 both had very particular connotations for the polity, peculiar to that time and in addition to the more general import of a royal funeral or a *lit de justice*. This book takes a non-normative, non-performative approach to ceremony: the assumption is that departure from a set order is interesting rather than deviant. There is no such thing as 'bad' ceremony:[50] there are contested, misfiring ritual moments, there are misinterpretations by observers, and, there are furious negotiations followed by adequate performance, followed by recriminations and even attempts to rewrite the ceremonial record. Reasserting our rejection of the notion of ceremonies as re-enactments of past glories, the royal ceremonies of the later eighteenth century need to be treated just as seriously as those of earlier eras, *even if* historians are well aware of, for instance, the political writings of Rousseau and the approach of 1789. It would be difficult to say that there is a 'new school' of ceremonial study; there is, however, a discernable wave of new commentaries which bring fresh thinking to ceremonies and make their study ever more interesting and instructive.[51]

Though ceremonies are generally described in terms of stability of form and content, it is clearly the job of the historian to ask about the impact of change and controversy, whether that originates within or without the immediate ceremonial context. Innovations occur to meet novel circumstances, as the problem of royal death from smallpox reveals. Groups which expect to participate in a royal celebration proceed with their own plans even when they are overlooked initially by the royal organisers, as preparations for touching for scrofula associated with the coronation at Reims demonstrate. This last example also reveals the robust nature of ceremony; the elements of continuity and persistence. Through a detailed examination of a small number of central royal events and the many other incidents and practices associated with them, a rich picture of the reach of these celebrations beyond Versailles and beyond the immediate court circle will be constructed. The aim is to go further than the functionalist inclinations of some work on ceremony and to ask new questions about familiar events.

The present study deals with four main distinct types of ceremony – deathbed, funeral, *lit de justice* and coronation – and with linked minor ceremonies. There is no suggestion here that everything classed as 'ritual', as a distinct form of human behaviour, always looks or feels the same even when so closely bound together by time and, in many cases, by the identity of the participants. In each case under examination here, the distinctiveness of the occasion asserts itself both in the choreographed, scripted elements, in the preparations and in the wider social context. One purpose of this study is to disaggregate ritual behaviour as a category and highlight its specificity and contingency.

The prevalent yet under-critiqued idea of desacralisation has placed the relationship between king and people somewhere on a scale between non-existent and dysfunctional in the second half of the century.[52] Desacralisation could have serious implications for the study of royal ceremony and courts in the period since it suggests a fundamental shift in, and irreparable damage to, the nature and perception of monarchy at this time. However, the concept is founded on the assumption of a prior awe of the king based on a reverence for his sacral person that is then lost. There is little evidence for this reverence, or indeed for the fall from grace which is adduced from it.[53]

We can all agree with Marc Bloch that the sacred character of kingship predated Christianity. Bloch went on to suggest that Christianity, in fact, fatally undermined the notion of royal sacredness by trying to render it dependent on the church. He suggested that more ramifying 'pagan' ideas of sacredness persisted.[54] We should be wary of taking theoreticians of royal power at their word: is it a surprise that clerics claim the king for themselves as the first son of the church or seek to convince him that his power is mediated by them? Or, that lawyers lay hold of him as the prime legislator who they, and only they, are privileged to honour with their advice? The king in his wisdom accepts both these labels and many others, as well as the rituals required to enact these functions. This is power play pure and simple, and on all sides. By the eighteenth century, royalty was defined by a muddle of contradictory inherited axioms that demonstrate more than anything the multiplicity of royal power.[55] This complexity derived from competing theoretical visions of monarchy driven by a fundamentally anthropomorphic approach to power but also, importantly, from the magpie-like tendencies of monarchy to lay hold of all and any sources of legitimacy that seemed available to it – and to never let go. Monarchy accumulated attributes of power and was not overly dependent on any one source. The king was head of a dynasty, head of a government, a religious figure, a warrior, a peacemaker, a judge, a patron of the arts and sciences, a hunter, a healer, a father. Whatever theorists and publicists wrote, and it will be noted that they rarely agreed among themselves, the human experience of monarchy was not defined solely, or even mostly, by sacrality. Indeed, as we will see in the body of this book, in the 1770s, the king was envisaged as a benefactor within the terms of the popular sentimental discourse, another example of projection from one side and co-optation on the other of a potential source of legitimacy. William Doyle concludes that the desacralisation hypothesis has been a 'massive and unnecessary detour in our understanding of how eighteenth century monarchies and their courts worked'.[56] While one has sympathy with the riposte that the experience of royalty varied throughout Europe, Doyle's point certainly holds true for France.[57] Infinitely more useful and preferable here is the model of emotional communities, proposed in a different context by Barbara Rosenwein, since it accommodates sincerity, adherence and, importantly, flexibility.[58] Love for the king today does not preclude jokes about the king tomorrow and adulation or indifference the day after. The present work resists the idea of a unidirectional slide in popularity or affection for the monarchy towards 1789 and seeks to capture the multi-faceted and dynamic nature of both royalty and ceremony in 1770s France. Early modern people were equally as loyal and critical towards the seemingly unassailable status quo as modern people: restoring their agency in their relationship to monarchy is an important part of the revisionist critique of absolutism.

Self-evidently, power is the key concern in discussing monarchy and ceremony in this period since, as David Cannadine elegantly encapsulated it, '[r]itual is not the mask of force, but is itself a type of power'.[59] The ability to stage ritual on a grand scale, to marshal visual and aural effects, to draw crowds, was a key attribute of early modern power. Monarchical power fed on diverse sources of strength, as many in fact as were available, and ritual was one of these. Included among them was the sort of cohesive 'social magic' Pierre Bourdieu perceived in the forging of the twentieth century *noblesse d'état* and which we will see had central importance for the princes of the blood, the old and new members of the Paris Parlement, and the monarchy itself, in their negotiations around the funeral of Louis XV.[60] Discussing the English constitution of the nineteenth century, Walter Bagehot wrote that the monarchy's 'mystery is its life. We must not let in daylight upon magic.'[61] He did not, of course, mean to suggest that Queen Victoria was a sorceress, but rather that royalty, even in its comparatively pared down Victorian form, exercised at least some of its power through intangible means incapable of rationalisation, a term which, in standard Weberian terms, implies the progressive disenchantment of the world and the shedding of notions of magic and, by analogy, the desacralisation of the king, as noted above.[62] In the same vein, Marc Bloch described the royal touch for healing scrofula as an example of 'marvellous royalty': this phrase emphasises a facet of royalty exercised through marvels and wonders, a way of wielding influence which highlights the multi-faceted, contingent nature of royal power in this period. Bloch links the term particularly to the persistence of ideas about the power of kingship over time, a notion particularly apt for a study that deals closely with the change in the person of the king, as Louis XV died and Louis XVI came to the throne. Given that in 1774–75, sixty years had elapsed since the last king's funeral, fifty years since the previous coronation and decades since the last royal healing touch, we do well to pay attention to that cyclical aspect of power, and to the endurance of practices in spite of their abeyance, an endurance which drew on that special aspect of monarchy which is well captured by Bloch's word, 'marvellous', used here not in an overtly positive manner but to recall how royalty was, still at this juncture, something people marvelled at, particularly in its public ceremonial outings. The overall aim of this book is to examine how ceremony was used both to communicate and to lay claim to sources of power and legitimacy, and how ceremony worked in society for the monarchy and for other actors.

Defining the question

The present author has much sympathy with Jeroen Duindam's assertion that historians have dwelt too much on lofty considerations of civilisational shifts rather to the detriment of work on the 'concrete outlines of most European courts and their ceremony'.[63] The intention of this study is to look at precisely these contours of ceremony and how they related to the world around them, to look at ritual from the inside and the outside, preparations and also 'the working of ceremonial in society'.[64] In doing so, it will tread a middle path between the neo-ceremonialist approach of examining a single ceremony of decades or centuries and more inclusive projects[65] by taking a main sample of what are easily identified as royal ceremonies, unified by their proximity in time, by their main actors, and by their political context. The term 'public ceremonies' used in this work derives from Jean Rousset de Missy's 1739 compilation of European court ceremonial practices.[66] He lists 'les cérémonies publiques' of France as royal birth, baptism, coronation (he uses the term *couronnement*, not *sacre*), marriage, funeral, entry processions into towns and *lits de justice*. He provides a compilation of accounts of such ceremonies held in honour of different individuals. Rousset de Missy draws on the works of father and son Théodore and Denis Godefroy[67] and the manuscripts of Louis XIV's *maître des cérémonies*, Nicolas de Sainctot, as well as less well-known sources such as the *cérémonial de la chambre des comptes* (for his description of the birth of the dauphin in 1601, the future Louis XIII). He presents a collation of accounts of different events and not, as underlined above, a series of templates for ideal ceremonies. Precedent, what actually had transpired in past performances of a ceremony rather than a Platonic ideal of a ceremony, was what mattered to Rousset de Missy's potential readers – those organising and enacting ceremonies. In this, his work in turn follows a precedent set by the Godefroys.

To allow for rich examinations of public ceremonies, this study will draw selectively on Rousset de Missy's list, looking in detail at the death and funeral of Louis XV in the summer of 1774, the *lit de justice* of November 1774 and the coronation of Louis XVI in June 1775. The shared political context and proximity in time of these events make them an attractive sample of public ceremonies. These ceremonies share the important characteristic of bringing the theatre of royalty into public space: the king, living or dead, appears on streets, in cathedrals and at the Palais de Justice. The preparations made to receive the king into these places meant that enclosed spaces were physically taken over and remoulded to best fit their ceremonial purpose, in particular church buildings at Saint Denis – for the funeral of Louis XV – and in Reims – for the coronation of Louis XVI. As such, these public ceremonies are creative of ceremonial spaces specific to their ritual purpose. The wider social context of each ceremony will be explored, revealing the extent to which each of these ceremonies provoked specific reactions. Linked to these grand ceremonies, the study will also be sensitive to ritualised moments on all scales, overt and covert, implicit and explicit. As such, the first chapter brings a ritual lens to the social, political and emotional stakes involved in the deathbed of Louis XV. This exception to the rule of the well-defined ceremonies illustrates the ramifying and contingent nature of ritual in early modern France.

Public ceremonies leave a variety of traces in the historical record. While the records of ceremonialists are the logical first point of call for the historian, these are not systematically preserved. The last great ceremonial compilation of the eighteenth century was that published by Rousset de Missey in 1739, though even this was not an exhaustive account of rituals carried out in previous years, as it omits problematic rites; for example, the death of the grand dauphin from smallpox in 1711 for which other sources had to be sought in the archive.[68] Overall, the records of ceremonialists are rather dispersed with no single comprehensive cache of documents covering this period. While in the seventeenth century, the *maître des cérémonies* Nicolas de Sainctot kept a voluminous register which served as a reference for his successors as well as for compilers and historians since,[69] neither the eighteenth-century *maîtres des cérémonies* nor their counterparts at the royal household department of the *menus plaisirs du roi* have bequeathed their working files to the researcher, if those could even be said with certainty to have been maintained systematically.

The study begins with an account of the oft-misunderstood deathbed of Louis XV where, it will be seen, an eye to ceremony transforms our understanding of these events. This is a scene-setting chapter, demonstrating my original approach. Chapters 2 and 3 deal with the funeral of Louis XV and with the *lit de justice* of November 1774. It will surprise some readers to see the funeral matched with the *lit de justice* in this way but, as I will argue, the political tension around the Maupeou parlement and the potential recall of the old parlement was a determining factor in conduct of the funeral ceremony as well as in the events leading up to the *lit de justice*. These two chapters share several thematic threads with politics and ceremony inextricably intertwined in the summer and early autumn of 1774. Chapters 4, 5 and 6 deal with the coronation of Louis XVI in June 1775 at Reims. Chapters 4 and 5 cover the preparation and conduct of the coronation ceremony itself, while Chapter 6 deals with the royal touch for scrofula, demonstrating the less rational, mechanistic aspects of royalty; the persistence of beliefs and forms that attached people to the monarch.

As an original contribution to the new court history, and to the wider revisionist project, this book recovers contemporary attitudes to and involvement in the public ceremonies of the reign of Louis XVI. The ceremonies of the late Bourbon court have not been studied in such depth nor in such a manner. This innovative approach will reveal much about political, social and cultural life which will be of interest to historians of ceremonies and courts as well as historians and interested readers more generally. As a study of power, it demonstrates the voracious and indiscriminate appetite of monarchy for attributes of legitimacy and the emotional power of those claims. As a study of politics, it shows public engagement in ceremony as an aspect of current affairs. The 'marvellous', the uniquely royal mingling of parade and prestige, the best show in town, intangible yet binding, emerges as a motor of ceremony and of monarchy, a usually forgotten dimension which knitted a polity together.

Notes

1 Robert Darnton, *The Literary Underground of the Old Regime* (Cambridge and London, 1982), 11.

2 James H. Johnson, *Listening in Paris: A cultural history* (Berkeley and London, 1995), 60.

3 Guillaume Chrétien de Lamoignon de Malesherbes (1721–94) was born into a Parisian legal dynasty. He took the role of royal censor from 1750 and permitted the publication of the *Encyclopédie*. He was an enthusiastic botanist. He was briefly a minister under Louis XVI. He emerged from a long period of retirement to lead the king's legal defence at the end of 1792, and was guillotined in 1794.

4 Sarah Grant, *Toiles de Jouy: French printed cottons 1760–1830* (London, 2014), 95, plate 49, 'Detail from *the Tomb of Jean-Jacques Rousseau*. Linen, c 1778–83'.

5 Nigel Aston, *Religion and Revolution: 1780–1794* (Basingstoke, 2000); Darin McMahon, *Enemies of the Enlightenment: The French Counter-Enlightenment and the making of modernity* (Oxford, 2001); David Sorkin, *The Religious Enlightenment: Protestants, Jews, and Catholics from London to Vienna* (Princeton, 2008).

6 Denis Diderot (1713–83) letter to the Princess Daschkaw, Paris, 3 April 1771, in *Memoirs of the Princess Daschkaw, Lady of Honour to Catherine II* (London, 1840) volume 2, 164.

7 Joël Félix, 'Monarchy', in *The Oxford Handbook of the French Revolution*, David Andress (editor) (Oxford, 2015), 58.

8 Jay M. Smith, '"Our Sovereign's Gaze": kings, nobles and state formation in seventeenth century France', *French Historical Studies*, 18:2 (Autumn 1993), 396–415.

9 Munro Price, 'Politics: Louis XVI', in *The Short Oxford History of France: Old Regime France* (Oxford, 2002), 223.

10 See Ambrogio A. Caiani, *Louis XVI and the French Revolution* (Cambridge, 2012).

11 Geoffrey Koziol notes the unproductive nature of such separation in his 'The dangers of polemic: is ritual still an interesting topic of historical study?', *Early Medieval Europe*, 11:4 (December 2002), 386. Koziol is responding to Philippe Buc's highly polemical, *The Dangers of Ritual: Between early medieveal texts and social scientific theory* (Princeton, 2001). Buc replies unapologetically in 'The monster and the critics', *Early Medieval Europe*, 15:4 (November 2007), 441–52. See also Alexandra Walsham's review article, 'The dangers of ritual', *Past and Present*, 180:1 (2003), 277–87, among others. Both Koziol and Walsham describe aspects of Buc's project as 'nihilistic'.

12 Julian Swann, *Provincial Power and Absolute Monarchy: The Estates General of Burgundy, 1661–1790* (Cambridge, 2003), 9.

13 Arlette Jouanna, *Le Pouvoir absolu: naissance de l'imaginaire politique de la royauté* (Paris, 2013); Yves-Marie Bercé, *La Naissance dramatique de l'absolutisme, 1598–1661* (Paris, 1992); and, above all, the illuminating study

by Fanny Cosandey and Robert Descimon, *L'Absolutisme en France: histoire et historiographie* (Paris, 2002).

14 Ronald G. Asch, *Sacral Kingship between Disenchantment and Re-enchantment: The French and English monarchies, 1597–1688* (New York and London, 2014), 3.

15 Fanny Cosandey, 'L'insoutenable légèrté du rang', in *Dire et vivre l'ordre sociale en France sous l'Ancien Régime* (Paris, 2005), 184.

16 The princes of the blood feature in Chapters 1–5 below, particularly in Chapters 2 and 5.

17 See Pierre Bourdieu, in particular *La Noblesse d'État: Grandes Écoles et esprit de corps* (Paris, 1989).

18 Here we join Sydney Anglo in applying a 'tincture of scepticism', *Images of Tudor Kingship* (London, 1992), 4.

19 Giesey the functionalist argues against intentionalist Elias in his 'The king imagined', in *Rulership in France, 15th–17th Centuries* (Aldershot, 2004), 219–37; Dougal Shaw, 'Nothing but propaganda? Historians and the Early Modern royal ritual', *Cultural and Social History*, 1:2 (2004), 139–58.

20 William Beik, 'The absolutism of Louis XIV as social collaboration: *Louis XIV and the Parlements: The assertion of royal authority* by John J. Hurt', *Past and Present*, 188:1 (August 2005), 195–224.

21 Giora Sternberg, *Status Interaction during the Reign of Louis XIV* (Oxford, 2014), 10.

22 Jeroen Duindam, *Vienna and Versailles: The courts of Europe's dynastic rivals, 1559–1780* (Cambridge, 2003), 12; see also Thomas Scheff, 'The distancing of emotion in ritual' (and comments and reply), *Current Anthropology*, 18:4 (September 1977), 483.

23 See the discussion of Turgot's suggestion to relocate the 1775 coronation in Chapter 4 below.

24 For an insightful analysis of the field, see Jeroen Duindam, 'Early modern court studies: an overview and a proposal' in *Historiographie an europäischen Höfen (16.–18. Jahrhundert) Studien zum Hof als Produktionsort von Geschichtsschreibung und historischer Repräsentation*, Markus Völkel und Arno Strohmeyer (editors) (Berlin, 2009). Individual works of note include Philip Mansel, *The Court of France, 1789–1830* (Cambridge, 1988); Ronald G. Asch and Adolf M. Birke (editors), *Princes, Patronage and the Nobility: The court at the beginning of the modern age, c 1450–1650* (Oxford and London, 1991); Gérard Sabatier, *Versailles ou la figure du Roi* (Paris, 1999); John Adamson (editor), *The Princely Courts of Europe 1500–1700* (London, 2000); J.H. Elliott and L.W.B. Brockliss (editors), *The World of the Favourite* (New Haven and London, 1999); Jeroen Duindam, *Myths of Power: Norbert Elias and the early modern European court* (Amsterdam, 1995) and *Vienna and Versailles*; Leonhard Horowski, 'Such a great advantage for my son', *The Court Historian*, 8:2 (December 2003), 125–71 and *Die Belagerung des*

Thrones: Machtstrukturen und Karrieremechanismen am Hof von Frankreich 1661–1789 (Ostfildern, 2012); Caiani, *Louis XVI and the French Revolution*; Giora Sternberg, 'Epistolary ceremonial: corresponding status at the time of Louis XIV', *Past & Present* 204 (August 2009), 33–88 and *Status Interaction*.

25 But see Caiani, *Louis XVI and the French Revolution*, and Marie-Lan Nguyen, *Les Grands Maîtres des cérémonies et le services des cérémonies à l'époque moderne, 1585–1792*, Mémoire de maîtrise sous la direction de M. le Professeur Lucien Bély (Paris, 1998–99) for a general account of the office holders and an overview of their tasks. Also, Pauline Lemaigre-Gaffier, *Administrer les menus-plaisirs du roi: l'état, la cour et les spectacles dans la France des Lumières* (Paris, 2016).

26 Jacques Le Goff suggests that Bloch might be considered the founder of anthropological history in his preface to the 1983 edition of *Les Rois thaumaturges: étude sur le caractère surnaturel attribué à la puissance royale particulièrement en France et en Angleterre* (Paris, 1983), first published 1924, II.

27 Peter Burke, *The Historical Anthropology of Early Modern Italy* (Cambridge, 1987), 3.

28 Clifford Geertz, 'Thick description: Towards an interpretive theory of culture', in *The Interpretation of Cultures: Selected Essays* (London, 1993), first published 1973, 6.

29 Ibid., 5.

30 Lucien Bély, 'Les cours européennes', in *Fastes de cour et cérémonies royales: le costume de cour en Europe, 1650–1800, sous la direction scientifique de Pierre Arizzoli-Clémentel et Pascale Gorguet Balesteros* (Paris, 2009), 23.

31 Bloch, *Les Rois thaumaturges*. See Chapter 6 below which deals with the ceremony of the royal touch for scrofula in 1775.

32 Fanny Cosandey, 'Instituer la toute-puissance? Les rapports d'autorité dans la France d'Ancien Régime', *Tracés, revue de sciences humaines*, 17 (2009), 44; Bourdieu, *La Noblesse d'Etat*, 157.

33 For an exhaustive definition of *la société des corps*, see Roland Mousnier, *Les Institutions de la France sous la monarchie absolue*, volume 1 (Paris, 1974), chapter 10.

34 For a more recent pan-European perspective on royal funeral rituals, see Juliusz A. Chrościcki, Mark Hengerer and Gérard Sabatier (editors), *Les Funérailles princières en Europe, XVIe–XVIIIe siècle*, three volumes (Paris, Rennes, 2012–15).

35 Many of Giesey's essays are collected in the volume *Rulership in France, Fifteenth to Seventeenth Centuries* (Aldershot, 2004): of note are 'The King Imagined', which originally appeared in K.M. Baker (editor), *The French Revolution and the Creation of Modern Political Culture, Volume 1, The Political Culture of the Old Regime* (Oxford, 1987), 41–59, and 'Inaugural aspects of French Royal Ceremonials', first in Janos M. Bak, *Coronations: Medieval and Early Modern monarchic ritual* (Berkeley, 1990), 35–45.

Another key work is *Cérémonial et puissance souveraine, France XVe–XVIIe siècles* (Paris, 1987). In the same year, *The Royal Funeral Ceremony* appeared in French as *Le Roi ne meurt jamais: les obsèques royales dans la France de la Renaissance* with a preface by François Furet.

36 Ernst Kantorowicz, *The King's Two Bodies: A study in medieval political theology* (Princeton, 1957); Alain Boureau, *Le Simple corps du roi: l'impossible sacralité des souverains français XVe–XVIIIe siècles* (Paris, 1988), 20–25; Fanny Cosandey, *La Reine de France: symbole et pouvoir, XVe–XVIIIe siècles* (Paris, 2000), 9–10.

37 Marina Valensise, 'Le sacre du roi: stratégie symbolique et doctrine politique de la monarchie', *Annales ESC*, 41:3 (1986), 546.

38 On the fruitfulness of abandoning the problem of constitutionality, see Gérard Sabatier and Mark Hengerer, 'Les funérailles princières: un outillage politique performant', in *Les Funérailles princières*, volume 3 (Rennes, 2015), 397.

39 Boureau, *Le Simple corps du roi*, 26. Catherine Bell echoes these sentiments in her work which attempts to remove rituals 'from their isolated position as special paradigmatic acts and to restore[d] them to the context of social activity in general'. See Bell, *Ritual Theory, Ritual Practice* (Oxford, 2009), 7.

40 Boureau, *Le Simple corps du roi*, p 25.

41 Bloch, *Les Rois thaumaturges.*

42 Jean Jacquot, *Les Fêtes de la Renaissance* (Paris, 1956), 2 volumes.

43 André Burgière, 'Processus de civilisation et processus national chez Norbert Elias', in *Norbert Elias: La politique et l'histoire, sous la direction de Alain Garrigou et Bernard Lacroix* (Paris, 1997), 145.

44 'Système de la cour', *L'arc*, 65 (1976), 21–35. A longer version was published under the same title in *Le Terroire de l'historien* (Paris, 1978), volume 2, 275–99. These are the seeds of the 1997 publication of the same name.

45 '[L']approche anthropologique, sociologique ou historico-ethnographique … [des Annalistes] … fut trop longtemps dominée, écrasée même par la problématique de Norbert Elias …'. Emmanuel Leroy Ladurie, in collaboration with Jean-François Fitou, *Saint-Simon ou le système de la cour* (Paris, 1997), 38.

46 Michèle Fogel, *Les Cérémonies de l'information* (Paris, 1989); Boureau, *Le Simple corps du roi*; Marin, *Le Portrait du roi* (Paris, 1981), and Jean-Marie Apostilidès, *Le Roi machine* (Paris, 1981), though published earlier, should be grouped with these.

47 As well as important articles by Alain Boureau, Alain Guéry, Marina Valensise cited above, monographs of interest include N. Pollini, *La Mort du Prince: rituels funéraires de la Maison de Savoie (1343–1451)* (Lausanne, 1994); B. Boissavit-Camus, F. Chausson and H. Inglebert (editors), *La Mort du souverain entre Antiquité et Moyen Age* (Paris, 2003); M. Gaude-Ferragu, *D'Or et de cendres: la mort et les funérailles des princes dans le royaume*

de France au bas Moyen Âge (Villeneuve d'Ascq, 2005); and Chriościcki, Hengerer and Sabatier, (editors), *Les Funérailles princières en Europe.*

48 Merridee L. Bailey and Katie Barclay (editors), *Emotion, Ritual and Power in Europe, 1200–1920: Family, state and church* (Cham, Switzerland, 2017).

49 Alain Gruber, *Les Grandes Fêtes et leur décorations à l'époque de Louis XVI* (Geneva, 1972) is a descriptive art historical work.

50 For a vivid discussion of this idea see Buc, *The Dangers of Ritual*, 8. See also note 11 above.

51 See works by Abby B. Zangler and Michael Wintroub in English, and Muriel Gaude-Ferragu, Alain Boureau and Pascal Lardellier in French.

52 For example, Dale Van Kley, *The Damiens Affair and the Unravelling of the* Ancien Regime (Princeton, 1984); Jeffrey Merrick, *The Desacralisation of the French Monarchy in the Eighteenth Century* (Baton Rouge, 1990).

53 Jens Ivo Engels, 'Beyond sacral monarchy: a new look at the image of the early modern French monarchy', *French History*, 15 (2001), 139–58; William Doyle, 'Desacralising desacralisation', in *France and the age of Revolution: Regimes Old and New from Louis XIV to Napoleon Bonaparte* (London and New York, 2013), 107. But see also Aston, *Religion and Revolution*, and Asch, *Sacral Kingship between Disenchantment and Re-enchantment*, which both suggest a more negotiated, even cyclical, sense of de- and re-sacralisation. The idea of linear desacralisation of the monarchy is umbilically linked to the classic Weberian model of a disenchantment of the world ushering in modernity, on which see the important article by Alexandra Walsham, 'The Reformation and the "disenchantment of the world" reassessed', *The Historical Journal*, 51:2 (June 2008), 497–528; Michael Saler, 'Modernity and enchantment: a historiographic review', *American Historical Review*, 111:3 (June 2006) 692–716, and Barbara H. Rosenwein, 'Modernity: a problematic category in the history of emotions', *History and Theory*, 53 (February 2014), 69–78.

54 Bloch, *Les Rois thaumaturges*, 55, 60.

55 Valensise, 'Le Sacre du roi', 548.

56 William Doyle, review of *Monarchy and Religion: The Transformation of Royal Culture in Eighteenth-Century Europe* (review no. 616), www.history.ac.uk/reviews/review/616. Accessed 10 December 2018.

57 Michael Schaich, Author's response to review, available at same location as the review.

58 Barbara Rosenwein, *Emotional Communities in the Early Middle Ages* (Ithaca, 2006).

59 Cannadine, 'Introduction: divine rites of kings', in David Cannadine and S.R.F. Price (editors) *Rituals of Royalty: Power and ceremonial in traditional societies* (Cambridge, 1987), 19.

60 Pierre Bourdieu, *La Noblesse d'Etat.*

61 Walter Bagehot, *The English Constitution*, edited by Paul Smith (Cambridge, 2001), 50.

62 See J.C.D. Clark's comments on Weber's use of the phrase 'disenchantment' in 'The re-enchantment of the world? Religion and monarchy in eighteenth-century Europe', in Michael Schaich (editor), *Monarchy and Religion in Eighteenth Century Europe: The transformation of royal culture in eighteenth century Europe* (Oxford, 2007), 47 and Walsham, 'The Reformation and the "disenchantment of the world" reassessed'.

63 Duindam, 'Ceremony at court: reflections on an elusive subject', *Francia*, 26 (1999), 140.

64 Cannadine, 'Introduction: divine rites of kings', 14.

65 Compare, for example, Richard A. Jackson, *Vive le Roi! A history of the French coronation from Charles V to Charles X* (Chapel Hill, 1984) with Alain Gruber, *Les Grandes Fêtes*, which includes everything from laying the cornerstone for the new church of Sainte Geneviève (1764) to the coronation of Louis XVI and the *fête de la féderation* in 1790. Gruber notes that he did not set out to sustain or refute any thesis but simply to bring to light an unknown aspect of art history.

66 *Supplément au Corps Universel diplomatiqe du droit des gens, tome quatrième, Le Cérémonial diplomatique des cours de l'Europe ou Collection des actes, memoires et relations concernant les Dignitez, Titulaires, Honneurs & Prééminences; les Fonctions publiques des Souverains, leurs Sacres, Couronnemens, Mariages, Batêmes, & Enterrements; les Investitures des grands Fiefs; les Entrées publiques, Audiences, Fonctions, Immunitez & Franchises des Ambassadeurs & autres Ministres publics; leurs Disputes & Démêlez de Préséance; et en général tout ce qui a rapport au Cérémonial & à l'Étiquette. Recueilli en partie par Mr Du Mont. Mis en ordre et considérablement augmenté par Mr Rousset, membre des Académies des Sciences de St Petersbourg & de Berlin. Tome Premier* (Amsterdam/The Hague, 1739). 'Public ceremony' was also a term favoured by Auguste Rondel, whose collection of printed works associated with theatre and ritual are now to be found in the Bibliothèque Nationale de France (BNF) Richelieu, see his *Fêtes de cour et cérémonies publiques* (Florence, 1927).

67 Théodore Godefroy, *Le Cérémonial de France, ou déscription des Cérémonies … observées aux couronnemens, entrées, et enterremens des roys et roynes de France et autres actes et assemblées solemnelles. Recueilly des mémoires de plusieurs sécrétaires du Roy, Hérauts d'Armes, et autres* (Paris, 1619); Denis Godefroy, *Le Cérémonial François* (Paris, 1649).

68 This is examined in Chapter 1.

69 The Dreux-Brézé, *grands maîtres* of the eighteenth century, made records on single sheets which easily became dispersed. See Nguyen, *Les Grands Maîtres*, 119.

1

The deathbed ceremonies of Louis XV, May 1774

Introduction

Louis XV fell ill on 28 April 1774 at the Trianon. He had been feeling unwell for about eight days and was unable to eat the night before.[1] He quickly returned to Versailles and took to his bed. The nature of his malady was unclear, but by the morning of 29 April it was evidently serious. Royal ministers cancelled all business.[2] Courtiers flocked to Versailles.[3] The 64 year-old king's health and life expectancy was the centre of all concern.[4]

The deathbeds of Bourbon kings of France were rare: in just under two hundred years of Bourbon rule, there had been only two by 1774. The assassin's blade denied Henri IV one in 1610; Louis XIII's was protracted in 1643; and, in 1715, Louis XIV died with dignity in spite of gangrene. By 1774, Louis XV was one of the very few still alive who had attended the deathbed of the last king, aged barely 5 years. In the intervening period, the deathbeds of ordinary people had been a flashpoint of religious controversy during the *billets de confession* affair of the 1750s and 1760s. The deathbed became an occasion on which French people were required 'to lie down and be counted'.[5] The deathbed of Louis XV promised to bring to crisis the king's own ambiguous religiosity and the vexed question of his salvation.

The uncertainties of the deathbed also roused strong currents of emotion. Anxieties were multiple: those of the duc d'Orléans whose letters reveal a real personal attachment to the king as a person as well as the head of the House of Bourbon; those of Madame du Barry, the king's mistress, who struggled to determine her best course of action; those, indeed, of the king himself, about the nature of his illness, and about preserving dignity in dying. Smallpox triggered disgust and fear tightly wedded to curiosity about the spectacle of the physical condition of the king.

Eighteenth-century deathbeds presented contemporaries with two urgent problems: how to deal with dying and dead bodies and, perhaps more importantly to them, how to save the soul of the dying person. When that person was also the king, these problems acquired special dimensions of ceremoniousness and dynastic and political concern, particularly when, as was the case in 1774, there was a significant unresolved and contentious political issue which divided not only the nation but also the members of the wider royal family: namely, the Maupeou Coup of 1771. What is more, the king was dying of smallpox, an illness controversial in its own right. The deathbed of Louis XV brought together political, religious and medical controversy with the added element of strong emotional engagement with the death of a monarch, and family member.

At the heart of this chapter lie the religious ceremonies that framed the passing of Louis XV and gave shape to the conduct of his deathbed. This is not a royal ceremony in the same way as the funeral and coronation that followed. Unlike such grand occasions, organised by teams of ceremonial staff, this scene was controlled by the king's own wishes and his knowledge of liturgical forms. Only the king could summon his confessor to his bedside and set the sequence of death rituals in train. In that sense, this chapter takes a liberty in widening the usual sense of ceremony.[6] It recognises discrete ritual moments occurring in the framework of the deathbed: the religious elements, certainly, but also the *amende honorable*, the accession of the heir, the convoy of the body – to name a few. Royal deathbeds, as well as more ordinary ones, were generally understood as set pieces, marking the end of a life in a fittingly solemn manner. As a royal deathbed, it also gave rise to dynastic rituals of attendance and succession. A new understanding of the deathbed yields a different estimation of the king's death and sets the tone for the analysis of subsequent ceremonies.

This chapter will address the specificity of the deathbed of Louis XV, providing the ceremonial, political, medical and religious context for a new understanding of this event. By looking at the rites that took place around the dying king – and in which, I will argue, the king himself took a leading organisational role – it will provide a new account of this event. It will describe and compare the three deathbed experiences of Louis XV:

his illness at Metz in 1744; the Damiens attack of 1757; and, the main focus of this chapter, his death from smallpox in 1774. This chapter will also offer a new reading of the transport of the king's dead body to Saint Denis, drawing on knowledge about royal deaths from smallpox and also the very specific meaning of the term '*sans cérémonies*' as applied to the funerals of monarchs, in order to show that this stage of Louis XV's obsequies was perfectly consonant with those of his predecessors and relations. The idea that Louis XV's remains were hastily got away from Versailles and unceremoniously bundled into the crypt at Saint Denis retains some currency in the historiography as a negative index of the popularity of the king and, indeed, the monarchy more broadly. This image, derived from the *Mémoires* of the baron de Besenval,[7] will be tested against the facts as set out in this chapter and found wanting.

The king's illness

In 1774, smallpox was the number one killer in France, decimating the population and leaving one in six survivors marked for life.[8] Inoculation against the disease, though reasonably well established elsewhere, was widely regarded with suspicion. By 1758, there were probably no more than two hundred inoculated people in the whole of France.[9] Following an epidemic in 1763, the Parlement of Paris banned the procedure in the city, due to concern that inoculated patients were spreading infection.[10] At the same time, the Parlement requested that the theological and medical faculties of the Sorbonne provide expert guidance on the moral and medical implications of the procedure. The duc de Luynes recorded the anxiety that inoculation was trifling with Providence – deliberately risking the death at age 5 of someone who would eventually have smallpox at 45 but live to be killed by something else entirely.[11] The theology faculty declared this conundrum outside its competence, leaving it entirely in hands of the medical faculty which remained deadlocked on the matter, in spite of vigorous debates, at the time of the king's death in 1774. Clearly, inoculation was not established in public or expert opinion as a risk-free prophylactic by the mid 1770s. Smallpox remained endemic; the general attitude towards it was fearful, familiar and fatalistic.

On 29 April 1774, Louis XV was bled twice. Some contemporaries were surprised. The duc de Croÿ,[12] a courtier of long-standing who was familiar with the king, was shocked to hear he had been bled: he knew that the first doctor, Lemonnier, was not an advocate of bleedings. The baron de Besenval suggests that this treatment was responsible for seriously undermining the royal health and may have caused his death.[13] This would be ironic if true, since Louis XV's childhood survival is often attributed to his guardians' refusal to allow doctors near him. The famous English smallpox inoculators, the Suttons, were heard to say in Paris that they knew all was lost when the second bleeding was performed.[14]

Smallpox was diagnosed on the night of 29 April. A light brought close to the king's face revealed eruptions on the skin and doctors, under a number of pretexts, made a closer examination.[15] The royal family were promptly informed that they could no longer visit nor have communication with the king. Of course, the reason for this was a matter of curiosity and very soon the nature of the king's illness was widely known. The dauphin and the rest of the royal family had been at the bedside only minutes before the diagnosis, much to the anguish of the duc d'Orléans.[16] Only the dauphine Marie-Antoinette had had the disease. Since none of the three grandsons was immune from smallpox and they were the last males of Louis XV's descendance, the succession to the throne was potentially in danger. Orléans' private correspondence demonstrates his concern for the king and his heirs and does not refer to the potential benefit to him as the next in line to the throne. He trembled for the House of Bourbon rather than rejoicing for the House of Orléans. Dynastic and personal loyalty ran deep.

There was room for doubting the smallpox diagnosis since it was widely believed, including by Louis XV, that he had survived the disease in 1728. Panegyrics were composed at that time in honour of his heroic vanquishing of the disease, without resort to the dubious procedure of inoculation.[17] On 30 April, the king was extremely worried and, in order to avoid distressing him, his doctors told him that he was suffering from a fever. The king on his sickbed was heard to exclaim 'if I hadn't had smallpox at eighteen, I would think I had it now!'[18] Outside his room, there was no doubt about his illness. The public bulletin on his health, published in Versailles on 30 April, baldly announced the diagnosis.[19]

At a quarter to eight that evening, Paris echoed to the tolling of the great bells of Notre Dame announcing the exposition of the Blessed Sacrament, there and in all churches throughout the city and suburbs, confirming the seriousness of the king's condition.[20] A planned memorial mass for the charitable princesse de Talmond, with a fundraising sermon in aid of the foundlings she supported, was postponed.[21] More mundanely, *traiteurs* were instructed not to have musicians performing and all theatrical performances were cancelled. The curtain came down in the middle of the fourth act at the Comédie Française: the ticket price was reimbursed to those who wished to claim it.[22] Siméon Prosper Hardy and his fellow parishioners were astonished to hear their new parish priest harangue them on their lack of assiduity at prayers for the king's health. Were they Christians? Were they Frenchmen? he fumed to a stunned congregration who felt, not chastened, but inclined to classify this latest outburst along with the *curé*'s other examples of indiscrete zeal.[23] Is this proof of Parisian indifference to the fate of the king? Surely not. Hardy records a ceaseless flow of rumour on all aspects of the deathbed, testament to a lively engagement in the unfolding events that simply refused to be channelled by a priest's version of appropriate behaviour.[24] Attendance or otherwise at religious services speaks only of indifference to those particular prayers, at least in Hardy's circles.

At Versailles, a new pattern for the king's day quickly emerged, reshaping the ceremonial life of the court. Mass was said around noon at his bedside and an abbreviated ceremony of *lever* was held thereafter with a *coucher* taking place around ten o'clock at night. In fact, Louis XV did not move from his bed and the duc de Croÿ refers to both ritual moments as *l'ordre*, something that was usually only a part of the longer ceremony. The king's bedroom was the site of daily formal interactions with his courtiers as well as religious and medical staff seeing to his other needs. Individuals attended and then mixed indiscriminately with the crowds that filled the palace, which was buzzing with gossip over many dinner and coffee meetings. Whatever the concerns about the disease, the dying king continued to be constantly surrounded by spectators and Versailles filled with the curious.[25]

Louis XV was not isolated on his sickbed; access to his apartments and the rest of the palace continued as normal. As his doctors opted for a cooling treatment, the windows of his apartments were wide-open to the people walking in the courtyards below. The dauphine, Marie Antoinette, shuddered in horror on observing that the king's soiled bed sheets were aired on a balcony overlooking the garden where the otherwise quarantined dauphin frequently walked.[26] The duc de Croÿ speaks of visiting the king's bedroom and examining the blood from the latest blood-letting which had been left on a side table. To allow fresh air to circulate, the connecting doors between the bedroom, the council room and the Hall of Mirrors were all left open. This passageway was frequently used to move soiled mattresses from the king's bed to be aired on the adjoining balconies, 'because the king was in the habit of not using a bedpan, just letting everything go where he lay. So that the gallery, through which everyone passes, is filled with bad air and all that is most gross, most disgusting

1 Print of Louis XVI as dauphin and his siblings. From left to right: the comte d'Artois, the comte de Provence, the dauphin (courtesy of Waddesdon Image Library, Bodleian Imaging Services).

and most risky …'.[27] This unsanitary set-up meant that some subsequent deaths were attributed to merely passing through the gallery.[28] Madame de Genlis gives a good sense of the fear the disease inspired, alleging that 'Monsieur de Letorière died because he peeped in the door for two minutes'.[29] These are powerful images of a corrupt body as a source of disease and death: they overlook the fact that smallpox made regular appearances at Versailles at that time of year and had already infiltrated the court before the king sickened. The general attitude to smallpox was both familiar and fearful. With the addition of post-revolutionary hindsight, Louis XV's illness later became an allegorical plague destroying France. In 1774, it was well known that the king had smallpox yet the announcement of his illness drew crowds to Versailles. In any case, according to the English ambassador, 'there is scarce a Palace to which the Court can go without Danger' from smallpox.[30]

Protective measures were thought of only for the immediate royal family. The precious male direct line, the dauphin and his two brothers, were formally forbidden to approach the monarch's apartments from 30 April.[31] With the exception of the prince de Conti,[32] all the princes of the blood had come to court immediately on hearing of the king's illness and kept vigil by the king's bedside, actions prompted by personal concern but also the performance of dynastic roles. The dauphin and his brothers benefitted from the childhood inoculation of the duc de Chartres against smallpox as Chartres shuttled between the bedside and their apartments, acting as a channel of information and as a human *cordon sanitaire.*[33] He had regular meetings with his father, the duc d'Orléans, who stayed by the king's side with the other princes of the blood. Chartres' absence from the king's side was so unexpected in a prince of the blood that the dauphin attempted to send him back to his rightful place and desisted only when the medical reasons were explained.[34]

The king's daughters insisted on their right to remain among the male entourage of their dying father, requisitioning one of the adjoining rooms where the princes of the blood gathered around them.[35] In an act reminiscent of the much-lauded custom of faithful wives closeting themselves with stricken husbands and dying, martyrs to their conjugal piety, the sisters – who had never had smallpox and had certainly not been inoculated – doggedly refused to be removed from the sick room. In his diary, the Président d'Ormesson de Noiseau hints at a touch of steel behind the sacrifice. He credits Madame Adélaïde with organising both the protective exclusion of the young princes and the attendance of the princes of the blood, 'avec beaucoup de présence d'esprit'.[36] As a 42-year-old woman, Madame Adélaïde effectively acted as head of the family, claiming her place caring for her father despite the dangers. Her courageous gesture was recorded in terms of filial piety and appropriate female sacrifice, particularly when she later sickened with smallpox. In the *Journal Encyclopédique*, Le Mierre wrote of the sisters 'forgetting their grandeur in favour of nature', high praise indeed in sentimentalist France.[37] Madame de Genlis described the sisters' relatively benign experience of smallpox as a miracle earned by their correct filial behaviour.[38] This rather gendered interpretation of the time is thrown into relief by the fact that, when Mesdames fell sick, the prince de Condé was among the men who remained with them in seclusion at Choisy.[39]

Religion: the king's deathbed confessions, 1744, 1757

The historiography of the death of Louis XV relies heavily on the accounts left by the baron de Besenval and the duc de la Rochefoucauld-Liancourt, *grande maître de la garderobe*, though it is rarely remarked that both these men were partisans of the duc de Choiseul,[40] and personally ill-disposed towards the king. To achieve a balance of views in this description of the deathbed, I have also drawn on less usual sources: the journal of the duc de Croÿ; letters written by the duc d'Orléans; and the sole letter left by the king's confessor, the abbé Maudoux.[41]

Unlike his predecessor Louis XIV, Louis XV had not left off the dalliances of his youth and middle years to sustain a pious old age through secret marriage. In the youthful Madame du Barry, the 64-year-old king maintained a most scandalous official mistress, widely known to have risen by the king's favour from the lowest reaches of society.[42] Though Louis XV was widowed in June 1768, their liaison was technically adulterous since Madame du Barry was married, in a sham somewhat ironically arranged to permit her presentation at court in April 1769. Court politics generally granted power and prestige to official mistresses. Madame du Barry stood on less sure ground with even seasoned ministers, the duc de Choiseul and the comte de Saint-Florentin, expressing disapproval of her directly to the king.[43] What is certain is that the Catholic Church could not look favourably on a situation of fornication and adultery. As the king could not make a sincere confession while he continued his liaison with Madame du Barry, he made no confession at all. Thus, the king came to his deathbed in a state of sin, unshriven.

The ideas of confession and political change were twinned very early in the king's illness.[44] Croÿ records that the first thoughts about confession arose during discussions on bleeding the king on 29 April. It was said that the king believed it irresponsible to undergo a third bleeding without being prepared for a Christian death. Confession, and by implication penance, was a subordinate ritual allowing the king to take part in the main sacrament of the dying: he had made a confession in order to receive the eucharist. Two recent incidents of sudden death in his entourage had prompted the king to express his horror of dying like a dog, that is, without the sacraments. When others had serious illnesses, he was always concerned to know whether the sacraments had been taken.[45] In this, he shared a common concern of his age. The briefly raised prospect of a third bleeding therefore sparked speculation on the continued presence of Madame du Barry and the ministers linked to her, the duc d'Aiguillon above all. The eruption of spots on the skin shortly after the second bleeding put paid to the idea of a third operation.

Post-Tridentine Catholic last rites are composed of three different stages administered together or separately: confession and penance, anointing, and the *viaticum*, literally meaning provisions for the journey, the last eucharist. Confession is the only fixed element of this sequence since it is a requirement to receive the *viaticum*, which is considered the main sacrament of the dying. Extreme unction is often administered as the final religious act. The question of the king's confession loomed large in 1774, and with historians since then, because sincere contrition would require an intention not to commit the same sin again. It was well known that the king had not attended confession on a regular basis for decades. As he lay on his deathbed, sin was personified by his mistress Madame du Barry, who would have to be sent from his side.[46] The timing of the confession was therefore a matter of ongoing concern and is a leitmotif in the accounts of Rochefoucauld-Liancourt and of Besenval, both of whom describe a weak king manipulated by two competing factions: that of Madame du Barry and the duc d'Aiguillon facing down a less well-defined opposition who wished to see the king shriven. The duc de Croÿ was personally devout yet well disposed towards the king's mistress. He credits her with discretion and tact in a difficult situation: 'Madame du Barry remained only at the insistence of her supporters, because she said "the whole family dislikes me: I should like to go!" But the king was so used to seeing her that she felt she was useful to him, she seemed to sacrifice herself by staying …'.[47] The battle lines may not have been as crudely and decisively drawn as some supposed: Croÿ describes this 'parti politique', which completely shapes the narrative of other commentators, as 'a thing as strange as it is uncertain'.[48]

Many spectators in Versailles in 1774 remembered the scandal that occurred when the king had fallen ill thirty years earlier at Metz. The 'Jansenistically-inclined' first almoner,[49] Monsieur de Fitz-James, bishop of Soissons, in a shocking exaggeration of his authority,[50] threatened to withhold the *viaticum* from the king until his mistress, who had already been sent from the king's presence, left the town entirely.[51] The king had already confessed and commanded his mistress to leave him before Fitz-James intervened. No priest could, in good conscience, deny confession to a sick person who requested it.[52] Fitz-James arranged a proclamation that the Blessed Sacrament would be withdrawn from all churches in the town until she departed. Local people, gathered to pray for the king's health before the Sacrament in their parish churches, were outraged and vented their anger on the unfortunate Madame de Châteauroux and her sister as they left. The *viaticum* was administered and, afterwards, the king publicly asked the forgiveness of God and his people for the scandal he had caused, acknowledged his unworthiness to carry the titles of most Christian king and eldest son of the church and confirmed that the bishop's conditions regarding the exile of Madame de Châteauroux would be carried out. When the rite of extreme unction was mooted, Fitz-James again exerted himself, demanding an even greater distance between the king and Madame de Châteauroux. The Parisian diarist Barbier recorded that most people found the public nature of these measures to be merited, given the scandal the mistress had created by following the king to the battlefront. His own feeling was that Monsieur de Fitz-James' intervention was excessive because it reflected badly on the king:

> the king's reputation must be respected, he must be allowed die with religion but also with dignity and majesty. What is the use of this ecclesiastical show? It would be sufficient for the king to make a sincere inner repentance. It was right that Madame de Châteauroux should not longer appear, but her departure should have been better managed.[53]

In 1774, all were aware of the example of Metz. Many were aware of its sequel. Following the king's recovery, Madame de Châteauroux was invited to return to Versailles.[54] Fitz-James was ordered to retire to his bishopric in Soissons and lost all hope of further promotion. Other members of what Louis XV darkly referred to as the cabal of Metz were exiled – the dauphin's governor, the duc de Châtillon, with his wife, and the duc de la Rochefoucauld, father of Rochefoucauld-Liancourt who attended Louis XV in 1774. The memory of Metz had many ramifications and was not simply a tale of ecclesiastical blackmail of a royal sinner, of a frightened king in thrall to those threatening him with damnation. It was also a cautionary tale for courtiers and a demonstration of the king's will to shape his own public rituals. When, in 1774, Louis XV said he wished to avoid the scenes of Metz, it was to this persistent humiliation of his mistress that he referred.

The king's 'second deathbed' commenced on 5 January 1757, when one of the first medical efforts at assistance after his stabbing by Robert Damiens was to bleed him. It is not surprising that the king, who had already lost blood and was understandably shocked, felt weak and feared for his life. He requested extreme unction and, in order to receive it, made a forty-five minute confession. The king's confessor, Père Desmarets, remained at his side in the following days. The royal family gathered by his bedside and the king personally requested their forgiveness in the presence of members of his household. This again was a public acknowledgement of wrongdoing following on the heels of a deathbed confession. His reigning mistress, Madame de Pompadour, remained cloistered in her rooms in the palace. While she kept a low profile, she did not envisage withdrawing without an order to do so.[55] On 13 January, over a week after the attack, Louis XV called on Madame de Pompadour in her apartment. When his third deathbed came in 1774, the king was already well aware of the sequence of confession and apology which would be enacted, should he sustain consciousness for that long.

It is self-evident then that, in the case of serious illness, the king would wish to avail himself of religious ritual just as he had done at Metz in 1744 and after the Damiens attack in 1757, both occasions when he thought he might die. Unavoidably, this would mean a confession. The king had abstained from both confession and the eucharist for years, in line with Catholic teaching on the absence of absolution for a recidivist. He continued to hear mass every day. John McManners has described him as a man of simple faith, '[t]he formal religion of the chapel at Versailles was all his religion but within its limits he was sincere'.[56] Bernard Hours endorses and reads more into this point of sincerity. Louis XV, he suggests, insisted on his own form of spiritual probity, in that his attitude to religious ceremonies was dictated by his sense of personal sinfulness. There was no sense of royal entitlement.[57] Louis XV's avoidance of the sacraments reflects well on his orthodoxy and the seriousness of his personal faith since, in the absence of true contrition, he did not perform a charade of repentance and avoided profaning the sacraments. In April 1739, the first time it was known publicly that the king had abstained from the sacraments because of his personal life, the memorialist Barbier complained, saying it would be far better for the king to secure a papal dispensation to allow him to perform his Easter devotions, no matter what sins he had committed.[58] This was not Louis XV's way. As the duc de Croÿ put it, 'he was always very exact in his religious practice, except for the one point he believed he could not conquer, women'. [59] The duc d'Orléans agreed that 'the seed of devotion is not at all extinct in him as has been said'.[60]

'Nothing is so mad as to risk one's soul but nothing is so natural.'[61] Madame de Sévigné captured perfectly the dilemma of the worldly Catholic, seeking to balance how one wished to live with how one ought to die. Confession was the redemptive link between the two. Death in a state of sin was understood to mean eternal damnation or lengthy suffering in purgatory: confession at the right moment was crucial. Those who lived on after their confession were expected to demonstrate contrition. Suffering was understood as expiation. Contemporary mores predicted agonies for a sinner on his deathbed. The king had his own mental struggles on this point: 'it is widely reported that his confessor told him to offer up his pains to God in expiation, to which he replied: 'Oh if only it were enough, it is such a small thing! I would wish to suffer more!'[62]

Guidelines for confessors did not require them to withhold the opportunity for penance from even the worst offenders.[63] The Jesuit Père Crasset wrote comfortingly that 'one evil wish loses us heaven, but one good sigh regains it … it is never too late to convert'.[64] During the *billets de confession* affair, Louis XV opined that there should be nothing as freely available as confession.[65] When the marquis de Chauvelin collapsed in front of him in late 1773, Louis XV called out 'a priest! absolution! and though he was dead, the *abbé* absolved him conditionally and said that he could still feel a pulse, which relieved the king's distress'.[66] Taken together with his experiences at Metz and his confession following the Damiens attack, this is evidence of Louis XV's clear personal wish for confession in order to partake of the sacraments before death and of his absence of doubt that this would be provided on request. The question for those surrounding him was one of timing: when would the king's illness be sufficiently worrying for him to call his confessor? When would the sickbed become a deathbed, with all that implied?

The days of 30 April, 1 and 2 May passed without incident. On the afternoon of 3 May, the king finally spoke aloud the dread diagnosis that no one had yet admitted to him. Louis XV looked at the spots on his hands and said to his grand chamberlain, the duc de Bouillon: 'This is smallpox. It must be smallpox.' In the absence of any response, he said, as much to himself as anyone else, 'My word, that really is surprising.' What was surprising? Croÿ felt the king referred to his attendants hiding the nature of his illness from him: he could equally have been astonished by the fact of having the disease at all, given his belief that he had already had it. The king was now aware of the seriousness of his illness and, tellingly, it was the next morning, 4 May, that he told the duc d'Aiguillon to make arrangements for Madame du Barry to leave 'with dignity … avoiding all the cruelties of Metz'.[67] Her departure that afternoon was dignified and unobtrusive. The king knew she was comfortable and safe, and in the care of a minister he saw regularly. It would be easy to recall her at will. His strength seemed to improve during the day and he asked to get up. Walking was too much for him. He was carried back to his bed in a dead faint. When he revived, he seemed basically strong, his head was clear. The public bulletins on his health, while providing some details on his physical suffering, continued to insist that all was as well as could be expected.[68]

In Paris, on 5 May, the municipal authorities held a solemn mass and commenced a novena at the church of their patron saint, Sainte-Geneviève, for the king's recovery. It did not seem impossible: 'I am beginning to hope' wrote the duc d'Orléans to Madame de Montesson.[69] Printed invitations were distributed to the merchants' solemn mass for the king at the Oratory on rue Saint-Honoré on 6 May.[70] Signs of any development, either physical or spiritual, were anxiously awaited. Rumours circulated that the bulletin posted at the Tuileries reported preparations for the sacraments that presaged death: the king had requested to lie in his bed of state and the text for the ceremony of the *viaticum*.[71]

On Saturday 7 May, three days after the departure of Madame du Barry and hours before the ninth day – commonly held to determine the course of the illness – began, around quarter past three in the morning, the king told the duc de Duras to fetch his confessor. Abbé Maudoux arrived at four o'clock and stayed for sixteen minutes on this first visit.[72] Senior members of the royal clerical staff arrived soon after, the grand almoner, cardinal de la Roche-Aymon, and the first almoner, bishop of Senlis. The king then sent for his daughters and gave instructions for the royal family's participation in the ceremony of the *viaticum*.[73] Events moved quickly once the king had decided to confess in order to receive the sacraments. The ceremony took place at seven o'clock in the morning, just four hours after Louis XV first called for his confessor.

Louis XV specified the arrangements for the *viaticum* himself. The duc de Penthièvre, always interested in ceremonial, took a detailed note of proceedings.[74] The royal guards knelt and presented arms along the route from the chapel to the king's apartments. That part of the royal family that was excluded from the king's presence went to the chapel to accompany the sacrament in procession. The sacrament was attended by the royal household clergy led by the cardinal de la Roche-Aymon and the bishop of Senlis. There was no time to make the usual arrangements in the chapel: there were no prie-dieus, no cushions to kneel on (*carreaux*). The dauphine and her sisters-in-law were accommodated on plain chairs. The dauphin, his brothers and their wives together with the younger princes and princesses of the blood, the duc de Chartres, the duc de Bourbon, and their wives with the comtesse de la Marche and Madame de Lamballe, were all present and conducted the sacrament towards the king's chamber. The princesses' trains were carried by pages. Liveried servants bore flaming torches before the sacrament itself.

This procession stopped at the end of a set of stairs: the dauphin and his brothers were forbidden to approach any closer to the king who was waiting impatiently, saying to his confessor 'I have always believed in Jesus Christ: you know how profoundly I worshipped him at Mass and at Benediction.'[75] They remained kneeling at the foot of the stairs, participating in the ceremony from afar. The sacrament was met at the top of the steps by the duc d'Orléans, the prince de Condé, the comte de la Marche and the duc de Penthièvre. Orléans and Condé had spent the night in the king's chamber, de la Marche and Penthièvre had been summoned from their rooms elsewhere in the palace. The processional canopy over the sacrament was handed from Swiss guards to the captains of the guards and the gentlemen of the bedchamber at this point. The princes of the blood escorted the sacrament through the guard room, where they were joined by mesdames, the king's daughters, who gathered their skirts around their feet as they were without attendants to carry their trains.

In the bedroom, a circle of clergy formed around the bed with the duc d'Orléans and the prince de Condé having the honour of holding the communion cloth. The king's ministers were also present. The cardinal de la Roche-Aymon made a brief speech before administering communion to the king. Once the formal religious ceremony was completed, the cardinal moved to the door of the Council room and addressed the assembly on the king's behalf, in another ritual moment familiar from the king's earlier deathbed experiences.

'Some edifying words regarding the scandal His Majesty may have caused and on his attitude to religion' is the duc de Penthièvre's laconic description of the cardinal's speech.[76] For him, the importance of the event lay in the religious ceremony, the great respect intended and enacted towards the sacrament, and in the king's reception of this sacrament. 'He repented publicly' wrote the abbé Maudoux, surely best placed to know the intention behind this scene. Every morning from then until his death, the king renewed his promise to dedicate his life to making reparations for his past, presenting his life as an offering to God.[77] The duc de Croÿ rendered the substance of what was said as:

> Gentlemen, the king has directed me to say that he asks pardon of God for having offended him and for the scandal he caused among his people: if God returns him to health, he will devote himself to doing penance, to supporting religion, and to the relief of his people.[78]

The king wished he had had the strength to say it himself. His inability to speak loudly enough to make his own announcement as well as the fact that he thought he could feel 'something' in his mouth indicate sores in his mouth and throat.[79] He said to his daughter, Adélaïde, that he had never felt so calm. Low mass was said as usual at the king's bedside around noon that day. There appeared to be some improvement, the crucial ninth day was felt to begin well. His confessor remained constantly at his bedside.[80]

The duc de Croÿ's description of this moment as 'a kind of *amende honorable* that the confessor obliged the grand almoner to carry out, and that the king firmly supported' hints not at reluctance from the king but from the cardinal.[81] Translating '*amende honorable*' simply as a bland 'apology' is misleading.[82] *Amende honorable* is one of the sentences listed in the Grand Criminal Ordinance of 1670. It is placed at the milder end of the spectrum of punitive sentences, taken to range from a death sentence through permanent banishment and public whipping to an *amende honorable*.[83] The 1762 fourth edition of the dictionary of the Académie Française defines it as a 'a kind of punishment of infamy ordered by Justice, & which consists of publicly recognising one's crime, & asking pardon' with the example 'making an *amende honorable*, a torch in the hand and a noose around the neck'. An *amende honorable* carries with it the sense of expiation through publicity since the offender, usually to some degree stripped of clothing and with a rope around his neck, was required by the sentence to be led by the executioner to a public place, often a specified church, in order to beg forgiveness on his knees. The *amende honorable* was usually made moments before death. Measures to ensure notoriety as part of the sentence meant that the names of those sentenced in their absence were always displayed either in a public square or posted on their usual residence. The key elements of the *amende honorable* were publicity, religion and, crucially, honour. The *amende honorable* was, as the term clearly implies, a 'fine of honour' in which the offender sacrificed a portion of his honour through public humiliation in order to restore the honour of those he had offended.[84] The phrase *amende honorable* was also used to describe the king's short speech at Metz that he had been strong enough to deliver himself.[85] The use of this term clearly indicates how seriously contemporaries took these speeches.

These speeches were part of the formal cycle of religious ritual around Louis XV's three deathbeds. It is of vital importance to realise that in 1774 the king knew that such a speech would be made after his confession, that it was not a surprise to him and is unlikely to have been forced upon him.[86] This shifts our perception of power at the deathbed. The king, after all, had had the benefit of dress rehearsals in 1744 and 1757 and could draw on experience in his arrangement of proceedings. He was also a believer who fervently wished to partake in the sacraments of his church, once he had cleansed himself of sin through confession and penance. This was no mere apology but a ritualistic gesture of public penance heavy with religious significance. An *amende honorable* should be understood as a public ceremony of contrition.

The king's health worsened the next day (8 May). He experienced some delirium and, when the duc de Croÿ attended his bedside as usual around noon, 'all his loyal servants were frightened by his face … there was a general terror'.[87] He suffered with fever and, by 9 May, the encrusted spots on his skin began to turn black. At mass that day, he gave few signs of life though his mind still seemed clear. This was the first day the usual ceremonies at his bedside were cancelled. Rumours were circulating in Paris that the king had already died. Cloth sellers were going door to door with samples of black fabric for mourning clothes. Parisians continued to engage in religious ritual, playing their part in the national drama. A pamphlet of prayers for the king's recovery was sold at the doors of churches, comprising a translation from the Latin of the prayers for Benediction, and featuring a preface in which the king seemed to speak directly to the reader, recognising that he had not kept the promises of Metz.[88] At Notre-Dame the blessed sacrament remained exposed as an aid to prayer for the king's recovery.[89]

At the king's request, the ceremony of extreme unction, or anointing of the sick, was performed by the bishop of Senlis at quarter to nine on the night of 9 May.[90] This was the same prelate who preached the sermon on Holy Thursday 1774 which appeared to foretell the king's death and who would give his funeral oration in July 1774. He delivered both correctives and comforts. The duc de Croÿ recorded that all those courtiers with the right to enter the king's bedroom attended. They remained standing around the bed while the bishop stood beside the king enunciating the prayers and administering the holy oils. An assisting priest held a crucifix before the king's eyes and then presented it to him to kiss. The duc de Croÿ saw very little movement from the sick man but, as the prayers ceased, the king was heard to say 'amen'. As he left at the end of this ceremony, Croÿ found a crowd had gathered outside the room 'who seemed to be truly affected by the horror of what we had just seen'.[91]

It seemed, about an hour later, that the king was on the verge of death. The windows of his apartments were open, as part of his cooling treatment. Crowds gathered below and at the windows around the marble courtyard awaiting the declaration of his death, lingering into the early morning. The princes of the blood remained in their day clothes until five in the morning.[92] The king remained in the same state, 'as though unconscious, but still aware', well into the next day with his doctors continuing different, contradictory treatments. As 10 May dawned in Paris, the entire clergy of the city were taking part throughout the day in a sequence of processions to the relics of Saint Geneviève, imploring the saint's intercession for the king's health. 'A prodigious multitude' flocked to join them, according to Hardy.[93] At one o'clock, in Versailles, the death-agony commenced. Abbé Maudoux asked him if he felt pain: 'oh! oh! oh! very much!' came the response. The abbé was sure the king remained lucid until the very last moments. With the bishop of Senlis, the confessor led the prayers for the dying which continued until the king passed away at about quarter past three on 10 May 1774.

The doors of the bedroom were opened wide to allow the curious to view the corpse. In the Oeil-de-Boeuf, a steward announced: 'le Roi est mort'.[94] Priests arrived to perform the vigil with the corpse, sitting around the king's bed and reciting psalms just as had happened for his predecessors. Soon afterwards, the cast-iron gates of the palace were hung with black mourning drapes.[95]

2 Portrait of Louis XV, De Launay (engraver) after Jean-Michel Moreau. Louis XV is shown in this mourning portrait in profile on a medallion with a weeping figure of France.

Kingship passed immediately to the dauphin with no more ceremony than the duc de Chartres informing him of the death of his grandfather, saying 'I am leaving for Paris and I have come to take Your Majesty's orders'. This low-key form of accession to the throne was entirely normal, in keeping with the legal maxim that 'death seizes the living'.[96] Following Louis XIV's death in 1715, the senior prince of the blood, Philippe d'Orléans, had led the princes to see the dauphin and to inform him of his new status. The pronouncement of the word 'Sire' by Orléans had reduced the child Louis XV to tears.[97] Given the necessity of quarantine, the senior princes who had been with the dying Louis XV were not with the dauphin in 1774, but those who were with Louis XVI – his wife, his brothers Provence and Artois and their wives, his sisters Clothilde and Élisabeth, the younger princes and princesses of the blood and courtiers – knelt, rendering the first homage to the new king.[98]

In a satisfyingly dramatic sketch of this moment, Madame de Campan famously suggests that there was an uncontrolled exodus from Louis XV's quarters to those of Louis XVI at the moment of the death. Her vivid version of events, written after the Revolution, is laden with ominous portents: the thunderous noise of the approaching courtiers was the first sign of the ill-starred new reign, a powerful image which historians have often repeated. The devout young couple fell to their knees, shedding copious tears and crying 'Oh God, guide us, protect us, we are too young to reign!'[99] According to Jacob Nicolas Moreau, also writing some time later, on hearing that there was no hope for his grandfather, the dauphin said: 'Oh! My God, I am the saddest man in the world! I can see that God has decreed what will be: it is decided. It remains to me only to give religion the protection it badly needs, to send away from me vicious and frivolous people, and to provide relief to my people.'[100] Croÿ concurs that the young king cried out and lamented his youth and lack of experience, though without mention of religion or rushing crowds. Within thirty minutes of his grandfather's death, Louis XVI was giving orders, choosing his regnal name, setting a date for his first meeting with this ministers.[101] Both Madame de Campan and Moreau relay a stylised picture of the event, emphasising what was important to them and heightening the sensational content of the inaugural moment of a reign that ended in trauma. The quarantine observed by the dauphin, and which continued for nine days after his grandfather's death, renders several elements of this traditional picture rather dubious. Anxiety about his new responsibilities and distress at his grandfather's death are understandable. The new king met with his household officers and ministers from 19 May at

La Muette.[102] The dignified eventuality of Chartres conveying the news was a fittingly sober gesture for the passing of command rather than a tumult of tears and forebodings.[103] It was important that a sufficiently high-ranked individual be on hand to pass this momentous news of what was, after all, a dynastic event: the continuation of the House of Bourbon. This minor but deeply important moment signalled the complexity of the role of the new monarch; a bereaved person expected to shoulder immense burdens of business.

The convoy to Saint Denis

Another dark and dramatic image of Louis XV's death is that of the convoy bringing his body to Saint Denis by night and in haste, in no small part thanks to the following description by the baron de Besenval on which many historians have relied:

> the convoy most resembled the transport of a burden which one hastens to be rid of, not the last respects rendered to a monarch.[104]

In truth, the dead king received a full and solemn send-off. Misunderstanding of the nature of the ceremonies performed around his corpse immediately after his death has produced this image of disrespect. This misunderstanding stems in the main from the king's death of smallpox, coupled with a readiness to detect decay in the edifice of monarchy at this juncture.[105] Yet Louis XV was not the first member of the royal family to die of smallpox in the eighteenth century, and examination of the ceremonies held in their honour sheds light on this historiographical problem. Louis XV's grandfather, the grand dauphin,[106] and his daughter, Élisabeth of Parma, both fell victim to smallpox and died at court. Cause of death, particularly when it was virulently contagious disease, could and did have ceremonial consequences.

The grand dauphin's death was a mercifully swift one. He fell ill at Meudon on 9 April 1711 and died on the 14th, 'at a time he was believed to be safe from this dangerous disease'.[107] Since his father, Louis XIV, had had smallpox, he remained at Meudon during the illness but took the precaution of ordering the next in line to the throne, his grandson the duc de Bourgogne, to stay at Versailles with his family. Among their number was the baby duc d'Anjou who would, all too soon and most unexpectedly, become Louis XV. Once the death of his son had occurred, Louis XIV withdrew to Marly where he was advised by his ceremonial staff that 'due to the kind of illness which killed Monseigneur, it would be pointless to render him the honours he is due at Meudon, because no one would come'.[108]

Meanwhile, at Meudon on 16 April, our narrator, the *maître des cérémonies* Michel Ancel Desgranges, records that the remains were placed in the usual double coffins by the officers of the prince's household. In the next paragraph, he admits his disingenuity: 'I say he was placed in the coffin by the officers of his chamber because that is what should have happened.'[109] In reality, he confesses, confusion reigned. The moment Monseigneur expired, the apothecary and the surgeon left Meudon to follow the king, leaving no one to carry out an autopsy or an embalming. Desgranges wrote to the medical staff to have them sent back but before this could be done another apothecary, Beaulieu, asked the king directly whether he wished the body to be opened. Louis XIV's doleful 'non' was taken as an order and the apothecaries avoided approaching the body. Since they would not go to Meudon, Desgranges was obliged to call in the neighbouring Sisters of Charity to deal with the remains. Monseigneur was buried bedded in bran from the nearby village.[110]

The body was taken to Saint Denis the next day 'without ceremony save the usual solemn ceremonies due to a prince of this rank'.[111] In keeping with this idea of *sans cérémonies*, the funeral convoy from Meudon to Saint Denis was minimal for a person of his rank in this period. Two of the king's bodyguard led twenty-six pages carrying torches and a further twenty guards with torches who accompanied two carriages, one with the body and the other with the bishop of Metz, the duc de la Trémoïlle, first gentleman of the king's bedchamber nominated to accompany the corpse, and the ceremonial staff. At Saint Denis, the coffin was carried into the church by eight guards and the bishop of Metz formally gave it into the care of the religious of Saint Denis, who waited at the main door, candles in hand, for the party to arrive. Following the usual prayers, the coffin was placed directly in the crypt. The solemn ceremonies in his memory were held subsequently.

The royal family was lucky, given the prevalence and virulence of the disease, to be spared another adult smallpox fatality until 1759. In that year, Élisabeth of Parma, Louis XV's only married daughter, travelled to Versailles to visit her family and was infected, dying on 6 December. The treatment of Élisabeth's remains confirms that public health concerns were foremost in cases of royal smallpox and led to alterations in the normal ceremonies. On the day she died, the grand master of ceremonies wrote to the lieutenant general of police regarding the customary mourning closure of the theatres, adding that 'Madame's body will be transported from here directly to Saint Denis without pomp due to the sickness of which this Princess died.'[112] He also wrote to the abbess of Val de Grâce that, in spite of her request, her community would not have the honour of hosting the princess's embalmed heart since 'the illness of which this Princess died does not permit the opening of her body, therefore she was carried and buried immediately at Saint Denis'.[113] Her body was transported swiftly to Saint Denis the day after her death by a convoy of twelve royal pages who were not dressed in mourning for the occasion, presumably through lack of time to furnish such clothes.[114]

Smallpox dictated certain measures in relation to even a royal body: rapid inhumation without autopsy and reduced funeral processions. Bearing in mind widespread misapprehensions regarding Louis XV's funeral solemnities, it is important to point out that, as with Monseigneur, for Élisabeth ceremonial accoutrements were not spared for subsequent memorial services. These were all carried out with due ceremony and solemnity. Reduction in some parts of the funeral solemnities for public health reasons did not mean disrespect or neglect of the deceased. A service, complete with ornate catafalque, was held for Élisabeth of Parma at Notre Dame in February 1760. The parlement was invited by the grand master of ceremonies in person, accompanied by heraldic officers, the king-at-arms and four heralds in costumes of deep mourning, in the usual ceremony known as *sémonces*. As we shall see in the next chapter, the *sémonces* for the funeral ceremony of Louis XV were also a public occasion and they gave rise to a sharply political display of disrespect for Maupeou's parlementaires.

Though Louis XV was the first king to die of smallpox, it is clear from the procedures followed for the grand dauphin and for Élisabeth of Parma that concerns about possible contagion dictated the avoidance of all traditional death rites involving exposure to a corpse, which seemed in the eyes of contemporaries to be almost more threatening than the infected, living royal body.[115]

A further cause of misunderstanding of these rites is the recurrence of the term *sans cérémonies*. This is often taken at face value to mean, simply, that no ceremony was observed, which would be a clear sign of disrespect for the dead king if true. However, this phrase had a long pedigree in royal funerals, reaching back to 1643 when Louis XIII caused a revolution in kingly funerals with his express command that he be buried 'without the usual ceremonies'.[116] Master of Ceremonies Sainctot gave two reasons for this decision: the king's piety and his aversion to expense 'taking into account the poverty of his people'.[117] The term *sans cérémonies* is taken to apply specifically to the period of lying in state at the royal palace and to the processional transfer of the body to Saint Denis. In practical terms, this amounted to the cancellation of the elaborate cycle of events in Paris revolving round the effigy of the king, as had been practised at the funeral of Henri IV and some, but not all, of his predecessors.[118] Rather than the corpse and effigy being exposed for forty days at the Louvre with the attendant procession through the capital's streets, grand service at Notre Dame and subsequent procession back through the city towards Saint Denis, the king was 'shown simply and without ceremony on his death bed, & attended during this time by churchmen, with prayers and masses continuously said, & taken from Saint Germain to Saint Denis without pomp'.[119] The king's wish for simplicity meant that Saint Denis became the main focus for his funeral rites, placing the events around his death firmly in the religious arena. In a reversal of the ceremonies observed for his father, Henri IV, Louis XIII's remains were displayed for a short time at the royal palace and for a much longer period, six weeks, in the church of Saint Denis. This pattern was taken as a template for the funeral of Louis XIV, also celebrated *sans cérémonies*.[120] Master of Ceremonies Michel Ancel Desgranges received the order 'to do as was done for Louis XIII' from the duc de Bourbon, grand master of the royal household, after the duc had conferred with the new regent. The reduction in ceremony was explained by Desgranges as a consequence of the location of death. His assertion that 'the grand ceremony … is only used when the king dies at Paris' is absurd given that Henri IV and Louis XVI, the only Bourbon kings to die in Paris, died violently. Nonetheless, it indicates an awareness that a different sort of ceremony was being performed for the king. Princes and princesses of the blood continued to observe elaborate forms for stages of the funeral which were now more or less omitted for kings.

The funeral of Louis XIII holds a special place in the history of French royal funerals, creating in a single public ceremony a high level of novelty consciously observed and recorded by contemporaries. The suppression of elements of display at the royal residence, together with the increased emphasis on religious aspects, removed some opportunities for the involvement of secular bodies from outside the king's household, such as the Parlement of Paris, in the ritual. The military side of the household remained closely involved, in some ways preserving the notion of the undying king in their ceaseless vigil over the body from the time of death to the day of burial in the crypt. They were the only secular group of household officers guaranteed a place at the dead king's bedside. The convoy, which had previously been the site of much dispute over precedence and proximity to the effigy, became, as the parlement lost its dedicated place beside the effigy, an exclusively religious, household and military matter. With secular bodies from outside the royal household excluded from the bedside and the convoy, their role was reduced to attendance at the grand service at Saint Denis. This is one reason why there was such an intense focus by the political classes on the funeral service for Louis XV in July 1774, as we shall see in the next chapter.

Two days after Louis XV died, on 12 May, his remains were taken directly to the Royal Abbey at Saint Denis in the evening, as had happened for Louis XIII and Louis XIV at the end of their brief periods of lying-in-state at the palaces where they had died. It was about seven o'clock when the convoy left the palace of Versailles, led by the first gentleman of the bedchamber, the duc d'Aumont, and the first almoner, the bishop of Senlis, with eighteen liveried pages lighting the way with torches and about one hundred guards on horseback. The clergy of the two parishes of Versailles and local Franciscan monks conducted the convoy to the town limits of Versailles. When the convoy arrived at the gates of Saint Denis at eleven o'clock, it was met by the governor of the town, the comte Danès, at the head of the assembled ranks of municipal and judicial officers and clergy.[121] The convoy continued to the Abbey, at the door of which the bishop of Senlis formally deposited the late king's remains into the care of the Benedictines. Prayers for the dead continued through the night and into the next day. The body was immediately placed in the vault,[122] just inside the entrance to the Bourbon crypt on a stone ledge carved into the thickness of the wall, two feet from the ground. It was traditional for the coffin of the last dead king to be placed there, awaiting the death of his successor.[123]

Louis XV's funeral convoy copied those of his predecessors, Louis XIII and Louis XIV, in taking place at night by torchlight. While, in London, night burials may have had have some lingering sense of shame attached into the eighteenth century,[124] this was not the case in France. Indeed, Vanessa Harding suggests that the elaboration of funerals in late seventeenth-century France was strongly influenced by the wish to express a religious identity forged by the Counter-Reformation. The placement of Louis XV's coffin in the wall of the crypt, rather than among the remains of his ancestors, was also normal. While Louis XIII, for example, left explicit instructions that he be buried between his mother and father, this did not occur until Louis XIV's remains were brought to the Abbey.[125] Neither night burial nor deposit in the side vault were gestures of disrespect towards the late king.

Conclusion

A reinterpretation of the deathbed and burial of Louis XV has been offered in this chapter by focusing on the importance of circumstance in shaping ceremony. This account bears witness to Louis XV's religious practice and to the close involvement of the princes of the blood in these events, in spite of their ongoing political estrangement from the king due to the 1771 exile of the parlement. The king's two previous experiences of such a situation meant he was less open to manipulation than is often thought and, indeed, that he took a central role in the conduct of his deathbed rites.

The convoy transporting the king's corpse from Versailles to Saint Denis is the most widely referred to aspect of Louis XV's death rites in the historiography, but it is too often used as a metaphor for a clichéd appraisal of his reign and for a monarchy already doomed in the 1770s. Two key aspects of this convoy have been overlooked: the evolution of the idea of burial *sans cérémonies* and the impact of smallpox on his death rites. Contextual examination of these two dimensions reveals that the convoy was carried out with respect and, importantly, in conformity with those of his predecessors.

Once the king had been buried at Saint Denis, preparations began for his funeral. However, he had died without resolving the key political question of the day – the exile of the Paris Parlement in 1771 and its wholesale replacement. His political, if not personal, relationship with the princes of the blood remained strained by this controversy. Yet both the parlement and the princes would be needed to perform his funeral solemnities. This daunting ceremonial and political problem, the subject of the next chapter, faced Louis XVI as soon as he came to the throne.

Notes

1 Emmanuel de Croÿ, *Journal Inédit Du Duc De Croÿ, 1718–1784*, volume 3 (Paris, 1906), 83; Siméon Prosper Hardy, *Mes Loisirs, ou Journal d'Evénéments tels qu'ils parviennent à ma connoissance*, 30 avril 1774, f 327.

2 Croÿ, *Journal*, volume 3, 107.

3 Ibid., 87. 'Versailles est plein comme un oeuf' according to Jacob Nicolas Moreau, *Mes Souvenirs* (Paris, 1898, 1901), 2 volumes, volume 1, 348.

4 Elements of this discussion appeared as my 'The deathbed of Louis XV', *French History*, 29:4 (December 2015), 451–509.

5 John McManners, 'Death and the French historians', in *Mirrors of Mortality: Studies in the social history of death*, Joachim Whaley (editor) (London, 1981), 107.

6 Geoffrey Koziol, 'The dangers of polemic: is ritual an interesting topic of historical study?' *Early Medieval Europe*, 11:4 (December 2002), 387.

7 Pierre Joseph Victor, baron de Besenval, *Mémoires de M le baron de Bésenval … Écrits par lui-même, imprimés sur son manuscrit original et publiés par son exécuteur testamentaire [i.e. Viscount A. J. P. De Ségur]*, 3 volumes (Paris, 1805), volume 1, 85.

8 Pierre Darmon, *La Variole, les nobles et les princes: la petite vérole mortelle de Louis XV 1774* (Bruxelles, 1989), 20.

9 Ibid., 61.

10 Catriona Seth, *Les Rois aussi en mouraient: les lumières en lutte contre la variole* (Paris, 2008), 57.

11 Luynes, Charles Philippe d'Albert, duc de, *Mémoires du duc de Luynes* (Paris, 1860–65), volume 14, 470–71.

12 Emmanuel de Croÿ, 1718–84.

13 Besenval, *Mémoires*, 60.

14 Croÿ, *Journal*, volume 3, 107.

15 This is why the duc d'Orléans says 'on s'est aperçu de la petite vérole hier … en regardant sa langue.' Gabriel de Broglie, 'La mort de Louis XV d'après des lettres inédites du duc d'Orléans', *Nouvelle revue des deux mondes* (March, 1974), 562.

16 '[C]ela fait trembler' he wrote on 1 May. Ibid., 562.

17 'Retourne en Circassie, au-delà de ces mers / D'où l'art d'Inoculer t'accrut dans l'univers', Jacques Martineau de Solleyne '*Les Voeux de l'Europe et de la France pour la santé du roi*', 1729, in Seth, *Les Rois aussi en mouraient*, 77.

18 Croÿ, *Journal*, volume 3, 90. Louis XV's son-in-law, Philip of Parma, was the victim of the same '[f]uneste certitude qui a conspiré à sa perte' in 1765, see Carmelina Biondi 'Il "variolico veleno" alla corte di Parma' in *Un viaggio infinito … salute, malattia e morte percorsi di lettura tra Belgio, Francia e Italia in ricordo di Paola Vecchi*, Carmelina Imbroscio (editor) (Bologna, 2001), 78.

19 'Dernière maladie de Louis XV: mort et funérailles', *Revue des documents historiques* (Paris, 1873–74), 156.

20 Hardy, *Mes Loisirs …* , 30 avril 1774, f 327.

21 Hardy, *Mes Loisirs …* , 2 mai 1774, f 328.

22 The actor Brissard announced '[m]essieurs, quoique Sa Majesté ne soit pas plus mal, nous venons cependant de recevoir l'ordre de cesser les spectacles'. Moreau, *Mes souvenirs*, volume 1, 344. The Comédie Italienne also closed. Hardy, *Mes Loisirs …* , 30 avril 1774, f 327, 330.

23 Hardy, *Mes Loisirs …* , 8 mai 1774, f 333.
24 See chapters on the coronation below, where I argue that similar efforts by religious to put their spin on the coronation were unsuccessful.
25 'Toute la cour se rendit au château; l'oeil-de-boeuf se remplit de courtisans, le palais de curieux …'. Jeanne Louise Henriette de Campan, *Mémoires sur la vie privée de Marie-Antoinette, Reine de France et de Navarre, suivis de souvenirs et anecdotes historiques sur les règnes de Louis XIV, de Louis XV et de Louis XVI* (Paris, 1822), volume 1, 77–78.
26 Moreau, *Mes Souvenirs*, volume 1, 355.
27 *Journal du President d'Ormesson de Noiseau*, Archives Nationales (Paris) (AN) 144 AP 120, volume 5, f 944.
28 More than fifty, according to Campan, though this number should be treated with caution given her polemical ends in writing. Campan, *Mémoires sur la vie privée de Marie-Antoinette*, volume 1, 76.
29 Stephanie Félicite de Genlis, *Les Souvenirs de Félicie L**** (Paris, 1808), volume 1, 188.
30 Viscount Stormont, Ambassador, to the Earl of Rochford, National Archives (Kew) State Papers Foreign (NASPF), SP 78/292/87, Paris 25 May 1774.
31 The duc d'Orléans records the comte de Provence saying 'avec la plus grande force sur ce que l'on ne pouvait prendre trop de précautions pour la santé de M le dauphin …': de Broglie, 'La mort de Louis XV', 573.
32 Conti sent his first footman with instructions to send word every three hours. Hardy, *Mes Loisirs*, 2 mai 1774, f 328.
33 The dauphin was in seclusion during this time, 'renfermé dans son plus petit intérieur…il vivait en famille …': Rochefoucauld-Liancourt, 'Louis XV', 537.
34 Ormesson, *Journal*, volume 5, f 944.
35 Ibid.
36 Ibid.
37 Le Mierre, 'Sur la maladie de Mesdames', *Journal Encyclopédique Dédié à Altesse Sérénssime Mgr le Duc de Bouillon, Grand Chambellan de France, &c, &c, &c* (Bouillon, 1774–5), volume 5, partie II, juillet 1774, 319.
38 Genlis, *Les Souvenirs*, volume 1, 196.
39 Casimir Stryenski, *Mesdames de France, filles de Louis XV, documents inédits* (Paris, 1911), 347.
40 Étienne François, duc de Choiseul (1719–85), Foreign Minister 1758–61, 1766–70. Disgraced at Christmas 1770 in a prelude to the Maupeou Coup, he became a fashionable rallying point for those opposed to the Coup.
41 Pierre Joseph Victor, baron de Besenval, *Mémoires de M le baron de Bésenval … Écrits par lui-même, imprimés sur son manuscrit original et publiés par son exécuteur testamentaire [i.e. Viscount A. J. P. De Ségur]*, 3 volumes (Paris, 1805); François Alexandre Frédéric duc de Rochefoucauld-Liancourt, 'Relation inédite de la dernière maladie de Louis XV', in Charles Augustin

de Saint-Beuve, *Portraits Littéraires* (Paris, 1848), volume 3, 512–40; Gabriel de Broglie, 'La Mort de Louis XV d'après des lettres inédites du duc d'Orléans', *Nouvelle revue des deux mondes* (mars 1974); Antoine de Lantenay (Antoine Louis Bernard), 'L'Abbé Maudoux: confesseur de Louis XV' in *Mélanges de biographie et d'histoire* (Bordeaux, 1885), 485–87. Abbé Maudoux burned many of his papers, including his journal, shortly before he died.

42 Jeanine Huas, *Madame du Barry* (Paris, 2011); 'Mémoires de famille de Robert de Saint-Vincent', in *Un Magistrat janséniste du siècle des Lumières à l'Émigration, Pierre-Augustin Robert de Saint-Vincent*, critical edition presented by Monique Cottret, Valérie Guittienne-Mürger and Nicolas Lyon-Caen (Bordeaux, 2012), 382.

43 Creutz, Gustav Philip, comte de, *La Suède et les lumières: lettres de France d'un ambassadeur à son Roi (1771–1783)* (Paris, 2006), 129–30; 'Mémoires de Robert de Saint-Vincent', 382.

44 Joseph Alphonse Véri, *Journal de l'Abbé Véri* (Paris, 1928), 2 volumes, 89.

45 Ibid., 86.

46 Besenval, *Mémoires*, volume 2, 61, 66.

47 Croÿ, *Journal*, volume 3, 90.

48 Ibid., 86. Rochefoucauld-Liancourt describes the anti-du Barry party as composed of 'gens honnêtes' who engaged in no intrigues, begging the question of whether it should be understood a group, 'Louis XV', 527.

49 John McManners, *Church and Society in Eighteenth Century France* (Oxford, 1998), volume 1, 40.

50 McManners points out, '[t]he curé's latitude to refuse the sacraments was very limited. A parishioner who had been duly shriven was entitled to receive them. Inquiry could not be made behind the fact of absolution … And to the theologian, absolution was the narrow gate, the point at which the verdict of the Church had been given.' John McManners, *Death and the Enlightenment: Changing attitudes to death among Christians and unbelievers in eighteenth-century France* (Oxford, 1981), 259.

51 My account relies on Michel Antoine, *Louis XV* (Paris, 1989) 372–80 and Edmond Barbier, *Journal historique et anecdotique du règne de Louis XV* (Paris, 1847–56), volume II, 405–06.

52 *Pace* Jeffrey Merrick, 'Louis XV's deathbed apology', *European History Quarterly*, 38 (2008), 205–26; 206.

53 Barbier, *Journal historique*, volume II, 406.

54 She never returned to Versailles as she died suddenly in Paris on 8 December 1744.

55 According to Antoine, *Louis XV*, 715.

56 John McManners, 'The religious observances of Versailles under Louis XV', in *Enlightenment Essays in Memory of Robert Shackleton*, Gilles Barber and C.P. Courtney (editors) (Oxford, 1988), 187.

57 Bernard Hours, *Louis XV: un portrait* (Toulouse, 2009), 620.
58 E. Barbier, *Journal historique et anecdotique du règne de Louis XV* (Paris, 1847–56), vol. 2, 224.
59 Croÿ, *Journal*, volume 3, 108.
60 Duc d'Orléans to Madame de Montesson, 8 mai 1774, in de Broglie, 'La mort de Louis XV', 573.
61 Madame de Sévigné, quoted in Henri Bremond, *Histoire littéraire du sentiment religieux en France, tome 9, la vie chrétienne sous l'Ancien Régime* (Paris, 1968), 332.
62 Croÿ, *Journal*, volume 3, 103; Moreau, *Mes Souvenirs*, volume 1, 360.
63 McManners, *Death and the Enlightenment*, 245–46.
64 Bremond, *Histoire littéraire*, 375.
65 McManners, *Death and the Enlightenment*, 187; Antoine, *Louis XV*, 655.
66 Croÿ, *Journal*, volume 3, 97.
67 Ibid., 94. The duc d'Aiguillon gave a different version, see Véri, *Journal*, 88.
68 'Dernière maladie de Louis XV', 152–72.
69 Duc d'Orléans to Madame de Montesson, 5 mai 1774, de Broglie, 'La mort de Louis XV', 569.
70 Hardy, *Mes Loisirs*, BNF Manuscrits Français (Ms Fr) 6681, f 330.
71 Ormesson, *Journal*, volume 5, f 946.
72 After the Damiens attack, *abbé* Soldini spent three-quarters of an hour with the king to hear his confession and then remained by his side until replaced by Père Desmarets, his confessor, who arrived later. The king was evidently physically stronger then. Antoine, *Louis XV*, 713.
73 Even the minor daily religious observances of the royal family were the subject of ceremonial processions, as Giles Barber makes clear in his 'Il fallut même réveiller les Suisses': Aspects of private religious practice in a public setting in eighteenth-century Versailles' in *Religious Change in Europe 1650–1914: Essays for John McManners*, Nigel Aston (editor) (Oxford, 1997), 75–101. The title refers to the debate on proper accompaniment for queen Maria Leszczynska when she performed early morning devotions in the royal chapel before the king was awake.
74 AN K 138, no 12 (3).
75 Bertrand/Lantenay, *Mélanges*, 485. This hints at a close relationship between king and confessor.
76 AN K 138 no 12 (3).
77 Bertrand/Lantenay, *Mélanges*, 485.
78 Croÿ, *Journal*, volume 3, 101.
79 Hardy, *Mes Loisirs…* , 9 mai 1774, f 333; Duc d'Orléans to Madame de Montesson, 8 mai 1774; de Broglie, 'La mort de Louis XV, 573.
80 Bertrand/Lantenay, *Mélanges*, 486.
81 Croÿ, *Journal*, volume 3, 110.
82 *Pace* Merrick 'Louis XV's deathbed apology'.

83 Grand Ordinance of 1670, title XVI, article 13.

84 Diane Claire Margolf, *Religion and Royal Justice in Early Modern France* (Missouri, 2003), 165. This sort of public humiliation is presumably what the creators of the pamphlet *L'Amende honorable de Louis le dernier* (Paris, 1793) had in mind. It purports to contain a text given to Louis XVI to recite as penance and expiation.

85 Barbier, *Journal historique*, volume II, 405. When he confessed after the Damiens attack in 1757, Louis XV requested forgiveness of his family in the presence of his household, according to Jean-Christian Petitfils, *Louis XVI* (Paris, 2005), 128.

86 Besenval, *Mémoires*, volume II, 82, Merrick, 'Louis XV's deathbed apology', 212.

87 Croÿ, *Journal*, volume 3, 101.

88 Ormesson, *Journal*, volume 5, f 948.

89 Hardy, *Mes Loisirs*, f 333. When the king received extreme unction at Metz, the whole town of Metz 'hors la populace' were permitted to attend. Barbier, *Journal historique*, volume II, 405.

90 For an analysis of his sermons and wider role, see Hermann Weber, 'Das *Sacre* Ludwigs XVI vom 11 Juni 1775 und die Krise des Ancien Régime', in *Vom Ancien Régime zur französischen Revolution: Forschungen und Perspecktiven*, Erich Hinrichs, Erberhardt Schmidt and Rudolf Vierhaus (editors) (Göttingen, 1978), 539–65.

91 Croÿ, *Journal*, volume 3, 105.

92 Moreau, *Mes Souvenirs*, volume 1, 361.

93 Hardy, *Mes Loisirs…* , 10 mai 1774, f 334.

94 Croÿ, *Journal*, volume 3, 106.

95 Moreau, *Mes Souvenirs*, volume 1, 364.

96 'La mort saisit le vif'. See Richard Bonney, *L'Absolutisme* (Paris, 1989), 49. Ormesson, *Journal*, volume 5, f 952.

97 Philippe de Courcillon, marquis de Dangeau, *Mémoire sur la mort de Louis XIV* (Paris, 1858), 32.

98 Hardy, *Mes Loisirs*, f 337.

99 Campan, *Mémoires sur la vie privée de Marie-Antoinette*, volume 1, 78, though Louis XVI was the first adult to accede to the throne in 150 years.

100 Moreau, *Mes Souvenirs*, volume 1, 362. See also Joël Félix, *Louis XVI et Marie-Antoinette: un couple en politique* (Paris, 2006), 99.

101 Croÿ, *Journal*, volume 3, 115.

102 Ibid., 115.

103 Ormesson, *Journal*, volume 5, f 944.

104 Besenval, *Mémoires*, volume 2, 85. See Seth, *Les Rois aussi en mouraient*, 251; Durand Echeverria, *The Maupeou Revolution: A study in the history of libertarianism, France 1770–1774* (Baton Rouge, 1985), 31; see also Véri, *Journal*, 90.

105 See also Darmon, *La Variole, les nobles et les princes* and Seth, *Les Rois aussi en mouraient.*
106 Louis, dauphin de France (1661–1711). Son of Louis XIV, a prince who never became king.
107 *Pompe funèbre de Monseigneur le Dauphin, 1711*, AN O[1] 1043 (67).
108 Ibid.
109 Ibid.
110 Ibid. Simeon Prosper Hardy recorded that bran was also used in the burial of Louis XV to absorb fumes of decay. Hardy, *Mes Loisirs*, f 337.
111 *Pompe funèbre de Monseigneur le Dauphin, 1711.*
112 *Lettres expédiés à l'occasion de la mort de Mme Infant*, AN O[1] 1042 (133).
113 Ibid.
114 AN K 1717 no 10 (1). Jules Michelet, *Histoire de France au dix-huitième siècle 17. Louis XV et Louis XVI* (Paris, 1867), 11, gives a lurid account of this death, in which his disgust for the monarchy produces a repugnant description of the bodily decay produced by smallpox.
115 The 1760s debate on the location of graveyards reveals a contemporary dread of putrefaction, on which see McManners, *Death and the Enlightenment*, 310.
116 *Mémoire touchant la reception des corps des Roys Reines Princesses de la Maison Royale par les Religieux de l'abbaye royalle de St Denis en France*, AN K 1716 no 2 (7).
117 Rousset de Missey, *Supplément au Corps Universel de diplomatique de droit des gens* (Amsterdam/The Hague, 1739) 401.
118 See Ralph E. Giesey, *The Royal Funeral Ceremony in Renaissance France* (Geneva, 1960).
119 Jean Rousset de Missy, *Supplément au Corps Universel diplomatiqe du droit des gens, tome quatrième, Le Cérémonial diplomatique des cours de l'Europe ou Collection des actes, memoires et relations concernant les Dignitez, Titulaires, Honneurs & Prééminences; les Fonctions publiques des Souverains, leurs Sacres, Couronnemens, Mariages, Batêmes, & Enterrements; les Investitures des grands Fiefs; les Entrées publiques, Audiences, Fonctions, Immunitez & Franchises des Ambassadeurs & autres Ministres publics; leurs Disputes & Démêlez de Préséance; et en général tout ce qui a rapport au Cérémonial & à l'Étiquette. Recueilli en partie par Mr Du Mont. Mis en order et considérablement augmenté par Mr Rousset, membres des Académies des Sciences de St Petersbourg & de Berlin. Tome Premier* (Amsterdam/The Hague, 1739), 401.
120 *Pompe funèbre de Louis XIIII, mort à Versailles le premier septembre 1715, par Desgranges*, Bibliothèque Mazarine (BM), MS 2346.
121 'Maladie et Mort du Roi', *Mercure de France*, juin 1774, 222–24.
122 Ibid., 223.
123 'Rapport sur l'exhumation des corps royaux à Saint Denis en 1793 par dom

Germain Poirier', published as Annex I in Alain Boureau, *Le Simple corps du roi: l'impossible sacralité des souverains français – XVe–XVIIIe siècle* (Paris, 2000), 80.

124 Vanessa Harding, *The Dead and the Living in Paris and London, 1500–1670* (Cambridge, 2002), 196.

125 Marie de Medici died in 1642, one year before her son. Though she died abroad, as a sign of forgiveness, Louis XIII permitted her remains to be transported back to Saint Denis, where they arrived shortly before his death.

2

The funeral of Louis XV, July 1774

Introduction

The death of Louis XV ripped open the barely healed wounds of the Maupeou revolution. In 1771, the political landscape had abruptly changed with the replacement of the parlements and mass exile of their members. Opposition was vocal and public, included the highest nobles in the land, and had not disappeared by 1774. The funeral of Louis XV brought confrontation.

This chapter examines the political background to the funeral rites of Louis XV. It provides a discussion of the relationship between the princes of the blood and the parlement, essential to understanding the context of Louis XV's funeral, the main ceremony addressed here. With the subsequent chapter on the *lit de justice*, these chapters together provide a revised discussion of the place of ceremony in encounters between the king and the parlement as well as some new reflections on the 1774 recall of the *parlements* and their conduct down to the Revolution.

Though most historians have concluded their account of Louis XV's funeral with the removal of his body to Saint Denis on 12 May, this was not the last of his death rites. The term *sans cérémonies* applied only to the convoy and there followed several weeks during which services took place throughout the country and, more mundanely, the *Gazette de France* sold commemorative engravings of the dead king.[1] This led to the ritual of the catafalque, the ceremony at which all the elements of French customary constitution came together to pay their final respects to the dead king on 27 July 1774. From the time of his death in May, this ceremony was the object of negotiations and the stuff of daily rumour, its importance as the public enactment of the constitutional settlement obvious to all and a clear example of the vitality of ceremony in late eighteenth-century public life.[2] The ceremony itself raises questions about scales of publicity: it was conducted for a closed set of corporate groupings yet attracted much wider public attention, its audience expanded far beyond the élite figures within the Abbey walls, not only to those who stood outside on the day but also to those who had participated in rumour-spreading and speculation in the preceding weeks.

The catafalque ceremony was a hybrid of politico-religious and heraldic ritual set in a gorgeous decorative display honouring the rank of the deceased. It was also an occasion of physical enactment of the constitution by assembled corporations gathered around the body of the dead king. Like all funeral ceremonies, its ostensible object was the dead person but the true protagonists were the living.[3] Yet this event does not appear in the historiography of the recall of the parlement and is rarely mentioned in accounts of the first months of Louis XVI's reign. The ceremony dictated that the princes of the blood should 'salute', meaning bow to, the assembled representatives of the new parlement, an institution they regarded as an unconstitutional imposition, and which remained highly unpopular with a vocal section of the public.[4] The catafalque ceremony reveals the instrumentalisation of ritual by political actors. While the number of participants in this ceremony was tightly controlled by invitation, restricted to members of certain corporate bodies, curiosity and political passions generated a much wider network of interested persons,[5] subverting the idea of a sealed-off, élite representative culture since every move reverberated in wider public consciousness.

Thanks to the work of William Doyle and Julian Swann, new interpretations have placed the political conflicts of the early 1770s in a different light. The wholesale replacement of the parlement is no longer seen as a premeditated masterstroke of absolute authority but, rather, as an ad hoc reform made in response to a political situation spinning out of control.[6] The implications for 1774 have not been fully realised.[7] If the ministry is understood as having been surprised into reform, the ultimate reversal of that change must take on a different aspect. It is no longer the abandonment of a carefully calibrated advance in governance but the remedy for a persistent canker in the body politic. None of the studies of the parlements over several turbulent decades has said anything about the role of ceremony. Given the importance of ceremonial form, specifically but not exclusively the *lit de justice*, in every one of the clashes between monarch and parlement, this is a significant omission and one which this and the subsequent chapter will seek to address, looking at the crucial role of ceremony in the politically tense years of exile and eventual recall. To set the scene for our discussion of 1774, we will first examine the complex relationship between the princes of the blood and the parlement, a cornerstone of the complicated power dynamic at work between the magistrates and the crown.

The princes of the blood and the parlement of Paris

In the simplest terms, and most concretely, the princes of the blood were male members of the ruling dynasty who were apt to inherit the throne.[8] In the history of the French monarchy, peerage long enjoyed higher esteem. The rise of the importance of royal blood may in part be attributed to the massive contraction of the royal gene pool in the mid-1500s and a concomitant emphasis on the dynastic element of kingship.[9] Henri III's 1576 Ordonnance of Blois enshrined the status of prince of the blood, explicitly elevating the status of blood over peerage, no matter how venerable. In doing so, he lent royal approval to the accession of Henri of Navarre in spite of his Protestantism and distant cousinage to the king, and set him above such mighty and ambitious Catholic peers as the Guise. Though Henri IV did of course *eventually* convert in 1593, in this moment in 1576 dynastic trumped all other concerns including religious. For Guy Rowlands, this is a key moment in the evolution of France as a dynastic state.[10] In ceremonial terms, the consolidation of the princes' primacy shifted the meaning of royal rituals which became enactments of this dynastic understanding.[11] In Chapter 1, we have seen ritualistic dynastic behaviour around the deathbed of Louis XV in the princes' vigil and in the passing of power to Louis XVI. It is also discernable on more formal ceremonial occasions, such as funerals, when the princes take the role of chief mourners. Through their participation, the princes confirmed and performed a mystic, but fundamentally secular, primacy of Bourbon blood, incarnated in the person of the king and reflected in the dignities enjoyed by them.[12]

The Bourbon princes of the blood, and in many ways the prince of the blood is most prominently a Bourbon institution,[13] reckoned their descent through the male line from either Charles de Bourbon (grandfather of both Henri IV and Louis, prince de Condé) or Louis XIII (father of Louis XIV and Philippe d'Orléans). With each succeeding generation, their direct blood link to the throne was diluted and it was possible for their rank to diminish as new generations were born in the direct line. By the 1770s, due to the fecundity of the dauphin Louis-Ferdinand's marriage to Marie-Josèphe de Saxe, which produced three adult males in the direct line all seeming likely to produce heirs of their own, the princes of the blood were more distant from the throne than at any previous juncture in the Bourbon monarchy.

This distance was not only abstract. In his *Mémoires*, Louis XIV instructed the dauphin that 'the sons of France … for the good of the state, should never have any other retreat but the court'.[14] While this is usually read as a statement of intent about the nobility as a whole, what is actually articulated here is an aspiration in relation to the princes of the royal blood. Louis XIV's advice to his successors was to ensure that these royals remained physically close to the king by requiring them to be resident at court. Louis XV's small number of surviving relatives were easily accommodated when the court was re-established at Versailles in 1722, with the regent, as heir presumptive, allocated the apartment formerly associated with the dauphin.[15] As the century wore on, the relationship between blood and physical space grew ever more complex. Due to the demands of rank, procreation, long life and restricted space, as the king's family increased in number and the princes' own families expanded, there were several generations of royals requiring accommodation and the princes of the blood eventually found themselves ousted from the prestigious garden-facing apartments on the lower floors of the *Aile des Princes* in Versailles in favour of Louis XV's numerous children and grandchildren who all required sufficiently splendid accommodation. This became particularly problematic in the early 1770s as each of his three grandsons set up separate married households.

Just as the contraction of the royal gene pool in the mid-1500s prompted the promotion of consanguinity, the expansion of the direct line in the late 1700s implied the demotion of the existing princes of the blood. As the direct line continued to expand, the house of Orléans was set to lose its first prince of the blood status. When Louis Philippe I d'Orléans died in 1785, his right to retain the title and associated privileges during his lifetime lapsed. As had occurred a century earlier on the death of the Grand Condé,[16] the king (this time, Louis XVI) pronounced upon the matter and, again, it was decided that the title of first prince of the blood was not sufficiently lofty for a son of France and that the succeeding duc d'Orléans, best known to history as Philippe Égalité, should hold the title until the comte d'Artois' son, the duc d'Angoulême, in turn produced a son to whom it would be given.[17] The family realities of Louis

XVI prompted the revival of old titles last used for Philippe d'Orléans (1640–1701), the only brother of Louis XIV, and the incorporation of new gradations of distinction into ceremonies for the brothers of the king (*frères du roi*). The rule of primacy of blood held true: the closer to the king, the greater the distinction. Blood ties were emphasised in order to garner higher status. Louis XVI's nephews were styled sons of France (*fils de France*). The blood tie was not only an end in itself: practically, it brought wealth and honours; politicially, the treasured benefit of access to the monarch, and potential for influence, was the key attraction for the princes of the blood. This is why exile from the court really was a punishment, as Jacques Mathieu Augeard pointed out to the duc d'Orléans in May 1771: 'I beg you to pay attention to your position: you are exiled, and a prince of the blood who is no longer at the court has no credit for his person or for those of his house.'[18]

The princes of the blood were an integral part of the monarchy's self-conception, in theoretical and ceremonial terms. They were also central actors in the story of king and parlement in the years 1771–74. They were hereditary members of the parlement, sitting in it as members of the Court of Peers (*cour des pairs*) as well as at *lits de justice*. Writings on the constitutional importance of their role appeared periodically during the eighteenth century, most notably in the 1750s.[19] Throughout the 1750s and 1760s, the parlement repeatedly used invitations to the princes and peers to sit as the *cour des pairs* as one of their procedural weapons in times of conflict with the crown, usually coming after numerous deputations to the king, representations and remonstrances.[20] The princes' unique ties to the king were occasionally successfully exploited by the crown to turn an invitation from the parlement into an occasion to demonstrate publicly their approval of royal policy. In January 1760, for example, the princes consulted the king on receipt of an invitation from the parlement. Discussions resulted in the duc d'Orléans leading the princes to meet with the king and endorse royal policy, a clear victory for the crown.[21] Crown and parlement effectively competed to harness their political weight. Tactical decisions on managing these links were largely in the hands of ministers, and when they were not well managed – as in 1770–71 – the personal result was estrangement and the political impact devastating.

The princes' involvement in the travails of the parlement began the moment they were denied the right of assembly as the Court of Peers in June 1770. Their unique connections with the king and the parlement allowed both the duc d'Orléans and the prince de Condé to conduct behind the scenes negotiations in an attempt to break the stand-off between ministry and parlement in the winter of 1770–71. Following the expulsion from the ministry and exile of the duc de Choiseul on Christmas Eve 1770,[22] an attempt was made to stage-manage an agreed outcome at the beginning of January 1771.[23] There are several different interpretations of the motivations of those involved, though it is clear that the prince de Condé played a key role. While *lettres de jussion* of 4 January ordered the parlement to return to work, it was understood that the edict of discipline would effectively be suspended by the crown, neither withdrawn nor put forward for registration. Thus, both sides saved face. On 7 January 1771, work did indeed resume and judgement was rendered in the case of Condé's mistress, Madame de Monaco.[24] This was the last case involving a prince of the blood heard by the parlement. Condé's equivocal role in seeking a middle path,[25] and the clear element of personal interest, tainted his reputation. The session was pointedly nicknamed the *Parlement Monaco*.[26]

The members of the parlement did not demonstrate the restraint implicit in an agreement to let matters lie as, at the Monaco session, they adopted a new *arrêté* that, while it announced their intention to return to work, reiterated their complaints about the edict. Efforts for peace consequently failed. The allusion to the edict prompted a royal reaction: the government reasserted that the king would not abandon the edict. When the parlementaires voted on 15 January to continue their strike, it seems Maupeou's need to produce a compliant parlement, whether to ensure the goodwill of the king or of du Barry and d'Aiguillon, robbed him of the political judgement to secure an agreeable one. The shocking tactic of magistrates being questioned at home by armed musketeers on the night of 19–20 January 1771 was the tipping point: where fifty-eight magistrates to fifty-three had previously voted to resume judicial service, now all voted to continue the strike. *Lettres de cachet* were issued, not only sending the parlementaires into individual exile but also, scandalously, confiscating their offices to the profit of the king.[27] The princes continued to plead the parlement's case with the king. They publicly declared their allegiance to the exiled parlementaires in the *Protestation des Princes du Sang* which they signed and officially lodged with the civil clerk of the *parlement*, Sieur Étienne Ysabeau, on 12 April 1771.[28] Sieur Ysabeau was requested to inform all officers of the court, including those sitting in the place of the exiles, of the content of the document. On 15 April, having failed to attend the new parlement's first meeting, they received letters forbidding them to enter the king's presence until new orders were forthcoming. The wedding of the king's second grandson, the comte de Provence, took place in May 1771 with only the comte de la Marche, the prince de Conti's son, in attendance.[29] De la Marche never evinced political differences from the monarch, allegedly remarking 'when one cannot mobilise 100,000 men, it is better not to resist the will of the king'.[30] The protesting princes were gradually attracted back to the court. The prince de Conti alone remained aloof, having been on bad terms with the king since the conclusion of the Austrian alliance in 1756 severely undermined his political aspirations.

The Condés returned to court first, at the beginning of December 1772. This was perhaps in response to the overtures of the comte de la Marche, apparently in league with Chancellor Maupeou, though other rumours suggested that the duc d'Aiguillon, seeking to undermine the chancellor, encouraged their return.[31] The spectre of self-interest, or perhaps enticement, again was associated with Condé's position, given his son's induction into a high chivalric order soon after their return. Equally, the prince may simply have tired of the long-running dispute with the king. He wrote to him on 6 December 1772:

> we desire to return to your good graces, Sire, even more ardently because we are unhappy that our distance from the Court could be used as a pretext for even the slightest disturbance in your kingdom. The maintenance of your authority is essential, love for your person is deeply written on our hearts.[32]

Condé requested the other princes to sign his letter, as they had all signed the joint Protest of 1771, and to accompany him to court. They did not. His prompt return to favour – received by the king the day after his letter was delivered by the comte de la Marche[33] – probably encouraged the Orléans to try a similar path. On the evening of his return to court on 7 December, Condé hosted the duc d'Orléans to supper; Orléans and Chartres returned to court soon after, on 29 December.[34] The Orléans' unrepentant stance, reiterating their original protest while seeking to receive grace, was seen as audacious.[35] Given their close contacts with the exiled magistrates, they were at pains to make clear their return did not mean a change in their opinion, not least by publishing explanations of their movements. They did not, having returned to the court, have any dealings with the new parlement and, significantly for their public image, it was said that they had returned to court to better negotiate the return of the old parlement.[36] This approximate kind of dynastic unity was crowned on New Years' Day 1773 by the induction of Condé's son, the 16-year-old duc de Bourbon, into the Order of Saint Michel, a stepping-stone to the illustrious Order of the Holy Spirit. The dauphin and his brother, Provence, who were close to him in age, acted as his sponsors to the king's great joy.[37]

The death of Louis XV called into question this uneasy settlement reached at the end of 1772. The face-saving modus vivendi was thrown into crisis. The Orléans and the Condés had been allowed to return to court on the understanding that they would not have to attend the new parlement. What they called their 'submission' entailed no public act or statement implying that they accepted the institution. Louis XV did not seek to force them to do such a thing. His death meant that Louis XVI might have to.

Preparations for the funeral of Louis XV

The *menus plaisirs de la chambre du Roi* was the department of the king's household that oversaw arrangements for everything from royal funerals to operas to carnival balls.[38] The king's four first gentlemen of the bedchamber had ultimate responsibility for the running of the department, dividing this duty between them with one taking main responsibility each year. In 1774, it was the duc d'Aumont's turn.[39] They were assisted by the *intendant des menus plaisirs.* From 1762 this was Denis Papillon de La Ferté, who kept a frank journal of his business as a reference for himself, and potentially others, calling it a 'preservative against the Bastille'.[40]

Once Louis XV died, the *dessinateur des cabinets du roi*, Charles Michel-Ange Challe, was instructed to begin work on sketches for a temporary funerary monument, known in 1770s France as the catafalque.[41] This large but ephemeral artefact, rather less well known than the effigy, was used in élite French funerals from about 1685. The last king's funeral which used an effigy was that of Henri IV and the first one with a catafalque was that of Louis XIV. The traditional services in commemoration of the deaths of foreign monarchs were performed throughout the eighteenth century around a catafalque. This was a well-practised element in the ritual vocabulary of the king's servants, though each one was different and designed for the occasion. Challe had designed several important catafalques in the preceding ten years – those of the queen Maria Leszczynska, her father Stanislaus Leszdzynski, the dauphine Marie-Josèphe de Saxe, Louis XV's son-in-law Philip, duc of Parma, Elisabeth Farnese, queen of Spain, and Charles Emmanuel

III, king of Sardinia – and he has been praised for developing the art by introducing classical elements and giving these monuments a more architectural aesthetic.[42] The economically-minded intendant resolved that materials which had been used in the several catafalque ceremonies conducted in recent years should be reused as much as possible.[43] This did not mean that Louis XV's catafalque merely reproduced what had gone before, and we shall see below the grandiose scale of that ceremony thanks to a little-known account of the décor.[44] By 23 May, Papillon de La Ferté had the new king's handwritten comments on his memorandum about the funeral, with plans drawn up for ceremonies at Saint Denis and in Paris. The king decided that the décor at both sites should be of the same standard as that for Louis XIV.[45]

As practical preparations proceeded, thoughts turned to the political implications of the ritual. Both the parlement and the princes of the blood had ceremonial roles to play at the solemn funeral service for Louis XV. The ceremony was contentious because the princes of the blood were required to bow to the parlementaires in the course of the service. The prospect of this encounter prompted a flurry of speculation and political horse-trading in May, June and July 1774. The exiled parlement had not been forgotten and it was believed that this potential confrontation would be a moment of truth when the new king would have to declare himself in favour of old or new.[46] This was a tense moment in the early days of Louis XVI's reign, analysis of which adds much to our understanding of the recall of the parlement and its conduct in the 1770s and 1780s.[47]

From his exile on his estates at Orly, Louis II François de Paule Lefèvre d'Ormesson de Noiseau, a senior figure in the old parlement given his status as *président à mortier*, kept a detailed record of everything he heard about both the king's death and the negotiations surrounding the funeral ceremonies. Scion of a great parlementaire dynasty, a magistrate of thirty years standing, d'Ormesson was 'one of the most distinguished judges of the court', known for his impartiality.[48] He avidly followed the activities of the princes of the blood who had sided with the parlement at the time of the Maupeou Coup, in part through his direct contacts with members of the duc d'Orléans' household.

The king's death had immediate ritual impact on Ormesson as, in a compelling conjunction of death rites and constitutional status, he felt that it was important for his household to take mourning to demonstrate his continued position as a parlementaire.[49] The adoption of mourning personally and for one's household was a well-observed social convention. The topic was debated with his colleagues who were all convinced that taking mourning was an important act with social meaning and not merely a cosmetic exercise in etiquette. The question was complicated by the fact that all the members of the old parlement had come under pressure to liquidate their offices, that is, to accept reimbursement of the capital sum that made them owners of their offices. The liquidation question was fiercely debated during the parlement's exile, including in pamphlet form. A letter from Ormesson to the king was among this mass of printing.[50] Rather typically, the exiled magistrates debated the terms: either the offices had been confiscated to the king and therefore could not be resigned by their former holders; or liquidation could be understood as the abolition of venality not of offices, an alteration of fiscal arrangements with no other consequences for the office-holder.[51] The financial aspect was not forgotten by pamphleteers who sarcastically wondered how the chancellor had performed the magical act of endowing the treasury with sufficient funds to reimburse offices at 10,000 livres a head.[52] While the chancellor repeatedly extended the deadline by which the exiles were to submit or lose their capital, ultimately it was clear that liquidation should be resisted as a further humiliation maliciously intended to serve as a form of forced resignation. Force was the key word: the chancellor stood accused of extorting liquidations in return for granting reasonable requests for variations in exile orders. One Monsieur de Bretiginères died in exile on 22 April 1772 rather than liquidate, his request to travel to Paris for healthcare having been denied.[53] All this created special sensitivities in the discussion on mourning for Louis XV. D'Ormesson was among those who had taken a middle path regarding liquidation.[54] He stubbornly maintained, however, that his office had not altered and would not agree with some who argued that they should all take the same level of partial mourning. He concluded that not to take full mourning would constitute public acceptance that his status as a member of the parlement had changed. He resolved to take mourning as a ritual signal of his continued status. If this was unfavourably received at Court, 'for the last three and a half years we have not been able to please the Court. It demands our recognition of being stripped of our offices and this would indirectly do so'.[55]

As early as 12 May, two days after the king's death, another exiled magistrate, Clément de Barville, drafted and circulated to the princes of the blood a letter on the parlement question. However, the princes were not ready to proceed. They and the king's ministers were barred from his presence due to quarantine restrictions.[56] Work had already begun in the duc d'Orléans' household on a memorandum for the new king.[57] On 21 May, ten days after the king's death, d'Ormesson received intelligence that the duc d'Orléans would definitely attend the catafalque ceremony to properly pay his respects to the king, but would certainly not bow to the assembled members of the new parlement. His informant, Belleisle, a senior member of the duc d'Orléans' household who had been working on the document for the king, put this in the context of the king not summoning a *lit de justice* to inaugurate his reign with the subtext that, since the ultimate ceremonial showdown was to be avoided, the princes would show willing for the funeral. The political and ceremonial were inextricably linked. The grand master of ceremonies would, as usual, indicate to the princes to whom they should bow and when. When the parlement was named, the duc would remain standing straight and slowly turn towards the next intended recipients of his bow, the *chambre des comptes*. Belleisle warned Ormesson that it would be impossible to dissuade the king from receiving a deputation from the new parlement in the early days of his reign, and foolish to attempt it. Louis XVI was well aware of the faults of the new parlement, had no respect for them, but was wary of lobbying against them. Persuading him to recall the old parlement would be 'a long-term project'.[58] Other commentators agreed that the young king distrusted the new parlement but added that he feared the old.[59]

A deputation from the Maupeou parlement, reduced in numbers at the king's request from forty-two to thirteen, made the customary visit to congratulate the king on his accession to the throne on 5 June.[60] Their reception by the royal couple was thoroughly parsed: despite the best efforts of commentators there was little remarkable in the brief, anodyne responses made by the king and queen. What really seemed to be an indicator of their status was the king's lack of response to their formal petition that he visit the parlement at Paris and show himself to his people. This had been publicly requested by the Maupeou parlement shortly after the death of Louis XV in mid May.[61] By not summoning a *lit de justice* to inaugurate his reign, though the reigns of his three predecessors had been endorsed in their earliest days at the Palais de Justice, Louis XVI not only avoided close association with the Maupeou parlement but also spared the princes of the blood, and himself, a confrontation over their attendance. Ceremony served politics. The new parlement was being kept at arm's length, though for what reason remained unclear. The funeral was set to be a crucial moment in the political battle that had been raging since 1771.

At the beginning of June, the uncensored *Gazette de Leyde* sounded a note of caution regarding the exuberance of the rumour mill:

> those who mistake their desires for reality, have already spread many rumours on this subject: but the example of the new king's conduct, the prudence of which rejects all haste, renders these rumours very doubtful in the eyes of the less credulous … nothing is yet decided, for or against.[62]

By mid June, the usual six weeks between death and burial of a king had almost expired yet the date of the ceremony was still uncertain.[63] It was bruited as 27 July, or the first days of August, with d'Ormesson recording that this was so that the dead king's grandsons, Provence and Artois, could recover from their inoculation against smallpox and be present. A memorial service for Louis XV in Rouen, where the parlement had also been exiled, witnessed the nobility snubbing the members of the new regional parlement.[64] At the same time, as the threat of being summoned to a *lit de justice* had receded, the senior princes of the blood changed their position on attendance at the funeral ceremony. It now seemed to Ormesson that neither the Orléans nor Condé princes would attend, leaving only the comte de la Marche, the prince who had not protested. There was a tempting rumour, which came to nothing, that the catafalque ceremony might be abandoned altogether on the basis that Louis XV had left a will requesting to be buried *sans cérémonies*.[65] Given that even the deaths of foreign monarchs were marked in France with a catafalque ceremony, this would have been an extraordinary step and, as noted in Chapter 1, *sans cérémonies* had a special meaning in relation to royal funerals.

At the same time, and inextricably bound up with discussion of the funeral, the duc d'Orléans was presenting the young king with a series of memoranda on the subject of the return of the old parlement. While it is reasonable to assume that Orléans and his household would seek to influence the young king on the question to which they had devoted so much energy, the quite unexpected advent of Maurepas at the heart of power may have encouraged them since, as Joel Félix has suggested, Maurepas' own long disgrace and exile may have predisposed him to sympathise with their position.[66] Orléans asked that the king not pass the text to Chancellor Maupeou and received a promise that it would be examined by someone in whom he had confidence. By 15 June Maurepas had already had several working meetings with Orléans' adviser Belleisle on the matter. Though he felt this augured well, Ormesson, perhaps thinking of Maurepas' reputation for frivolity and seemingly unaware that he might favour the cause, feared it was a delaying tactic that the king 'simply asked M de Maurepas to examine the memorandum to delay any discussion on it'.[67]

At the end of June, associates of the Palais Royal were in a fever of expectation of the prompt recall of the old parlement. Conversations between the king and the duc d'Orléans were scrutinised: a jest over a game of billiards seemed to mean that the king would soon recall the parlement. By 26 June, it was noticed that, although the traditional forty days, or approximately six weeks, had passed, there was no public discussion of arrangements for the funeral at Saint Denis.[68] This was attributed to the difficult situation vis-à-vis the princes of the blood, the duc d'Orléans in particular.[69] On 29 June, the rumours were at fever pitch, producing the enticing perspective that to avoid problems with the princes, none of the law courts would be invited to the ceremony. This raised the prospect of a ceremony stripped of its corporate element, rendering it a household event, truly a revolution in royal funeral ritual.

Inevitably, such heightened expectations were disappointed and no such revolution occurred. By the beginning of July, the unity of Orléans and Condé seemed no longer assured,[70] and the pressure on their political stance increased as the ceremony drew nearer. On Friday 8 July, thanks to his inside sources, Ormesson heard that the catafalque would go ahead on 27 July with the new parlement. The interested public knew only two things with any certainty: that Orléans had presented a memorandum to the king; and that it had been passed to Maurepas.[71] Signs and portents waxed important: it was recalled that the birth of the young king had taken place shortly before the recall of the parlement from the exile of 1754. A commemorative engraving from that time was about to be reprinted.[72] On the same day, Parisian bookseller Hardy copied into his journal a pro-parlement verse that was circulating in Paris:

> Young Louis, your reign barely begun,
> You are called Titus, and Henry the Fourth
> Return what your grandfather took
> I'll not hesitate to call you God.[73]

At this point, Chancellor Maupeou's supporters, invoking respect for the dead king, recalled that he had said he would never see the old parlement again and it would be unseemly to flout him directly by arranging their presence at his funeral.[74] The *Journal historique* reported that, on the same day, the duc d'Orléans had taken a copy of a 1754 engraving, which celebrated both the return of the parlement and the royal birth, to

Marly to show the king.[75] Clearly the fate of the old parlement was not yet decided.

In mid July, efforts were in train to cool temperatures. Police spies were spreading the word in cafés that it was forbidden to speak of either the old or new parlement.[76] By 15 July, it was clear to d'Ormesson that the Palais Royal was working to disperse the rumours of immediate return with the aim of calming the Maupeou party and softening any reaction. The duc d'Orléans spent some days at Saint-Cloud cultivating an air of leisure. Maurepas was at his country retreat. This was part of a planned subterfuge that seemed successful. Public speculation diminished and the *Journal historique* observed 'nothing new on the parlement'. Low-key negotiations continued.

In line with this new approach, d'Ormesson was told on 16 July that Orléans would claim an attack of gout in order to avoid attending the catafalque with the new parlement and thereby avoid directly flouting the king by refusing to attend. Orléans had used this stratagem to absent himself from the memorial ceremonies held for Charles Emmanuel III, king of Sardinia, in 1773, where the prince de Condé had participated.[77] Orléans' 'attack' was well-publicised. On 22 July, the *Gazette de Leyde* mentioned his 'several attacks of gout which will perhaps prevent him from going to this Ceremony'.[78] While Hardy heard on 18 July that the whole ceremony had been postponed until September,[79] d'Ormesson was reasonably sure that the catafalque would go ahead on 27 July, though no one was sure what would happen there.[80] When the marquis de Dreux, the grand master of ceremonies, went to Marly to receive the king's orders for the ceremony, it was widely noted.[81] The tantalising rumour circulated that the king had written a letter excusing the new parlement from attending the catafalque, which the chancellor was delaying delivering.[82] Eye-witnesses reported (mistakenly) that the preparations inside Saint Denis did not include any seating for the Maupeou parlement.[83] This trend was not long-lived as, on 18 July, it was decisively known that the chancellor had announced 'avec joie' to the new parlement that they would shortly receive an invitation.[84] Meanwhile, the affair was so present in popular consciousness that people were telling jokes about it: the duc d'Orléans, having agreed to attend the ceremony, was asked by the king about his bow to the parlement. 'Sire!' Orléans replied, 'of course, but I only bow in church.'[85]

D'Ormesson was rattled by the news of 22 July that Orléans and Chartres, having refused in writing to attend the catafalque, had been ordered to stay away from the court. Though he was calmed by the idea that this may have been part of a plan ('there is something mysterious, perhaps organised about this development'), his raw nerves were jangled by the insistent briefing from Maupeou supporters that the young king was punishing the princes who dared to defy his authority and uphold the new parlement.[86] D'Ormesson broke the terms of his exile by risking a trip to Paris later that day and heard, from Augeard among others, of disputes within the royal family and of a series of attempts during July to devise an acceptable form for the princes' attendance.

Earlier in the month it had been decided to postpone the catafalque until 13 August, implying the recall of the old parlement.[87] The king's aunts had exerted pressure for the ceremony to take place sooner and insisted that the king's burial needed to be witnessed by the parlement, he must be buried like his ancestors.[88] This point was ceded, with the innovation that the Offertory would be suppressed so that the princes of the blood could avoid having to bow to the parlement. The clergy refused to countenance a mass without an Offertory. This series of attempts to accommodate the princes having failed, the duc d'Orléans then again came under pressure to attend the unaltered ceremony. He was given plenty of time to consider. The king's strong wish for his presence was made known to him several times directly by Louis XVI and by Maurepas.[89] Warned in advance by Grand Master of Ceremonies Dreux that he was coming to invite him formally to the ceremony, Orléans had time to prepare a reply in writing. It was delivered by Belleisle to Maurepas, the very pair who had been working so closely on the pro-parlement memoranda. The letter contained an agreement to attend the ceremony allied to a refusal to bow to the parlement.[90] The king's anger was diverted by Maurepas who convinced him to express it by forbidding the Orléans' his presence until further notice, thus avoiding exile and with the additional benefit of excusing the Orléans from attendance at the second catafalque ceremony in Paris in September.[91] This order seemed rather shocking and was unexpected even to well-informed observers. D'Ormesson, as we have seen, was discomfited. The English ambassador, Stormont, scrawled an urgent note to London. His subsequent letter attests to his incredulity at what he perceived to be inconsistency, since the appointment of Turgot around the same time had led him to believe the way was smooth for the return of the old parlement. This is to reckon without the problem of the ceremony and, perhaps, without a personal blunder by Orléans who upset the king by appearing to reverse previous assurances about his attendance.[92] The comte d'Artois's attempts to align himself with the Orléans' posture were firmly squashed by the king.[93] On

25 July, Ormesson's visitors spoke calmly about the ban not interfering in the least with future plans for the return of the old parlement. Moreau later commented, 'no exile ever had a lesser appearance of disgrace than that of the duc d'Orléans'.[94] If this was exile without disgrace, it was clearly motivated by the king's wish to prioritise the funeral ceremony rather than by disagreement over the parlement.

Negotiations over the princes' involvement in the funeral ceremony of Louis XV were fevered but seemed, at the end of July, fruitless for the Orléans and their allies. The new parlement should have emerged as a winner: having secured its place at the first public ceremony of the new reign its position should have been consolidated. Yet, the absence of Orléans and Chartres, for publicly known reasons, and the light sentence imposed on them by their young king undermined this seeming triumph just as effectively as the mockery of some of the participants in the ceremony. The outright winner of this political battle may have been the new monarch. The young king ensured that his grandfather received the appropriate ceremonial honours without being forced to decide on the knotty parlementary quarrel with ministers he did not plan to retain.[95] The ceremony was given priority, the Orléans allowed to maintain their dignity and the question of the parlement postponed at the king's pleasure. Louis XV was buried, fittingly and with dignity, by the constitutional order he had created.

The funeral: invitation to the parlement and the catafalque at Saint Denis

The ceremonies for the solemn funeral service of Louis XV began on 23 July with the ritual invitation to the parlement, known as *sémonces*. This ceremony was conducted as usual, preserving all traditions and customs just as though there had been no change in parlement.[96] Like many other ceremonies in the Palais, it was held in public and watched by an audience of interested people.[97]

That Saturday morning, at the end of the usual session, the *gens du roi* announced that the *aide des cérémonies*, the most junior member of the grand master's staff, was waiting to address the court. Preceded by eight hooded heralds at arms, marching two by two, and a king-at-arms with his baton of office, the sieur Watronville[98] – holding his own baton of office and with his sword belted at his side – entered the chamber clothed in a long mourning robe with a train and a furred hat.[99] He was followed by twenty-four sworn criers, also dressed in black, with the arms of France and Navarre embroidered on their garments, carrying bells in their hands. The heraldic officers bowed to the assembly and Watronville took his place to read aloud the letter of invitation to the funeral.

The letter commanded the attendance of the parlement at the ceremonies in Saint Denis and at Notre Dame de Paris, wearing their traditional red robes. It had been signed and dated on 1 July, a sure indication that ongoing negotiations had delayed its delivery, and, since it made no mention of a date for the ceremony, Watronville was obliged to add that it would be held at Saint Denis on 27 July, at eleven in the morning. The *premier président* responded that the king's orders would be obeyed. At this, the king-at-arms called out to the criers to execute their task. They rang their bells twice. One of them advanced to the entrance to the parquet and called on those present to pray for the repose of Louis XV's soul. Another peal of bells, another shouted injunction from the king-at-arms, and the crier continued, declaiming the king's qualities, his date and place of death and the arrangements for the service. The procession then left the floor of the parlement. One of the parlementaires carried the message to colleagues in other courts.

The heraldic ceremony proceeded smoothly, yet in the background an incident had occurred which made this public ceremony a focus for the expression of anger against the new parlement. Hostility, and even violence, towards the new parlement was not novel. Maupeou's interim parlement, meeting from 24 January 1771, found it could not function without armed protection – the moment this slackened the court was invaded by clerks and others who shouted at, insulted and even laid hands on the new officers.[100] Though the new parlement fulfilled its functions, with famous advocates such as Linguet pleading before it – and, as we have seen, could attract crowds of the curious – the new institution functioned in an atmosphere of disrespect.[101] Court clerks were heard to whisper behind the Maupeou parlementaires' backs 'that robe does not belong to Monsieur X'.[102] A felon facing a death sentence, by custom asked if he would pardon his judges, responded that he could not complain since he had been judged by his peers. The Maupeou magistrates were alleged, in their ignorance, to condemn the innocent and let murderers walk free, with the punchline that since one should have been punished and one freed, it was all equal, except to the man who had been broken on the wheel.[103] Physical threats were not unusual. Walking in the Palais-Royal in 1774, a member of Maupeou's parlement was approached by a stranger who shook his fist in his face, saying 'You bastard, you'll be dismissed along with all those other idiots.'[104]

Public attendance at the ceremonies of the parlement was normal.[105] To mark the inauguration of the Maupeou parlement proper, which took place under armed guard in April 1771,[106] refreshments were set out for invited guests. No one came: the occasion was celebrated by an anonymous crowd of ne'er-do-wells mustered from street-corners.[107] In July 1774, many went to the parlement to see the *sémonces*, taking their chance to witness the latest act in the drama leading up to the catafalque ceremony.[108] Among them was a young man called Micault, nicknamed the daring young man (*le jeune homme téméraire*) by several chroniclers, who found himself ejected from his seat in one of the screened stalls known as *lanternes*. He initially ceded his place but when he learned that he had been humiliated by officers of the new parlement, he returned and angrily confronted them. Antoine Jean Jacques Désirat,[109] councillor of the *chambre des enquêtes*, though also a mere spectator at the ceremony, had evicted Micault from his seat by claiming precedence. When Micault returned to challenge him, Désirat called the ushers to arrest the young man. Since the court was already in session, a hearing was held once the invitation ceremony was over. The sole evidence was a statement by Désirat. Micault was tried, sentenced, fined three livres, cautioned and allowed to go, all within three hours of his alleged offence. The crowd had remained to hear this brief trial and Micault was escorted from the Palais de Justice by a sympathetic company.

The incident was known all over Paris by the evening. The prompt arrest and conviction of Micault was taken as yet another example of the despotism of the new parlement. Popular opinion was firmly on Micault's side, particularly when it was alleged that his belongings had been searched for incriminating documents. Désirat was ridiculed in scenes reminiscent of the charivari folk rituals inflicted on those who failed to observe their proper station in life. Walking in the Tuileries gardens in the following days, he found himself surrounded by a hostile crowd who sneered at his insistence on his rank, shouting 'Salut, honneur à M Désirat!' and making elaborate mocking bows, even kow-towing to him, until he fled the gardens – or was escorted from them by the Swiss guards and locked out, according to Hardy. Above all, these events demonstrate the disdain a good portion of the populace felt for the members of the new parlement, as Hardy observed at the time.[110] This was an inauspicious start to the funeral ceremonies for the members of the Maupeou parlement.

The catafalque ceremony on 27 July was celebrated 'with great pomp', lasting around five hours, and with the assembled ranks of clergy, parlement, *chambre des comptes*, *cour des monnaies*, representatives from the Châtelet and from the university and municipal officers, all attending on foot of formal invitations.[111] At eight o'clock in the morning, a group of fifty-nine members of the Maupeou parlement, comprising presidents and councillors from the *grand'chambre* and the *enquêtes* as well as the *gens du roi* and ushers, assembled at the Palais de Justice.[112] They processed solemnly in their red robes to their carriages, the ushers rapping their staffs of office on the floor as they went, and took their places in order of rank and seniority. Three coaches-and-six belonging to the *premier président* led the way in a procession of carriages closed by two brigades of mounted police whose presence was, effectively, decorative since the roads were kept clear for the parlementaires' passage by other detachments. On arriving at Saint Denis, they saw that the exterior of the building, from the towers down, was draped in black cloth and hung with black velvet banners bearing the king's arms and monogram.[113] A false entrance had been constructed over the main door: several angels leaned in attitudes denoting grief on a shield with the crowned arms of France and Navarre. They were covered by a black-veined grey marble arch, which in turn supported a lapis lazuli funerary urn surrounded by white marble figures holding branches and garlands. Similar false façades in matching grey marble had been created around the lateral doors, surmounted by funerary urns. These doors were decorated with azure scrolls on which golden lettering spelled the late king's initials. The parlementaires were conducted into the chapterhouse for a breakfast prepared by the royal kitchens and were joined by the duc de Brissac, governor of Paris, who was dressed in a long, hooded mourning cloak and wore the chain of the Order of the Holy Spirit. There they waited until midday when the chief mourners arrived. It was time for the parlementaires to take their places in the choir of the Abbey.

The Abbey was plunged into gloom by extensive black draperies covering all the windows. Painted in naturalistic colours, around the nave stood life-sized figures of young men, representing angels, bearing scrolls of the king's arms and initials. Four hundred paupers dressed in grey and holding flaming torches lined the walls of the nave,[114] and the parlementaires proceeded along the aisle between two rows of sworn criers who rang their bells as they passed through. Dividing the body of the church from the sanctuary and choir, a pyramid of red porphyry had been erected with columns at each corner bearing bronze funerary lamps. Inscribed on the pyramid in gold were the words 'a day of distress and anguish, a day of trouble and ruin, a day of darkness and gloom, a day of clouds and blackness'.[115] Above this inscription loomed the white marble figure of death, shrouded and proffering a clock to symbolise the rapid passage of time. At his feet lay his scythe with items symbolic of earthly grandeur.

Through the grey granite base of this pyramid, the parlementaires reached the sanctuary of the church. The royal tombs had been draped in black and the rest of the space transformed by temporary architecture in the classical style. The stalls were undecorated and now formed the foundation for a row of blue marble Iconic pilasters on a background of black-veined grey marble which enclosed the choir, rood loft and sanctuary. Each pilaster was a marvel of *trompe l'oeil* painting with the blue marble standing on a plinth of amethyst, decorated with garlands, lances and military 'spoils' in gold in commemoration of the dead monarch's triumphs in the field. They were topped with more blue stonework bearing further copies of the king's monogram and arms on a black background surrounded by ermine. The spaces above the aisles were also decorated in this manner. Mirroring the double semi-circle of marble pillars in the apse, this construction completed the circular space that would be the site of the solemn funeral ceremony, with temporary seating forming an amphitheatre centred on the catafalque. Here, the parlementaires took their seats in the left-hand stalls of the choir beside the officers of the university, who were already in place but rose and bowed on their arrival as did the officers of the police, the Châtelet and the *election*. Facing them in the right-hand stalls were the representatives of the *chambre des comptes*, who entered after the parlement, as well as the *cour des monnaies*, the king's parlementary officers and the provost and aldermen of Paris. Previous ceremonial occasions had seen the replacements of the old parlement incontrovertibly snubbed to public cheers.[116] Thus far, it appeared, the Maupeou parlement was having a good day.

The catafalque faced the altar from the centre of the semi-circle of temporary pillars, placed on a platform that brought these two centres of attention to an equal height. This temporary monument to Louis XV was in the form of a temple. Four columns, in the shape of Roman fasces, marked the corners of the monument where funeral lamps burned dimly. Six steps led up to a platform where four groups of veiled caryatids seemed to gather their own tears in the funeral urns they carried, performing at the same time the function of columns supporting an oval ceiling over a draped sarcophagus. Atop the monument were positioned two more female figures, representing France, arms raised to heaven, and Navarre, head on her knees, in mourning. On two sides of this oval roof were the words of Psalm 102: 'my days are consumed like smoke … my heart is smitten and withered like grass'.[117] The sarcophagus itself was covered in the royal pall with a crown wrapped in black crepe placed on a black velvet cushion fringed with silver. The sceptre and other royal honours also lay on top of the tomb. At its foot was a golden urn decorated with the likeness of the deceased king. On a small table before the catafalque, the king's royal cloak, arms and chain of the Order of the Holy Spirit were laid out. The purple velvet banner and the blue pennant of France, both decorated with golden fleurs-de-lys and golden fringing, were raised in the sanctuary on velvet-covered lances wrapped in black crepe. The whole catafalque stood under the enormous canopy suspended from the vault of the Abbey. The ceiling of the canopy, as one looked up, was decorated with a silver moiré cross and embroidered arms of France. From the edge of the canopy hung massive black velvet curtains, stitched with silver tears, golden fleurs-de-lys and bands of ermine, which reached down to the floor. These curtains were suspended from the vault of the Abbey by golden-fringed ropes. An identical canopy and curtains was suspended over the altar, marking the two centres of ritual attention. Challe's classical temple doubled as a baroque *chapelle ardente*, hundreds of candles creating a focal point of light in the otherwise sombre church.

The sheer scale and ambition of the decorative scheme belies the usual perception of Louis XV's burial as a furtive, hurried occasion, and, since it is usually overlooked, it bears description here. It demonstrates that the Renaissance funeral described by Ralph Giesey had been replaced by 1774 by a no less ritualistic, respectful and artistic display of grief. Its key difference from the effigy-centred Renaissance funeral was the adoption of a monumental scale. This had become possible as the processional part of the funeral had diminished in importance with the changes in funeral ritual introduced by Louis XIII and preserved in a characteristic form by later Bourbon royal funerals.[118]

The heightened sense of drama and the prolific use of human figures in the decorative scheme, together with the combination of religious, secular and heraldic elements in the ceremony itself, created a ritual which was undeniably impressive. It was such a resilient ritual form that it was able to accommodate artists' novel impulses, including the gradual transition in tastes through the Rococo to the neo-classical, without detracting from its overall function and power.[119] These rituals were important cultural expressions, their temporary nature and, since it was all achieved with *trompe l'oeil* painting, the relative cheapness of the

3 and 4 Views of Louis XV's funeral monument at Saint Denis, 27 July 1774, designed by Charles Michel-Ange Challe, from *Description du mausolée érigé dans l'église de l'abbaye royale de Saint Denis, le 27 juillet 1774, pour les obsèques de Louis XV*.

material allowing free rein to the artist's imagination in capturing artistic trends of the day.

Around the catafalque were grouped heraldic and household officers who had parts to play in the ceremony.[120] A herald dressed in mourning stood at each corner of the catafalque and the king's bodyguards lined the sides. Two seats to the left and right of the catafalque were occupied by the duc de Bourbon, the prince de Condé's son, performing the office of *grand maître de France*, with his baton of office wrapped in black crepe and the duc de Bouillon, *grand chambellan de France*, holding aloft the banner of France. The king-at-arms, Bronod de la Haye, with four of his heralds sat on a bench beside the catafalque and, in front of him, the prince de Lambesc, *grand écuyer de France*, was seated with the royal sword and several more heralds. In front of the prince de Lambesc were several officers carrying the royal insignia – the spurs, gloves, shield and flag – alongside the bishop of Senlis, who was to deliver the funeral oration.

Closer to the altar were places for the chief mourners, the comte de Provence, the comte d'Artois and the prince de Condé, with their train-bearers. The first gentlemen of the bedchamber and the captains of the royal guards together with other representatives of the royal household were already seated. The royal musicians were also in place, ready to play Delser's *Messe des morts* and a *De profundis* composed by Mathieu, master of the king's music.[121] The ceremony thus brought together the diverse aspects of royal power: princes, parlement, city, civil and military households, heraldry, religion and art.

At half past midday, the grand master of ceremonies, the marquis de Dreux, led the chief mourners, Monsieur, the comte d'Artois and the prince de Condé, to their seats. They bowed to the altar and to the catafalque before taking their places. Once the Cardinal de la Roche-Aymon had been led to the altar by Dreux, the ceremony began. The fact of being escorted was a mark of respect rather than a practical expedient. The order of entry into the body of the church was another such marker: the most important came last and waited least.

Set within this elaborate framework of ritual and decoration, the religious core of the funeral ceremony took the usual form of a mass, though this one was on a grand scale, conducted by a cardinal assisted by four bishops. After the reading of the Gospel, the numerous celebrants were seated for the first time as the Offertory took place. The king-at-arms rose and bowed to the altar, the catafalque, the clergy, the three princes individually, the parlement, the *chambre des comptes*, the *cour des monnoyes*, the Châtelet, the *élection*, the aldermen and the university. This was the fixed order of precedence for the *saluts* about which there had been so much trouble. The king-at-arms then stood before the altar holding a candle embellished with gold coins, symbolising the offerings being made.[122] Each prince was guided by a member of the royal ceremonial staff in their execution of the contentious *saluts ordinaires* in this same order, first Provence, then Artois and finally the prince de Condé.[123] Ormesson, who of course did not attend, was told that no bow made to the new parlement went beyond the strict minimum necessary.[124] The comte d'Artois bowed but with an air of mockery and a grimace. The prince de Condé made a particularly brief bow to the parlement and, immediately afterwards, a particularly elaborate one to the *chambre des comptes*.[125] Days before the ceremony, some commentators had already begun to say that these bows were in fact inconsequential with the explicit intent of exculpating any of the princes of the blood who did bow.[126] The *président* d'Ormesson rejected this analysis and was dismayed by the idea that there would be no difference at all between the treatment of the old and new parlementaires.[127] The popular verdict was captured in rhyme:

> Chancellor Maupeou warned his company,
> as a good protector, about the ceremony
> Each prince will make to you a bow
> Confirming your position and my influence[128]

The *saluts* were taken as confirming the Maupeou parlement's status. The exiles remained in limbo.

The bishop of Senlis gave his funeral oration and the main religious portion of the ceremony concluded with censing of the catafalque. The king's household and the peers of France enacted heraldic death rites.[129] The king-at-arms threw his jacket embroidered with the arms of France and his hat into the crypt and called forward in ritual sequence those carrying objects to be placed beside the dead king.[130] The banners of four companies of royal guards – *cent-suisses*, two companies of *gardes de corps* and the *gardes écossaises* – were deposited in the crypt by their captains. Four royal footmen together brought the royal spurs, gloves, shield and jacket embroidered with the coat of arms. The ceremonial helmet and pennant were brought to the crypt. The prince de Lambesc, *grand écuyer*, carried the royal sword, the duc de Bouillon, *grand chambellan*, the banner of France. Then came the most senior peers carrying the royal *honneurs:* the duc de Béthune, the hand of justice, the duc de la Tremoïlle, the sceptre and, finally, the duc d'Uzès with the royal crown. Each of these items was taken and solemnly placed on top of the coffin in the crypt. The duc de Bourbon, taking the part of *grand maître de France*, placed the tip of his staff of office in the crypt, a gesture symbolic of break-up of the household. The *maîtres d'hôtel* who accompanied him broke their staffs and threw the pieces into the sepulchre. The duc de Bourbon then said 'le Roi est mort'. The king-at-arms thrice repeated: 'the king is dead: let us all pray for the repose of his soul'. A prayer was recited and then the king-at-arms shouted three times 'Vive le Roi Louis XVI', his declaration of the new king joined by the shouts of the assembled dignitaries and the sounding of trumpets, drums and oboes in the nave.

While direct participation in the ceremony was limited to those members of élite corporate bodies present by invitation, the details of the ritual attracted the attention of those who remained outside. Hardy judged that, though the Maupeou parlementaires had set out to the funeral very proudly, they returned 'cut down to size and very humiliated'. The popular joke on the funeral was shouted at them by the roadside crowds.[131] More stories of subversions of ceremonial gesture came to d'Ormesson's receptive ears. This emergence of, and interest in, rumour from what was a closed ceremony points to the fluidity of the borders between public and private in these ceremonies. The commander of the mounted police, the *maréchaussée*, withheld the order for his company to salute the parlement as they passed on their way into Saint Denis. Instead of presenting arms smartly, the *gardes françoises et suisses* put them down when the parlement arrived at the Abbey. The duc de Fronsac was heard to comment that the bastards had come to their own funeral.[132] The bows to the parlement during the service were minimal: pointedly elaborate to the other bodies. The parlementaires' supposed colleagues from the *chambre des comptes*, the only body which had not had to bow to them that day, avoided all association with them, flouting protocol by leaving while the parlementaires were still eating.[133] Ceremonial gesture was repeatedly used to make the same disrespectful political point.

Conclusion

The drama around the *princes du sang*'s attendance at Louis XV's funeral went through two clear stages. The first part, just following Louis XV's death, consisted of direct lobbying for the return of the old parlement in time to take part in the catafalque. The second part, marked by a change of tactic, comprised lowering the temperature in negotiations around the new parlement and separating the question of the recall of the old parlement from that of the princes' attendance. A compromise was reached whereby the Orléans kept their dignity intact and the catafalque went forward as the young king wished. The ceremony was given priority, as the question of the parlement continued to wait on Louis XVI's pleasure. It was, in the end, fitting that Louis XV was symbolically buried by the members of the constitutional order he had helped create: his catafalque ceremony, involving the new parlement and lacking most of the princes of the blood, was an accurate representation of the state of the French constitution at the time of his death. Neither the reduced ceremony of the convoy nor the dispute around the catafalque should be taken as indications of a broken ceremonial culture since, after all, it was through another ceremony, the *lit de justice* on 12 November 1774, that Louis XVI instituted a new constitutional settlement. Moreover, our account of street rituals reveals the public involvement in these affairs that are often seen as divorced from the broader political culture of the time.

Louis XIV had particularly emphasised blood-based hierarchy at his court. The highest ranked were those with direct links to him, the children of France. Shared blood also granted elevated status to his cousins, the princes of the blood, who were the highest nobles outside of the direct royal family. Royal family demographics had an impact on the residential proximity of the princes to the king but they never lost their privileged role in the public ceremonies of the monarchy. In 1771, the exile of the parlement became, and remained, a political *cause célèbre* because of the public role of the princes of the blood. Even after they returned to court, their opposition continued and was well known. The notion of an all-powerful monarch is given the lie by the negotiation with the princes on the funeral ceremony in 1774 and by the light sentence imposed upon the recalcitrant Orléans. This accommodation in the name of dynastic harmony does not sit well with ideas of an absolute monarch and his servile courtiers. While funerals have been seen as tending to reinforce social order, reasoning that the honour of participation neutered the potential for disorder in rituals,[134] we have seen here that participation was neither automatic nor a guarantor of status, as the members of Maupeou's parlement were to discover. Ritual was responsive, shaped by contemporary concerns.

The close relationship between ritual and politics continued to be played out after the ceremony at Saint Denis as speculation on the return of the old parlement was linked first to the final commemorative ceremony in honour of Louis XV at Notre Dame in September and then, more accurately, with the parlement's own traditional *messe rouge* at Martinmas. The negotiations of June and July set the parameters for discussions on the exiled parlement: the king would clearly not be rushed or pressurised, yet he was open to discussion. What we have in the July catafalque ceremony is an accommodation of the prevailing tensions and use of ceremony to require acquiescence in the polity. Ritual is not a dumb witness or sideshow but rather an instrument of policy: that became even clearer when, in November of the same year, Louis XVI convened a *lit de justice* to abolish the new and recall the old parlement.

The public demonstrations of discontent, disrespect and violence towards the new parlement should give historians pause for thought. If, three years after its inception, this body was still the object of such opprobrium that its officers were unable to participate in public ceremonies without being humiliated, it seems unlikely that its position was well established or tenable. Such gestures of defiance and dislike towards the new institution surely show that it was not in practice a remedy for France's governmental ills, particularly in view of the ongoing boycott of the institution by the princes of the blood and the peers. This overt hostility makes it difficult to sustain arguments that Louis XVI made a 'mistake' in recalling the old parlement in November 1774. This was another key political moment of Louis XVI's early reign in which ceremony played a central part. It is discussed in the next chapter.

Notes

1 By 27 May, the *Gazette de France* was offering for sale 'Portrait de Louis XV avec la Vue sur la Place du même nom, prix 12f'. On the provinces, see Bernard Hours, 'Services funèbres provinciaux en France au XVIIIe siècle', in *Les Funérailles princières en Europe, XVIe–XVIIIe siècle*, volume 3, Juliusz A. Chrościcki, Mark Hengerer and Gérard Sabatier (editors), (Rennes, 2015), 161–75, as well as essays on French royal funerals in volume 1 of the same series.

2 William Doyle noted that 'the question of the parlements became … the central one in politics' but he did not remark on events around the funeral, in 'The parlements of France and the break-down of the Old Regime, 1774–1788', *French Historical Studies*, 6:4 (Fall 1970), 438.

3 See Thomas Scheff, 'The distancing of emotion in ritual', *Current Anthropology* (September 1977), 483.

4 Jacques Mathieu Augeard, *Mémoires secrets de J-M Augeard, secrétaire des commandements de la reine Marie-Antoinette (1760 à 1800)*, Évariste Bavoux (editor) (Paris, 1866), 76. *Journal de Monsieur le président d'Ormesson de Noiseau*, AN 144 AP 120, volume 5 f 969. See later in this chapter and Chapter 3 for examples of public hostility to the Maupeou parlement.

5 Joan B. Landes, *Women and the Public Sphere in the Age of the French Revolution* (Ithaca, 1988), 19.

6 Doyle, 'The parlements', 415–80; Jean Egret, *Louis XV et l'opposition parlementaire* (Paris, 1970); Bailey Stone, *The Parlement of Paris* (Chapel Hill, 1981) and *The French Parlements and the Crisis of the Old Regime* (Chapel

Hill, 1986); Julian Swann, *Politics and the Parlement of Paris under Louis XV: 1748–1774* (Cambridge, 1995) and 'Disgrace without dishonour: the internal exile of French magistrates in the eighteenth century', *Past and Present*, 195 (May 2007), 87–126.

7 Doyle is almost alone in discussing the broader ramifications, 'The parlements', 442 *passim*. In neither of his two volumes on the parlements under Louis XVI does Stone examine the recall of 1774. Swann's discussion halts in 1771. Overall, the events leading to the recall of 1774 are rarely discussed in detail.

8 Charles Loyseau, *Traité des ordres et des dignitez* (Paris, 1610), 81.

9 Richard A. Jackson, 'Peers of France and Princes of the Blood', *French Historical Studies*, 7:1 (Spring 1971), 38.

10 Guy Rowlands, *The Dynastic State and the Army under Louis XIV: Royal service and private interest, 1661–1701* (Oxford, 2002), 11.

11 See Jackson, 'Peers of France and Princes of the Blood', 39.

12 Marina Valensise, 'Le sacre du roi: strategic symbolique et doctrine politique de la monarchie', *Annales ESC*, 41:3 (1986), 547–48.

13 Loyseau, *Traité*, 84–85.

14 *Mémoires de Louis XIV pour servir à l'instruction du dauphin* (Paris, 1860), volume 1, 130.

15 William Ritchey Newton, *L'Espace du roi: la cour de France au château de Versailles, 1682–1789* (Paris, 2000), 31.

16 See note by Sainctot in Jean Rousset de Missy, *Supplément au Corps Universel diplomatique* (Amsterdam/The Hague, 1739), volume IV, 45.

17 Noël Laurent Pissot, *Le cérémonial de la cour de France* (Paris, 1816), 7; and, Isambert, Decrusy, Taillandier, *Recueil des anciennes lois françaises* (Paris, 1830), volume 27, 73 and 393.

18 Augeard, *Mémoires secrets*, 53.

19 See Julian Swann, 'Parlement, politics and the *parti janséniste*: the *grand conseil* affair, 1755–56', *French History*, 6:4 (1992), 455–57.

20 See Swann, 'The *grand conseil* affair', 450 *passim*, and 'Parlements and political crisis in France under Louis XV: the Besançon affair, 1757–1761', *The Historical Journal*, 37:4 (1994), 820.

21 Swann, 'The Besançon affair', 822–24.

22 See Doyle, 'The parlements', 418–20; Jules Flammermont, *Le Chancelier Maupeou et les parlements* (Paris, 1883), 161, 182, 185, 186; Swann, *Politics*, 344.

23 Jacob-Nicolas Moreau, *Mes Souvenirs* (Paris, 1898, 1901), volume 1, 244–45; Flammermont, *Maupeou*, 181, and *Remontrances du parlement de Paris au XVIIIe siècle* (Paris, 1898), volume 3, 174; Doyle, 'The parlements', 422; Swann, *Politics*, 345. While all offer different interpretations of what precisely happened and why, it is evident that there was an attempt to pull back from the brink. Swann writes that '[t]here is no single satisfactory

explanation for the conduct of the parlement in January 1771' (347) and the same might be said of Maupeou.

24 Pierre de Ségur, *La Dernière des Condés* (Paris, 1899), 220–25.

25 Ibid., 224.

26 Joseph Alphonse Véri, *Journal de l'Abbé Véri* (Paris, 1928), 72.

27 See Olivier Chaline, *Godart de Belbeuf: Le parlement, le roi et les normands* (Paris, 1996) 428–29, on dismantling of Rouen parlement in 1771.

28 This was reprinted in 1775 as part of the collection entitled *Les Efforts du patriotisme ou recueil complet des écrits publiés pendant le règne du Chancelier Maupeou, pour démontrer l'absurdité du despotisme qu'il vouloit établir, & pour maintenir dans toute sa splendeur la Monarchie Française … avec l'approbation unanime des bons & fidèles sujets de Sa Majesté Louis XVI*, which was associated with a larger series entitled *Maupeouana* or *Maupeouaneries*. See Durand Echeverria, *The Maupeou Revolution: A study in the history of libertarianism, France 1770–1774* (Baton Rouge and London, 1985), 23–24.

29 *Recueil des arrêtés, arrêts, etc., enregistrements d'édits, déclarations, et lettres patents du parlement de Paris, concernant les affaires publiques, ou les particuliers de distinction, des différens événemens qui y ont donné lieu, avec la description des différents prestations de serment, réceptions et installations; des cérémonies publiques, et des séances du Roy, princes du sang et ducs au Parlement 1765–1788*, par Regnault huissier au Parlement, Bibliothèque Municipale de Versailles (BMV), MS 120 G.

30 William Ritchey Newton, *L'Espace du roi* (Paris, 2000), 38.

31 Augeard, *Mémoires secrétes*, 57; Croÿ, *Journal*, volume 3, 30.

32 Ségur, *La Dernière des Condés*, 231.

33 *Récit exact de ce qui s'est passé au sujet du retour de M le prince de Condé à la* cour, a pamphlet printed in December 1772.

34 *Gazette de France*, du Lundi 11 décembre 1772; *Gazette de France*, du Vendredi 1er janvier 1773.

35 Croÿ, *Journal*, 30.

36 Augeard, *Mémoires secrets*, 71–72.

37 Croÿ, *Journal*, 33. *Gazette de France*, du Lundi 4 janvier, 1773.

38 On the administration of ceremonies by the king's household, see Denis Pierre Jean Papillon de la Ferté, *L'Administration des menus* (Paris, 1887); Alain Gruber, *Les Grandes fêtes et leurs décors à l'époque de Louis XVI* (Genève, 1972) 11–13; Marie-Lan Nguyen, 'Les grands maîtres des cérémonies et le services des cérémonies à l'époque moderne, 1585–1792', Unpublished mémoire de maîtrise, Université de Paris IV-Sorbonne, 1999; Ambrogio A. Caiani, *Louis XVI and the French Revolution, 1789–1792* (Cambridge, 2012), 49–55; Pauline Lemaigre-Gaffier, *Adminster les menus plaisirs du Roi: l'état, la cour et les spectacles dans la France des lumières* (Paris, 2016). On funerals, Pauline Lemaigre-Gaffier, 'Les Menus Plaisirs

et l'organisation des pompes funèbres à la cour de France au XVIIIe siècle', in *Les Funérailles princières en Europe*, volume 1, Chrościcki et al. (editors) 73–90.

39 The other gentlemen of the bedchamber were the duc de Duras, the duc de Richelieu and the duc de Fleury.

40 See Adolphe Jullien, *Un Potentat musical: Papillon de la Ferté son règne à l'Opéra de 1780 à 1790* (Paris, 1876), 16.

41 Gruber, *Les Grandes fêtes*, 110.

42 Richard P. Wunder, 'Charles Michel-Ange Challe: a study of his life and work', *Apollo* (January 1968), 28.

43 Papillon de la Ferté, *L'Administration*, 365.

44 *Description du mausolée érigée dans l'Abbaye Royale de St Denis pour les obsèques, qui se feront dans cette église, le 27 juillet 1774, de très-grand, très-haut, très-puissant et très-excellent prince Louis XV le Bien-Aimé, roi de France et de Navarre*, BNF Rondel Collection, Ra4 601.

45 Papillon de la Ferté, *L'Administration*, 365.

46 Croÿ, *Journal*, volume 3, 129.

47 The funeral is not mentioned in any of the following: Doyle, 'The parlements'; John Hardman, *The Life of Louis XVI* (New Haven, 2016) and *French Politics 1774–1789: From the accession of Louis XVI to the fall of the Bastille* (London, 1995); Munro Price, '*Politics: Louis XVI*', in *The Short Oxford History of France: Old Regime France* (Oxford, 2002); Stone, *The Parlement of Paris*; or Peter Burley, 'Louis XVI and a new monarchy: an institutional and political study of France, 1768–78', unpublished PhD thesis (University of London, 1981). It is mentioned in passing by Jean-Christian Petitfils, *Louis XVI* (Paris, 2005), 178. Joël Félix notes the importance of the ceremony to the young king, *Louis XVI et Marie-Antoinette: un couple en politique* (Paris, 2016), 115–16.

48 Swann, *Politics*, 338; and 'Disgrace without dishonour: the internal exile of French magistrates in the eighteenth century', *Past and Present*, 195 (May 2007), 94.

49 During their exile to Bourges in 1753–54, some parlementaries had worn mourning as their usual clothing to mark their peculiar status. Swann, 'Disgrace without dishonour', 108.

50 See *Les Efforts du patriotisme ou receuil complet des écrits pendant le règne du Chancelier Maupeou, pour démontrer l'absurdité de despotisme qu'il vouloit établir, & pour maintenir dans toute sa splendeur la Monarchie Française* (Paris, 1775), volume 2, which includes 'Lettre à un ami de Province, sur la liquidation des offices', 23–36, a letter from d'Ormesson to the king justifying his conduct, 37–41, and a series of false supplements to the *Gazette de France* on the subject, 132–435. See also the separate pamphlet known by its first line '*Je ne crois pas me tromper Monsieur*' (Paris, 1771).

51 'Mémoires de famille de Robert de Saint-Vincent' in *Un magistrat janséniste du siècle des Lumières à l'Émigration, Pierre-Augustin Robert de Saint-Vincent*, critical edition presented by Monique Cottret, Valérie Guittienne-Mürger and Nicolas Lyon-Caen (Bordeaux, 2012), 441; 'Lettre à un ami de Province' in *Les Efforts du patriotism* ..', 25, William Doyle, *Venality: The sale of offices in eighteenth century France* (Oxford, 1996), 126–29.

52 This was never the plan; rather, a rolling programme of annual payments was envisaged.

53 *Supplément à la Gazette de France*, 229.

54 Possibly due to concerns about wider family interests. His brother continued to progress in the royal administration. See *Gazette de France*, du Vendredi 24 janvier 1772, de Versailles le 22 janvier.

55 Ormesson, *Journal*, volume 5, f 951 and 975.

56 Ormesson, *Journal*, volume 5, f 950. Including, of course, Maupeou.

57 SP 78/292/183, Stormont to Rochford, 22 June 1774.

58 Ormesson, *Journal*, volume 5, f 968–69. Félix, *Louis XVI*, 110.

59 *Journal historique du rétablissement de la Magistrature: pour servir de suite à celui de la révolution opérée dans la Constitution de la Monarchie Françoise, par M de Maupeou, Chancelier de France* (London, 1775), 30.

60 Ibid., 48.

61 States Papers Foreign, SP 78/292/71, Stormont to Rochford, 18 May 1774.

62 *Gazette de Leyde*, Numéro XLVI, 10 juin 1774, Suite des nouvelles de Paris du 3 juin.

63 *Journal historique*, 77.

64 Ibid., 88.

65 The rumour was true to the extent that Louis XV's personal will, found on 6 June, had requested burial '*sans cérémonies*', in the special sense noted in Chapter 1.

66 Félix, *Louis XVI*, 126–27.

67 Ormesson, *Journal*, volume 5, f 1012.

68 Ralph E. Giesey, *The Royal Funeral Ceremony in Renaissance France* (Geneva, 1960), 163–64.

69 *Journal historique*, 79.

70 Ibid.

71 Ibid., 96.

72 Ibid. (8 juillet 1774) and 98 (10 juillet 1774). On 11 July, it is noted that nothing firm is known about conversations at Marly on the subject (100).

73 Simeon Prosper Hardy, *Mes Loisirs, ou Journal d'Evénements tels qu'ils parviennent à ma connoissance*, BNF Ms Fr 6681, f 374.

74 Ormesson, *Journal*, volume 5, f 1043.

75 *Journal historique*, 107–08. See also 100–01 where the image is described. Sadly, no copies survive.

76 Ibid., 102.
77 He maintained that he did so in his capacity as *grand maître de France* and not as a prince of the blood. This did not enhance his reputation with the pro-old parlement lobby. *Gazette de Leyde*, Numéro LX, vendredi 29 juillet 1774, Suite des nouvelles de Paris du 22 juillet.
78 Ibid.
79 Hardy, *Mes Loisirs*, f 378.
80 Ormesson, *Journal*, volume 5, f 1058.
81 Ibid., f 1057.
82 Ibid., f 1058. This might be a twisted version of the fact that the letter inviting the Maupeou parlement to the funeral was dated 1 July but not delivered until 23 July.
83 Ibid., f 1051.
84 *Journal historique*, 108.
85 'Sire, la bonne heure! mais hors de l'église point de salut.' Ibid., p 114; *Nouvelles à la main de Penthièvre*, le 25 juillet 1774. The joke is virtually untranslatable since it plays on the double meaning of *salut* as salvation and bow.
86 Ormesson, *Journal*, volume 5, f 1062.
87 Ibid.
88 Ibid.
89 Ibid. Thus, Orléans' refusal was not 'audacious' as Petitfils suggests but carefully planned. Petitfils, *Louis XVI*, 178.
90 SP 78/292/285, Stormont to Rochford, 27 July 1774.
91 Ormesson, *Journal*, volume 5, folio 1062.
92 SP 78/292/285, Stormont to Rochford, 27 July 1774.
93 Ibid.
94 Moreau, *Mes Souvenirs*, volume 1, 99.
95 SP 78/292/220, Stormont to Rochfort, 6 July 1774.
96 Regnault, *Recueil*, MS G 120, 321–30.
97 See John Rogister, *Louis XV and the Parlement of Paris, 1737–1755* (Cambridge, 1995). 255, on the *messe rouge* of 1754 when the stall keepers charged six or even twelve *livres* for a good place and the crowd applauded as the *présidents* executed their bows at the offertory.
98 I follow Regnault, who was present (*Receuil*, 321) rather than Hardy who suggests it was Desgranges the *maître des cérémonies* (*Mes Loisirs*, f 386).
99 See also Nguyen, 'Les grandes maîtres des cérémonies', 110, on the king's ceremonial officers and the parlement.
100 Echeverria, *The Maupeou Revolution*, 17.
101 Croÿ, *Journal*, volume 3, 20.
102 'Supplément à la Gazette de France, V, de Paris le 6 mars 1772' in *Les Efforts du patriotism* ... volume 2, 203.
103 'Supplément à la Gazette de France, IV, de Paris le 24 janvier 1772' in *Les*

Efforts du patriotism ...volume 2, 192. For other alleged incidents of incompetence, see 208–09 of the same volume. Whether true or not, clearly these stories would have exacerbated feelings against the Maupeou parlement.

104 Moreau, *Mes Souvenirs*, volume 2, 96.

105 Croÿ, *Journal*, volume 3, 6.

106 Michel Antoine, *Louis XV* (Paris, 1989), 933.

107 Moreau, *Mes Souvenirs*, volume 1, 250.

108 My account is based on the versions related in: Regnault, *Recueil*, MS G 118; *Journal historique*, 120; d'Ormesson, *Journal*, tome 5, f 1065; Hardy, *Mes Loisirs*, f 386–87.

109 Originally from Toulouse, Désirat had been a lawyer at the parlement of Paris since 1763. He became a magistrate as a Maupeou parlementaire in 1771 and, much later, was secretary to the Committee of Public Safety. Having been arrested as a noble, he was saved by the intervention of Carnot, Barrère and Billaud-Varenne. See Joël Félix, *Les Magistrats du parlement de Paris 1771–1790: dictionnaire biographique et généalogique* (Paris, 1990), 98.

110 Hardy, *Mes Loisirs*, f 386.

111 Croÿ, *Journal*, volume 3, 130; *Gazette de Leyde*, Numéro LXII, Vendredi 5 août 1774 de Paris, le 29 juillet; *Gazette de France*, Vendredi, 29 juillet 1774, de Paris, le 29 juillet 1774.

112 Regnault, *Recueil*, MS G 120, 332–36.

113 The details on the décor are derived from *Description du mausolée érigée dans l'Abbaye Royale de St Denis pour les obsèques, qui se feront dans cette église, le 27 juillet 1774, de très-grand, très-haut, très-puissant et très-excellent prince Louis XV le Bien-Aimé, roi de France et de Navarre*, BNF Ra4 601.

114 Regnault, *Recueil*, MS G 120, 338.

115 '[D]ies tribulationis et angustiae dies calamitatis et miseriae dies tenebrarum et caliginis dies nebulae et turbinis' from the book of Zephaniah, 1:15. King James version.

116 Swann, 'Disgrace without dishonour', 115.

117 [D]efecterunt sicut fumus dies mei ... percussus sum ut foeum et aruit cor meum ...' which the pamphlet wrongly attributes to psalm 101. King James version.

118 On similar developments in Sweden, see Mårten Snickare, 'De la Procession à l'oeuvre d'art totale: les transformations de la cérémonie funéraire royale dans la Suède du XVIIe siècle' in Chrościcki et al., *Les Funérailles princières en Europe*, 335–53.

119 Gruber, *Les Grandes fêtes*, 110.

120 Regnault, *Recueil*, MS G 120, 349.

121 *Gazette de France*, Vendredi, 29 juillet 1774.

122 Regnault, *Recueil*, MS G120, 388–89.

123 *Gazette de Leyde*, Numéro LXII, Vendredi 5 août 1774; De Paris, le 29 juillet; Regnault, *Recueil*, 388–89.

124 Ormesson, *Journal*, volume 5, f 1071.
125 Ibid.
126 *Gazette de Leyde*, Numéro LX, Vendredi 29 juillet 1774, Suite des nouvelles de Paris du 22 juillet.
127 Ormesson, *Journal*, volume 5, f 1056.
128 These verses circulated after the ceremony, according to Hardy, *Mes Loisirs*, f 389.
129 *Gazette de France*, Vendredi 29 juillet, de Paris, le 29 juillet 1774.
130 *Gazette de Leyde*, Numéro LXII, vendredi 5 aout 1774, de Paris, le 29 juillet.
131 'Hors de l'église point de salut'. Hardy, *Mes Loisirs*, f 390.
132 Ormesson, *Journal*, volume 6, f 1070.
133 Ibid., f 1071.
134 Jennifer Woodward, *The Theatre of Death: The ritual management of royal funerals in Renaissance England, 1570–1625* (Woodbridge, 1997), 24.

3

The *lit de justice* of November 1774

Introduction

Though the funeral ceremony for Louis XV at Saint Denis in July 1774 had been the focus of so much political wrangling, it was not the last act in the drama around the reinstatement of the parlement nor was it the last ritual heavy with political implications. Ritual was also deployed to political ends in the eventual recall of the parlement of Paris, in November 1774.[1] Historians examining the events between his accession and the recall have usually concluded that Louis XVI was skilfully manipulated into taking a decision on the fate of the Maupeou parlement that went against his inclination. Yet, just as was the case with the deathbed of Louis XV, a close look at the ceremonial rhythms of these events reveals more about the king's own intentions.

As dauphin, Louis XVI had been at his grandfather's side throughout the parlementary troubles of 1770 and 1771. Louis XV's anger when the princes of the blood publicly sided with the parlementaires was a clear indication of the kind of dynastic loyalty he expected, and usually received. While modern specialists on the parlement see the recall of 1774 as 'predictable, if not inevitable',[2] it has more generally been assumed that Louis XVI came to the throne with no intention of disturbing the status quo and, therefore, the further assumption has been made that the young king was manipulated during the summer and autumn of 1774 by seasoned political operators, most notably the comte de Maurepas, into adopting their agenda almost in spite of himself.[3] This is to disregard the subtleties of Louis XVI's attitude both to the parlement and to ceremony. The assumption of manipulation immediately casts the young king as a weak character surrounded by the strong and cunning, reducing him to something of a puppet, though as Joël Félix has pointed out and contemporaries confirmed, slow decision-making is not necessarily an indication of indecision but perhaps a recognition of the seriousness of the matter at hand.[4] There is other evidence of Louis XVI's readiness to implement in short order policies rather different to his grandfather's: the decision to inoculate himself and his brothers against smallpox at the beginning of the summer of 1774 stands in stark contrast to decades of inaction. The nub of the matter, for historians, is the absence of sources for Louis XVI's own views: the vast bulk of his surviving correspondence deals with foreign affairs and is said to show him in a 'very different light'[5] from the usual picture. Put plainly, the direct evidence paints a portrait of Louis XVI that significantly diverges from the usual one based on secondhand commentaries. It is worth bearing this distinction in mind and approaching with caution judgements that may be tainted by hindsight.

As experienced an observer as the English ambassador Viscount Stormont found the matter of the parlements perplexing, writing to London that 'the Point is of equal Defficulty (sic), and Importance, and would I think, embarrass a Man of the greatest Ability, and most consummate Experience'.[6] The exile, confiscation of offices, and replacement of, first, the parlement of Paris, and, then, other parlements around France from January 1771 was seen as an authoritarian move by the king and his ministers, applauded by some as an act of strong government, appalling to others as a symptom of despotism. The parlement had a dual judicial and political role. The judicial task was the processing of legal cases of all kinds. The political task was the registration of laws put forward by ministers: without this registration, laws were not deemed enforceable.[7] Ministerial attempts to restrain the political activities of the parlementaires were, of course, not new.[8] Their comments on laws, called remonstrances, were delivered publicly and could therefore be deeply irritating to ministers and to the king, particularly when reiterated. This very publicity meant that they were one of the few bodies in France with official standing that was vocally critical of royal policy. Crucially, the parlements always framed their criticisms in terms of their loyalty to the king and to the laws of the kingdom. Their vision of their place in the government of France placed the king among them as *primus inter pares*, an esteemed fellow judge to whom they owed the duty of advice.[9] Their rhetoric was not empty words as a cover for some other agenda but reflected their values of loyalty to king and law, and duty.

Remonstrances, to the parlementaires, were part of the fulfilment of their duty to advise the king. To ministers, they were an irksome intervention in their plans. Replacing critical parlements with more acquiescent bodies soothed irritated ministers but was not deemed a wholesome remedy by all parts of the body politic. As Stormont observed, it was difficult because the more pliable new bodies seemed desirable from the ministerial viewpoint yet lacked credibility, and important because the parlements played a vital role in the functioning of government in France. Dedicated meetings on this subject between the new king and selected ministers allowed the case to be rehearsed meaningfully for his benefit, something which sounds more like a serious attempt at debate and informed decision-making than a simple propaganda exercise and something which the young king apparently intended to pursue as early as the beginning of June 1774.[10] It was completely in character for a king who began his reign with 'great Attention and Application to business and the most earnest desire of being Informed. He puts a great Variety of questions to his ministers and minutes their answers.'[11] In the same vein, in the month after his accession, Louis XVI told the duc d'Orléans that 'he had already heard and thought a great deal upon the subject [of the parlement], that it was a matter of the highest importance, and must be thoroughly weighed.'[12] Chancellor Maupeou's reforms were attacked in Louis XV's council as early as 1772, when verses were already circulating on his imminent disgrace.[13] The durability of his coup was long contested.

The summer of 1774 was a pivotal time in the history of the parlement, closely entwined with royal ritual. This chapter will offer a new interpretation by emphasising the significance of ceremony in determining both the pace and nature of Louis XVI's decision to recall the parlements. Ceremony was skilfully deployed on the day of the recall *lit de justice* to send a clear message from the monarchy to the parlementaires about their mutual status. The use of the ceremony in 1774 did not follow precedent, since, on a previous analogous occasion, when the parlementaires had been exiled and replaced by a *chambre royale* in 1753–54, there had been no *lit de justice* to mark their return.[14] Ceremony was useful in 1774 to achieve a particular political effect. To develop a rich context, we will briefly examine the *lit de justice* as a ceremonial form in the eighteenth century and then look at other political rituals of summer and autumn 1774, street-level political actions as well as the last formal state commemoration of Louis XV, all of which reflect attitudes and enthusiasms on the burning political question of the day. With this background, we will then turn to the *lit de justice* of 12 November 1774, the first of Louis XVI's reign.

The *lit de justice* ceremony in the eighteenth century

The *lit de justice* ceremony was a curious entity. Louis XIV did not summon any between 1673 and 1715.[15] Given his experiences in the Fronde, Louis XIV was wary of the parlement and, determined to stymie any critical inclinations, from 1673, he required that registration of laws should precede remonstrances. When Louis XIV died, Philippe d'Orléans, as regent for the child Louis XV, restored rights of prior remonstrance to the parlement as a quid pro quo for cooperation in overturning Louis XIV's will in his favour at the famous *séance* of 2 September 1715.[16] This was not a *lit de justice*, since the king was not in attendance, and the records do not describe it as such. The *lit de justice* to inaugurate the regency was held on 12 September 1715 in Paris. The child-king was carried into the *grand'chambre* by members of his household, his governor and governess each holding one of the set of reins the child wore. The session lasted under an hour, serving simply to confirm the position agreed in the king's absence on 2 September.

Though the parlement could and did exercise its right of remonstrance in the absence of a *lit de justice*, the ceremony's use as a forum for expressing the king's wish for immediate registration of laws meant that any remonstrances offered subsequent to the ceremony were highly political since they directly flouted royal orders. Thus, remonstrances and *lits de justice* came to be closely associated in the eighteenth century, with the *lit de justice* often serving to heighten rather than defuse tension. Louis XIV's tight control of the remonstrance process coupled with his neglect of the *lit de justice* removed from the spotlight relations with parlement for much of his reign. The simultaneous revival of these two elements increased the scope for public clashes, as occurred in the 1730s, 1750s and 1760s. In his anger at the duc d'Orléans in 1771, Louis XV taxed him with this rash act of his grandfather's, the root of all his troubles.[17] However, the regency revival of the ceremony did not oblige Louis XV and his ministers to make use of the form as they did. Its survival during the Maupeou reforms – indeed, its use to inaugurate those new measures – is a testimony to the power this ceremony held for contemporaries. From the parlementary and public perspective, the appearance of the monarch in this forum lent it a special glamour and, by the 1770s, the *lit de justice* was incontrovertibly 'great state occasion …[one of the] most solemn rituals of the monarchy'.[18] The *lit de justice* was a major public occasion, one watched by the politically minded for key legislative developments and by the curious for the titillating spectacle of opposition to the king. In 1774, the question of Louis XVI's attendance at his first *lit de justice* as king was, due to the years of agitation about the Maupeou parlement, of deep political as well as ceremonial significance and for that reason merits discussion as one of the great public ceremonies of the first year of his reign.

While studies of the parlement and the broader 'world of law' have brought new colour to our vision of the eighteenth-century legal environment,[19] the central ceremony of this world – the flashpoint of so many political rows in the eighteenth century: the *lit de justice* – remains under-examined. It is important as it raises the central question of the exercise of power. While accounts of these encounters circulated freely at the time, in the form of printed *procès-verbaux*, their nineteenth-century compiler Jules Flammermont excised all detail of ritual conduct from his monumental work *Remontrances du parlement de Paris au XVIIIe siècle*, preserving only the speeches. As this has served as the major reference work for historians of the parlement, his decision has had a significant impact on our understanding of the broader nature of *lits de justice* and, perhaps, served to skew the development of the study of the parlements in a certain direction.[20] Historians have based their work on the parlement on what was *said* without reference to what was *done*.

In this chapter, the printed *procès-verbaux* have been used as a major, and untapped, resource for understanding the conduct of *lits de justice* and as a basis for examining what was done and how things were said.

Early moderns used the term *lit de justice* to describe the event of the king presiding over the assembled judicial court. As a ceremony, it is particularly interesting because the same forms could be used to serve distinct purposes. Unlike a funeral or a coronation, where the form of the ritual was specific to its purpose, the *lit*, a rather simple form it is true, was essentially the same no matter what business was transacted. Indeed, during the eighteenth century, the *lit* was regularly held outside the Palais de Justice, in the Tuileries or at Versailles, with the same forms observed. At the same time, it was not impossible for the government side to alter the shape of the ritual to achieve particular political effects, as occurred on 12 November 1774.

The broad outlines of a *lit de justice* were as follows.[21] The parlementaires assembled to await the king in the *grand'chambre* of the parlement building, the Palais de Justice on the Île de la Cité in Paris, wearing their

PROCÈS-VERBAL

DE CE QUI S'EST PASSÉ

AU LIT DE JUSTICE,

Tenu par LE ROI *à Paris, le Samedi douze Novembre 1774.*

A PARIS,

DE L'IMPRIMERIE ROYALE.

M. DCCLXXIV.

5 The cover page of the *procès-verbal* of the *lit de justice* of November 1774. Information on *lits de justice* circulated widely.

ceremonial red robes. The king, greeted on arrival by the princes of the blood, heard mass in the Sainte-Chapelle and then walked in procession to the *grand'chambre*. The *lit de justice*, from which the ceremony got its name, was a magnificent canopied chair, decorated with velvet hangings and elevated above the main body of the chamber atop seven steps.[22] The king physically overlooked and dominated the entire chamber. The *lit* remained in place even when not occupied by the king and, in the mythology of the parlement, was 'supposed always to be occupied by the King, and no one takes it in his absence'.[23] The chancellor or keeper of the seals served as intermediary between the lofty sovereign and the rest of the assembly, repeatedly climbing up and down the steps to ascertain the royal will and then communicate it to the meeting. He was the most mobile individual at any *lit de justice* since no one else moved around the chamber other than at the opening and closing of the session. To be sure, the court's clerk might move from his desk in order to read an edict intended for registration, but this was only at the chancellor's bidding. He did not circulate, as the chancellor did, through the ranks of peers and parlementaires, crossing and re-crossing the *parquet*.

Hats demarcated rank among the parlementaires.[24] The *premier président* and the nine *présidents à mortier* wore distinctive headgear to differentiate themselves from the rest of their colleagues. To these high round hats of black velvet, the *premier président* added the further distinction of two rows of golden braid where the other *présidents* had only one.[25] The *procureurs*, *gens du roi* and ushers wore square hats with obligatory *chaperons* for *procureurs* and staffs of office for the ushers.[26] Men's hats were key signifiers of respect in eighteenth-century French society. A wealth of status information could be conveyed by covering or uncovering one's head at appropriate (or inappropriate) moments, meaning that the wearing of a hat could become the source of some anxiety.[27] In 1720, business at the Palais de Justice ground to a halt over questions of hat-wearing on four separate occasions.[28]

At a *lit de justice*, the doffing and donning of hats was strictly controlled as one indicator of hierarchy and respect. The king removed and replaced his hat as a salute to the assembly before his opening words. He then spoke to the assembly while seated and wearing his hat. The chancellor removed his hat in order to consult with the king from a kneeling position. He then replaced it while addressing the gathering, usually sitting in his chair at the foot of the *lit de justice*. When the time came for one of their number to speak, the parlementaires all removed their hats and knelt. In the name of the king, the chancellor granted them permission

6 A rare image of a *lit de justice* in the reign of Louis XVI, this one at Versailles on 6 August 1787 by Giradet and Duparc. The king's elevated position is clearly visible as is raised seating for peers.

to stand. They remained standing, bareheaded, holding their hats in their hands, until their representative concluded his oration, watched by the seated ranks of hat-wearing princes of the blood and dukes-and-peers. This sequence of gestures of abasement was repeated on each occasion a parlementaire addressed the king. Their sometimes feisty rhetoric was uttered from an imposed position of physical humility, their standing bareheaded in contrast to the head-covered seated position of the king and his officers.

From the revival of remonstrances in 1715 to the parlement's twin remonstrances on the exile of the duc d'Orléans and the outcome of the *séance royale* in 1788, the relationship between the princes of the blood and the Paris parlement was complex and evolved over the course of the century.[29] On the death of Louis XIV in 1715, the princes turned to the parlement in order to inaugurate the regency at the *séance* on 2 September but also to strip Louis XIV's legitimated sons of their highest honours. These actions consecrated the parlement as *the* forum for the performance of the rank of prince of the blood since, in removing the title of prince of the blood from Maine and Toulouse, it was specified that they were henceforth to sit among the peers in the parlement ranked only in order of the venerability of their peerage. The legitimated princes never again enjoyed the right to cross the *parquet* and sit with the princes of the blood.[30] From the middle of the eighteenth century, the parlement and princes of the blood were increasingly allied on overtly political topics, in no small part thanks to the efforts of the prince de Conti after his falling out with the king in 1756.[31] The events of 1770/71 saw a clear majority of princes of the blood side with the parlement against the king, as discussed in the previous chapter. Again, a *lit de justice* proved the turning point as their refusal to attend the inaugural *lit* of the Maupeou parlement led to their banishment from the court and, though this was a less severe punishment than the exile experienced by the parlementaires, their position in that dispute had a large part to play in the political events of the early days of Louis XVI's reign.

No political stance could alter the fact that on ceremonial occasions such as a *lit de justice*, the princes of the blood sat with the king, in seats raised above those of the parlementaires though lower than that of the king. The princes of the blood faced the magistrates from the king's side and were expected to support the king's policy as it was announced.[32] The gesture of individual consultation of the princes was just that – a gesture, not an opportunity for oratory. Since the princes of the blood were some of the few who were allowed to cross the well of the court, the *parquet*, this stretch of floor formed a barrier between them and the rest of those in attendance. Many aspects of their position in the chamber symbolically captured the important political truth that, no matter how much they sided with the parlement, their status, their very existence as part of the body politic, depended directly on the king. The princes of the blood, followed by the dukes-and-peers, were always the groups most closely associated with the king's movements at any given ceremony and, if he were absent, were given the place of honour. From the 1750s, the princes of the blood were often invited when the parlement met with all chambers assembled to discuss laws and, when present, they always spoke first, thus influencing the shape of the debate. Even defiant meetings retained hierarchy as a badge of status. The physical arrangement of the ceremony depicted the political realities of overlapping and intersecting hierarchies and loyalties. The princes of the blood stood above the parlementaires but below the direct line, their loyalty to the House of Bourbon was complicated by their alliances with the parlement; the parlementaires' ultimate loyalty to the king and to the fundamental laws was entangled with their coalitions with the princes. The *lit de justice* could be an occasion for celebration and unity, or for confrontation, anxiety and fear.

Under Louis XV, legislative *lits de justice* were frequently presented by the government as a stage for royal anger, a policy discontinued under Louis XVI. The parlementaires invariably addressed this anger in their interventions as something they feared but which was wrongly applied to them, thus honouring the power of royal anger while exonerating themselves.

Overall, the physical staging of any *lit de justice* was one framed by permissions. The Palais de Justice was the magistrates' territory but their every act during this ritual was performed on foot of explicit permission from the king, communicated through the chancellor. There was no automatic right to speak, to stand or even to wear a hat. The parlementaires were told when they had permission to engage in these actions. In all appearance, then, the *lit de justice* illustrates the absolute power of the French monarch. Within these constraints on movement, however, there were set occasions to speak which the parlementaires exploited. In 1771, for example, at the *lit de justice* inaugurating the Maupeou parlement, Louis Antoine Séguier used his dedicated slot as *avocat du roi*, when he was theoretically obliged to support the king's position, to offer a defiant and lengthy public defence of his exiled colleagues to Louis XV. His speech and behaviour amply illustrate the particular mindset of the parlement and its emotional underpinnings.[33] Likewise, the ceremony did not require the king to be terse: Louis XV chose to speak only briefly but Louis XVI made some lengthy interventions at *lits*. Nonetheless, the ceremony was not a framework for debate and these exchanges did not lead to shifts in position or amendments to legislation on the day. The *lit de justice* offers a picture of the monarchy in miniature: an appearance of absolute control belied by the subtler workings of shared power, loyalty, anxiety, continuity and change.

By the time Louis XVI came to the throne, then, the *lit de justice* was established as the one of the most overtly political battlegrounds in the French polity. By 1774, the ceremony was firmly associated with Louis XV's efforts to oblige the parlement to obey and with his failure to do so, since attempts to bring the parlement to heel by convening *lits de justice* to register edicts of discipline were known to have failed in 1756 and again in 1770. In 1773, *Président* d'Ormessonn noted in his journal that only a *lit de justice* would consolidate Maupeou's new institution.[34] The new king's attendance at his first *lit de justice* was anxiously awaited since it would undoubtedly signal his intentions towards both the exiles and the members of the Maupeou parlement.

Political rituals of the summer and autumn of 1774

The summer of 1774 was full of incident – the many events to mark the passing of Louis XV, the young king's inoculation and recovery, the illness of his aunts, the drama over attendance at the catafalque ceremony – and, taking all these into account, it seems unsurprising that so serious a matter as the appointment of a new ministerial team was not completed before the end of August.[35] Historians have generally followed the abbé Véri's well-known account of the dismissal of Chancellor Maupeou and Controller General Terray, known as the Saint Bartholomew's massacre of ministers, according to which it was Maurepas' impatience that finally forced the young king's hand.[36] This account, which says nothing about Louis XVI's patience, is predicated on a summer largely devoid of events. It overlooks the importance of the funeral ceremonies at Saint Denis in July and in Paris in September, both of which required the participation of the parlement, and the entwined negotiations on attendance and recall, awareness of which adds depth to our understanding of relations between the monarchy and parlement in these months.

There was a clear sense that all offices and officers were open to change at the beginning of the reign. The ministry did not stagnate in the earliest days of the reign with several changes of personnel made in advance of the sensational dismissal of Maupeou and Terray in August. The first new arrival was the comte de Maurepas in early June, as adviser to the king.[37] Lieutenant General comte du Muy, a former *menin* of Louis XVI's father, took office as minister for war immediately after the duc d'Aiguillon's resignation.[38] A courier was dispatched to summon Charles Gravier, comte de Vergennes, from the French embassy in Stockholm on 6 June with reliable long-term member of the minstry, Henri Léonard Bertin, taking charge of the foreign affairs portfolio pending his arrival.[39] Anne-Robert de Turgot entered the marine ministry on 20 July, becoming controller general after Terray's departure. When Maupeou took the title of chancellor into exile with him on 24 August, he was replaced by 'one of his victims', Armand Thomas Hue de Miromesnil, a first *président* of the parlement of Rouen who became keeper of the seals.[40] Thus, there were three new ministers in place by the end of July, five by the end of August, as well as the important new minister without portfolio, the 'shadow of a meeting point', the comte de Maurepas.[41]

The timing of the dismissal of Controller General Terray and Chancellor Maupeou on 24 August is intriguing, given that it took place at a personally important juncture in the calendar for the monarch, between his twentieth birthday on 23 August and his name-day and feast of the patron-saint of the kings of France, Saint Louis, on 25 August. A flavour of contemporary thinking is found in the journal of Siméon-Prosper Hardy in Paris who greeted the news as epoch-making:

> Our young monarch, Louis XVI, could not better celebrate the anniversary of his birth and the feast day of one of his most illustrious predecessors, since he is at the same time his patron saint, than by spreading happiness and consolation in all hearts, these hearts which have for three years been restricted and oppressed by sadness begin now to expand with the news of a event which seems to announce a new order of things.[42]

News of the ministerial modification was known in Paris by six o'clock on the evening of 24 August[43] and was greeted by political rituals in the streets, with the jubilant public spirit even appropriating some planned festivities for the king's birthday. Fireworks in honour of that occasion at the Palais de Justice drew a huge crowd. Guards were summoned, as the crowd appeared to make a direct link between the ministers' fate and that of the Maupeou parlement and did not behave well towards them: 'the people are pitiless towards them'.[44] The next day the guard was increased at the Palais with more dispatched to protect Maupeou's Paris residence on Place Vendôme.[45] On the morning of 29 August, two straw figures with wax masks were found hanged near Sainte-Geneviève.[46] One of the effigies was dressed in a *simarre*, the characteristic gown of the chancellor, with the *cordon bleu* of the Order of the Holy Spirit and a wax face-mask of a distinctive orange colour.[47] As if this were not a clear enough indication of the intended victim, a placard reading 'Maupeou chancelier' was hung around his neck. The other figure bore the legend 'l'abbé Terrai (sic), contrôleur général des finances'. Both straw figures had their limbs dislocated as though they had been broken on the wheel. A crowd gathered before they were removed around six o'clock in the morning. This theatrical gesture was by no means the only one and several more participative demonstrations also took place. On the night of 30 August, there were further disturbances at the Palais de Justice. In the great tumult fireworks were thrown. At least one member of the *garde de la prévôté* and probably several others were injured.[48]

The ritualistic burning in effigy of the chancellor cannot be described as a spontaneous event since it took place on 31 August 'with the greatest pomp' and with an audience of more than twenty thousand souls.[49] The *Nouvelles à la main de Penthièvre* report an initial desire to burn the effigy in the courtyard of the Palais itself and in front of Maupeou's hôtel, and this is echoed by the *Journal historique*. Associations of spontaneity with unofficial rituals are sometimes used to denigrate them, rendering them as outbursts of unregulated emotion rather than planned demonstrations just as, paradoxically, ceremonies at the other end of the social scale are frequently portrayed as overly organised, lacking in real emotional content and therefore redundant. This occasion was a well-organised, theatrical display of political feeling of approval for royal policy: a *cérémonie de l'information* from below to above.[50] These events demonstrate that those beyond the parlementaires and the élite felt they had a stake in these political matters, and that, in the absence of representative mechanisms, ritual displays served to express these feelings. The parlement was part of a much larger, and more colourful, universe than the analysis of remonstrances, or even *lits de justice*, would lead us to believe, and politics stretched far beyond Versailles.[51]

The ceremony took place on the Place Dauphine, in the shadow of the Palais de Justice and under the watchful eyes of several squadrons of soldiers. An effigy of the chancellor was formally sentenced and had its hand cut off. It was required to ask forgiveness from the king, the queen, the princes of the blood, the magistrates and the nation. The effigy was robed in something resembling the chancellor's *simarre* and its torso stuffed with fireworks. It blazed as the crowd sang the *Salve* and danced round the bonfire. The ashes were then tossed to the winds – the usual procedure following the burning of heretics and witches – and fireworks continued until five in the morning amid shouts of 'vive le roi! Vive l'ancien parlement!'[52] Clearly, the exile of Maupeou was widely associated with an immediate dismissal of his parlement. It was rumoured that the government was well aware of the planned burning of the effigy and had permitted it to proceed. No one was surprised by this.[53]

Concern grew about the maintenance of public order around the Palais de Justice. On 1 September, the new lieutenant general of police, Lenoir,[54] requested the merchants, artists and artisans associated with the Palais to exert greater control over their workers. The sale of fireworks was forbidden and, on the same day, one sieur de Brai was fined fifteen livres for allowing others to set off fireworks from his windows.[55] Security was tightened appreciably inside the Palais itself. Most entrances were closed and passage through the complex was only permitted under armed escort. At the centre of the Palais, detachments of the *gardes françoises* were on standby. By dint of a slow walking advance, guards cleared the Pont Neuf where spectators had gathered. The crowd moved away peaceably but did not disperse. The soldiers and people laughed and drank together.[56] The ceremonial burning of an effigy of the abbé Terray planned for that night did not take place.[57] All in all there were about ten types of outrage perpetrated on the effigy of the chancellor in various places, including being pulled limb from limb by donkeys in an alarming schoolboy prank recalling the gruesome fate of regicides.[58]

Amid the hubbub, the king and queen enjoyed the acclaim of the unusually large crowds that waited for over three hours to cheer them on their return to Versailles from Compiègne.[59] The prince de Conti emerged from his somewhat notional seclusion, changing his usual practice of attending the Opera incognito for entering in grand style on 4 September. The other patrons obliged with a rapturous reception. It was rumoured that Miromesnil, the new keeper of the seals and former first president of the suppressed parlement of Rouen, had called on the parlementary prince.[60]

The dismissal of Maupeou from government translated the high level of public interest in the fate of the Maupeou parlement into public demonstrations of enthusiasm, through staged street ceremonies and through ritualised gestures, in this case, the recent innovation of hand-clapping at the Opera. Curiosity paired with political passion meant the public paid attention to the catafalque ceremony in July. Ceremonial farewells to the ministers were staged on the streets in August as further developments were awaited on the fate of the unpopular new parlement. As we saw in Chapter 2, the catafalque ceremony of July was a significantly more public event than the list of participants indicates; likewise the *lit de justice* of November was not merely a closed session in which the king addressed his legal officers. In fact, this event was the culmination of years of public political engagement at many different levels of society. As such, these public ceremonies reveal the shifting nature of the boundaries between public and private.

The tumult of popular applause for the exile of Maupeou did not mean that the incumbent parlement was instantly dismissed.[61] As the young king reportedly observed in late July, it simply wasn't possible to do everything at once.[62] Louis XVI met with a select group of ministers regularly in September to debate the pros and cons of the parlement question and, over the course of October, both Monsieur, the king's brother, and his cousin, the comte de la Marche, presented the king with memoranda in favour of preserving the Maupeou parlement, evidently confident that the question remained open.[63]

Meanwhile, the catafalque ceremony for Louis XV at Notre Dame on 7 September was attended by the members of the Maupeou parlement.

The royal master of ceremonies called at the parlement on 3 September to confirm orally their invitation to the ceremony on 7 September, giving some of the Maupeou parlementaires hope that they would be retained.[64] This was the last of the great public ceremonies related to Louis XV's death organised from Versailles, other than the regular annual anniversary masses said thereafter.[65] Other ceremonies in memory of the king continued without involvement from Versailles including one organised by the Sorbonne on 27 September.[66]

The cathedral was transformed for the event. An ambitious, if to modern eyes incongruous, false façade was erected, altering the external aspect from gothic to neo-classical by creating a line of corinthian columns topped with a pediment inscribed with an adapted version of a verse from the prophet Jeremiah: 'Judah mourns and the cry goes up from Jerusalem.' Contemporaries judged it 'magnificent'.[67] Internally, the layout of the cathedral was dramatically altered by the insertion of large wooden seating platforms for the distinguished guests and the entirety of the church was heavily draped in black. The focal point of the decoration was, of course, the catafalque. Like the catafalque at Saint Denis, this was designed by Challe and, though using many of the same architectural elements, he created a completely different effect for this separate ceremony.[68] The basic structure of the catafalque was, again, a four-columned, open-walled temple with several steps up to a platform on which was placed the bier. This was surrounded by sculpted female mourning figures, the bier covered in an ermine cloth, draped artistically to show the structure beneath. The dramatic difference in this design was on the roof of the structure where Challe placed not only large smoking funerary urns but also a massive victory column, 'raised to the loftiest height', inscribed with a spiral bas relief reminiscent of Trajan's column and topped with a winged figure of victory. This attracted popular admiration, though it was a perilous structure with at least two workmen killed during its elevation. The tone of the décor was in striking contrast to the lugubrious solemnity of Saint Denis, suitably marking the end of the cycle of grand mourning ceremonies.[69]

On the morning of 7 September, fifty members of Maupeou's parlement foregathered at the Palais de Justice in their red robes. From there they processed on foot to Notre Dame, escorted by *huissiers* rapping their staffs of office and by city guards.[70] The duc de Brissac, governor of Paris, clad in his long mourning cloak and wearing the collar of the order of the Holy Spirit, walked with them in the place of honour beside Bertier de Sauvigny, the first president. Among the parlementaires attending the

7 The false façade erected on the front of Notre Dame de Paris for the funeral ceremony of Louis XV on 7 September 1774, designed by Charles Michel-Ange Challe.

ceremony that morning was Désirat, the nemesis of the *jeune homme téméraire*, Micault.[71] Hardy noted in his journal that the large numbers of soldiers placed along the route taken by the parlementaires did not prevent catcalling on Rue Neuve and on the cathedral square. The *Journal historique* refers to 'some indistinct murmurs' as they passed.[72] The Swiss Guards and musketeers were on alert in case of trouble.[73] Clearly, public appearances of the Maupeou parlementaires provoked anxiety and the expectation of trouble in those charged with preserving order in Paris.

On the parlementaires' arrival at the cathedral, the large bell tolled and the *juré-crieurs* chimed in with their handbells. The parlementaires were conducted from a side door to high seats to the right of the altar beside the representatives of the university and, as at Saint Denis, their arrival was followed by that of the *chambre des comptes*. Once these dignitaries were seated, the clergy entered the cathedral through the main door. Around thirty-five archbishops and bishops took their places near the altar where the late king's first gentlemen of the bedchamber – the ducs de Fleury, Fronsac (for Richelieu), Aumont and Duras – were already seated, dressed in long mourning cloaks and wearing the insignia of the Order of the Holy Spirit. At midday the chief mourners, the comte de Provence, the comte d'Artois and the prince de Condé entered the cathedral by the choir door, in a solemn procession composed of the king- and heralds-at-arms, followed by members of the royal household. They were placed by the master of ceremonies in the seats closest to the altar and the service, celebrated by Christophe de Beaumont, archbishop of Paris, began.

The service in many ways mirrored that which had taken place in Saint Denis, including in the performance of ritual bows by the princes to the assembled corporate bodies, even the Maupeou parlementaires. Challe's dangerous catafalque caused much distraction when it caught fire during the funeral oration, though the conflagration was a minor affair, rapidly extinguished by soaked sponges on the end of poles. The service lasted three hours and ended with incensing of the catafalque. There was no heraldic element, no shout of 'vive le roi', since this had already been performed at Saint Denis in the presence of the king's buried body as tradition required. The participants then dispersed, the *premier président* taking his coach from outside the cathedral, the chief mourners being entertained at the archbishop's palace.

The occurrence of this final funeral ceremony at the beginning of September and the invitation to the Maupeou parlementaires goes some way to explaining the timing of the recall of the old parlement. If it was appropriate to hold the catafalque at Saint Denis with the new parlement, the same argument could be made for the catafalque at Notre Dame. Despite the paucity of sources on the king's thought processes, the ceremonial events of his early reign do reveal something about Louis XVI's approach to decision making. His dismissal of ministers aligned with personally significant dates. The recall of the exiled parlementaires also coincided with a significant and fitting date, Martinmas 11 November, the traditional day of their return to work from vacation, a feast day featuring the splendid ceremony of the *messe rouge* in the Palais de Justice when the parlementaires attended services in their red ritual regalia.[74] Work then usually resumed on 12 November.

Though no formal announcements on the Maupeou parlement's fate had been made, the president of the vacation chamber, Aymar-Charles-François de Nicolay, alerted his colleagues that persistent public whispers of an impending revolution in the constitution merited serious attention. They continued their discussions the following day and, since this gossip was judged to be fomenting 'a fermentation of minds which is prejudicial to the administration of justice and public peace', they instructed the *gens du roi* to raise their concerns directly with the king. On 24 October, they reported back that they had gained an audience with the king at Fontainebleau in the presence of Maurepas, Miromesnil and the ducs d'Aumont and de la Vrillière. The king's deadpan response to their concerns was telling: 'I am surprised, Sir, that the vacations chamber should make such a declaration on the basis of public rumour.'[75] The king was duping the Maupeou parlementaires. Letters recalling the exiled parlementaires had been signed by him at Fontainebleau on 21 October and, according to the *Nouvelles à la main de Penthièvre*, it was already known by some in Paris that they would be recalled the following week.[76] This is not the attitude of a monarch who was acting against his will and it is perfectly in tune with his policy, throughout his reign to date, of keeping the Maupeou parlement at a distance.

Regnault, the parlementary usher whose attention to proper procedure created the detailed records of proceedings we have today, is cited in the *Journal historique* for his insolence towards M. de Nicolay at this time. In the normal course of things, Regnault would precede such a distinguished officer, banging a staff of office to announce his passage. When Nicolay queried the absence of the staff around the end of October 1774, Regnault responded that it had been broken for four years.[77]

It was increasingly clear which way the wind was blowing. Maurepas, attending the Opera on 8 November, was applauded with such enthusiasm that he almost had to withdraw to allow the performance to proceed: on his departure, the duc de Chartres was observed giving the signal for further accolades.[78] By 9 November, the members of the old parlement had all returned to Paris as per royal command. The next day orders were delivered to their homes to present themselves, robed in red, at the Palais de Justice on 12 November.[79] The chief clerk of the court, Gilbert de Voisins, alone received instructions to go directly to the *grand'chambre* so that he could record the proceedings from the beginning.[80] On the morning of 11 November, the princes of the blood were invited by the grand master of ceremonies to attend the *lit de justice* on the following day. That evening, the duc d'Orléans attended the Opera for the first time since his withdrawal to the country, to great applause on his arrival and departure.[81]

'At last, these happy days have arrived …'[82]

At seven o'clock the next morning, 12 November, Louis XVI set out for Paris from La Muette accompanied by his brothers. At the entrance to Paris, they switched to a ceremonial coach and a mounted procession formed led by members of the grand falconry with troops from the grey musketeers and the black as well as the lighthorse and *gendarmes*, with the king's bodyguard positioned nearest to his coach. The French and Swiss Guards presented arms along the route. The royal party progressed slowly from the Porte de la Conférence through streets which echoed to cries of 'vive le roi!' and 'the most striking testaments of love and gratitude for all the good he seems ready to do for his people' to the Tuileries,[83] with the crowds projecting their hopes and aspirations onto the monarch. There they were greeted by the duc de Brissac, governor of Paris, who intoned a ceremonial address to the king on this occasion of his solemn entry into Paris and presented him with the keys to the city, just as had occurred on the occasion of Louis XV's first *lit de justice* and entry into Paris in 1715.

The procession continued on to the Palais de Justice where the princes of the blood welcomed the royal party at the foot of the grand staircase to the Sainte Chapelle.[84] They all entered together in order to hear mass and then proceeded to the *grand'chambre*. Leading the procession was the marquis de Clermont-Tonnerre, marshal of France, accompanying the king, who discreetly seated himself to the side while the king's brothers and the princes of the blood, those who had the right to walk across the *parquet*, moved to their seats. Monsieur and the comte d'Artois had special places between the king and the princes of the blood, thanks to their somewhat novel status as brothers of the king. Already seated were the provincial governors and lieutenants general as well as the knights of the Order of the Holy Spirit, although in theory they attended the *lit de justice* only as part of the king's entourage and were permitted only to accompany the king. The governors represented the king to his provincial parlements, presenting them with laws for registration in a format not dissimilar to a *lit de justice*. Every *lit de justice* summoned by Louis XVI was attended by at least some of these officers. They had also been present at the inaugural, and sole, *lit de justice* of the Maupeou parlement held at Versailles in April 1771 under Louis XV.

The king himself was accompanied by two royal ushers bearing silver maces and by six heralds-at-arms: these eight officers knelt in the middle of the *parquet* before the *lit de justice*. The duc de Bouillon, grand chamberlain, sat at the king's feet with the grand equerry, the prince de Lambesc – bearing the king's ornamental sword – seated on a stool to his right. On the left were the five captains of the king's guard as well as the provost of Paris, holding his white staff of office. At the foot of the steps to the *lit de justice* sat Miromesnil, the keeper of the seals. Ten counsellors of state, including Turgot as controller general of finance, and five masters of requests accompanied Miromesnil, all dressed in black satin robes. The other ministers, the duc de la Vrillière, Bertin, du Muy, Vergennes and Sartine were seated on a bench nearby. Though space was at a premium, the places usually occupied by the presidents, magistrates and lawyers of the parlement, including those of the *gens du roi* and the ushers, were left vacant. Contrary to time-honoured practice, possibly for the first time, the parlementaires were not present as the ceremony began.

Presiding over this assembly of the cream of the aristocracy and the representatives of his government at municipal, provincial and ministerial level, the king informed them of his plan to recall the old parlement and of his linked determination not to permit the dilution of his authority.[85] Miromesnil, having knelt before the king to receive his instructions, resumed his place and gave a more ample description of the planned changes. Once he had concluded, the king spoke again to reiterate the need for those assembled to lead by example in their obedience to his laws: 'I rely on your attachment and your zeal to demonstrate submission for all of my subjects.'[86]

It was exceedingly rare that the king should take possession of the main gathering place of the parlement in the absence of any its representatives.

In the usual course of a *lit de justice*, the parlementaires would be assembled prior to the king's arrival; it was most unusual for the king to use the space in this way.[87] Overlooking this novel element of the events of 12 November has led some to characterise the *lit de justice* as 'not a compromise but a surrender' by the monarchy,[88] a judgement with which it is difficult to concur in view of its staging. Ceremony was used effectively on this occasion to underline the significance of the powers at play.

The members of the old parlement, fresh from exile and returning to the Palais for the first time since 1771, were waiting in the chamber of Saint Louis, all in their red ceremonial robes with furred mantles for the presidents, who held their mortar-board hats in their hands, and furred hats for the councillors. The marquis de Dreux, grand master of ceremonies, entered and bade them to attend the king in the *grand'chambre* with the formula, no doubt momentous to his auditors, 'His Majesty calls you to him.'[89] They entered, making deep bows to the king, removing their hats. Once they had taken their places without distinction of office, the king lifted and replaced his hat and addressed the assembly: 'with no recriminations about the past, he spoke firmly'.[90] Invoking the shade of his grandfather, forced by their recalcitrance to ensure that justice was available to his subjects by other means, he informed the parlementaires that he was recalling them to duty. Duty was the keystone of his brief speech: the parlementaires were reminded of their duty to fulfil their role as magistrates but the king also referred to his duty to preserve the legacy of his predecessors. His promise to forget all was in fact the attempted promulgation of a law of silence on the Maupeou years rather than an act of clemency, echoing previous attempts to terminate debate on divisive subjects – such as the law of silence on the bull *Unigenitus*, issued by the regent in August 1720 and reiterated in 1754 by Louis XV,[91] and the law of silence on the d'Aiguillon affair which had so signally failed in 1770. Louis XVI ended his speech with a solemn warning to the parlementaires to occupy themselves only with their duties and pursuing his vision for the happiness of his subjects.

Louis XVI then personally announced the main office holders for the new parlement and robes swished around the *grand'chambre* as they took their places at his command. This treatment of parlementaires as individuals rather than as a corporation was also seen in the manner of their exile and of their summoning back to Paris – by personally addressed letter rather than to the group through the *premier président* – and could be regarded as a royal assertion of a right to police parlementaires individually, a direct challenge to the longstanding, and ardently defended, parlementary principle of corporatism, above all when combined as it was in 1771 with the confiscation of their offices to the profit of the king.[92] On this occasion, since it was to their advantage, the parlementaires acquiesced. The meeting had now taken on the traditional seating arrangements of a *lit de justice*.[93]

The legislative business of the day then commenced. The keeper of the seals, Miromesnil, dressed in a splendid purple velvet robe lined with crimson satin, climbed the seven steps to the king's lofty seat, knelt to receive his orders and then returned to his seat in an armchair, covered in the purple velvet carpet embroidered with golden fleurs-de-lys that extended from below the king's chair. He announced that the king had given permission for hats to be donned for the first time in the ceremony, marking the renewal of reciprocal respect. Proclaiming 'how happy I am to be at this moment the instrument of his supreme will', Miromesnil, who had also suffered in Maupeou's reforms, had the doors of the chamber opened and the edict re-establishing the parlement was read out by Gilbert, chief clerk of the court. Miromesnil then announced the king's permission for Étienne François d'Aligre, once more recognised as *premier président*, to speak on behalf of the parlement. The parlementaires rose and knelt as a body and were given permission to stand. They remained standing, bareheaded while all others had their hats on, for the duration of d'Aligre's speech. Though our central concern here is with the neglected ritual aspects of this ceremony, it is worth examining the main speeches from the parlementaire side to appreciate their corporate attitude as they returned to their functions.

D'Aligre took the floor, remarking that the king's praiseworthy motives at this assembly, 'to ensure the rule of law', were the only thing that could possibly enhance its splendour. The king's destiny and that of the parlement were clearly intertwined: his birth had seen them recalled from a previous exile; his accession could only give them hope. Quoting verbatim the promise that the king's magistrates would always advise him truly, made at the *lit de justice* marking the majority of Louis XV, and invoking the constitutional alliance of parlement, princes of the blood and peers copperfastened in the 1750s, d'Aligre declaimed that truth could come to the throne only through those voices.[94] D'Aligre accentuated precisely that combination of groups whose prohibited meeting in June 1770 had fanned the flames of the Brittany affair. Ministers were conspicuous in their absence from this advisory schema, though d'Aligre, and then Séguier, acknowledged their debts as well as the political reality by referring to the king's choice of ministers that had facilitated their recall. D'Aligre was careful to emphasise the king's personal role, encouraging him to live up to his widely reported principles of virtue: 'the heart of a prince who only wishes to rule with justice and goodness, is itself a temple to truth'.[95]

When d'Aligre finished, the keeper of the seals gave permission for the *gens du roi* to speak. Louis Antoine Séguier, Joly de Fleury and Barentin all knelt and, having received permission to stand, Joly de Fleury and Barentin remained standing, with their hats off, while Séguier took the floor. His opening phrases praised the king by comparing his virtues to those of his deceased father and suggesting that, even if Louis XVI had not taken the throne by birthright, the wishes of the people would have placed him there.[96] Having then offered a laudatory précis of the king's reign, including the renunciation of the *joyeuse entrée* levy, his inoculation against smallpox and the introduction of free circulation of grain, he evoked the calm after the storm, the summer of the king's reign, 'these happy days' which the king had inaugurated with the recall of the parlement, insisting throughout on the parlement's rectitude during their dispute with the deceased Louis XV.[97] He daringly continued by reiterating the principle of irremovability:

> the stunning setting and pomp which Your Majesty has dictated for this august ceremony, can only add a new support to the immutable law of property, and the political law of the irremovability of offices.[98]

The point was not lost on the public. Besenval noted this 'audacity' and felt that their recall served to confirm the principle.[99]

Both speakers were careful to describe the sovereign's duty to reign within the law, a description which, from their perspective, implied reigning in agreement with the parlement as the guardian of that law.[100] These were not conservative speeches of contrition but declarations of intent to continue to fulfil the parlement's duty as primary purveyor of unbiased advice to the king (whether or not he enjoyed the experience) and to do this as part of a body that included the highest aristocrats of the land exercising a clearly political function. 'It is so pleasing to us, Sire, to find ourselves again surrounded by the court of peers!' exclaimed Séguier, articulating parlementaire delight at their reunion with their high-ranking co-agitators. The parlementaires' characteristic vision of the king as the supreme magistrate continued to empower them to speak to him on their own terms, as a group of magistrates to an avowedly superior magistrate, all of whom derived legitimacy from the law. The repeated references to the king ruling in tune with the law and with justice were invocations of this shared foundation. As is proper for a group of magistrates, the law here should be understood a subject of interpretation and therefore of debate. This vision of the magistrates' relationship to the king was committed to the idea of constructive exchange and, as appropriate, remonstrances. Although this could be interpreted as aggressive rhetoric, the parlement under Louis XVI would prove much less argumentative than in the previous reign.

These speeches concluded, Miromesnil again kneeled at the king's feet before collecting the opinions of all the grandees in attendance, including the captains of the king's guards, as well as of the parlementaires. No one spoke aloud.[101] He then returned to the king's side and, having kneeled once more, he finally resumed his seat at the bottom of the steps, put his hat on, and declared that the king ordered the edict which had been read to be registered immediately by the court. This sequence of movements was rehearsed for each of the nine edicts and the one ordinance on discipline registered that day. The disciplinary text reiterated many of the limitations on parlementary behaviour found in the edict so unsuccessfully registered at the *lit de justice* on 7 December 1770 and prompted murmuring from the parlementaires. Séguier immediately indicated the parlement would appreciate more time to consider it but that it was inappropriate to do anything other than obey. Miromesnil ordered the measure registered immediately in the name of the king.[102]

When the registration of the edicts was concluded, the king spoke from his seat atop the *lit de justice*, reminding the magistrates that he expected them to act within the bounds of authority that he prescribed for them. After this brief speech, the king departed in procession, though without his brothers. The session had been lengthy. It was already two o'clock in the afternoon, but the business of the day was not concluded. Monsieur, the comte de Provence, proceeded to the Louvre where the members of the Maupeou parlement had been instructed to wait, clad in their black robes, since ten o'clock in the morning. He presided over a session of the *grand conseil* which heard again the edict transferring the parlementaires of 1771–74 to membership of that body and promising the *grand conseil* jurisdiction in the event of a judicial strike at the parlement, even though such strikes were banned on pain of forfeiture of office in the controversial edict of discipline registered that day.[103] The comte d'Artois, meanwhile, attended the *cour des aides* to oversee the registration of the edict re-establishing its members in their functions. They concluded their business around four o'clock and rejoined their brother at La Muette. This format, of the king holding a *lit de justice* and his brothers subsequently presiding over sessions of lower courts dealing with the same legislation, would be used again in 1776 when, following the *lit de justice* held on 12 March 1776 at Versailles to register Turgot's six edicts, Monsieur attended a session of the *cour des aides* in Paris on 19 March and the comte d'Artois was present at the *cour des comptes* on the same day.

The choreography of this unusual *lit de justice* must have been the object of some advance agreement. Certainly, d'Aligre had been spotted attending a long meeting with Maurepas as early as the beginning of September and, being too free in his speech on the sensitive topic, may have obliged Maurepas to request his withdrawal to his country estate in the middle of October.[104] Though both d'Aligre and Séguier had had years of exile to work on their speeches, it seems unlikely that the parlementaires as a body would have spontaneously seated themselves without distinction of rank, awaiting the king's indication of their new roles. Given their familiarity with the space, and years of habit, they would simply have taken up the places they were used to from 1771 and to which they returned on the king's word. Clearly, their movements were managed by the royal ceremonial staff to give maximum emphasis to their dependence on the king's goodwill and, in line with the king's speech, the idea that this was a new beginning, without reference to the past. They moved to their proper places only when given the king's explicit permission, taking up seats in order of rank, chamber and age, as usual.

For several nights after the *lit de justice*, the Palais de Justice itself and the streets of Paris were illuminated in public rejoicing at the return of the old parlement.[105] The fish-wives of Les Halles visited each of the parlementaires in turn to deliver their compliments, performing a song they had composed in honour of the occasion.[106] Wags noticed that 12 November was chancellor Maupeou's name-day and circulated the following acrostic verse, based on his first name, René:

> Receive for your gift, this new compliment,
> Enjoy, on this high day, the return of the Parlement,
> No, you couldn't make your feast-day more sweet,
> Except – give us your head, to make it complete.[107]

President d'Ormesson de Noiseau was publicly applauded on his first appearance at the Académie des Belles-Lettres since 1771.[108] Commemorative engravings were issued for sale such as the one reproduced in Figure 8. A series of monuments to commemorate the glory of

8 'The longed-for return', engraving by Wolckh.

the king and his great deed in recalling the parlement were mooted.[109] Charles François Lubersac de Livron presented the king with 10-foot high paintings of a massive obelisk he planned to site between the Seine and the Louvre, which were duly displayed at Versailles and the Tuileries.[110] These festive gestures of illumination and public acclaim bear comparison with those marking return from exile of other parlements, though there was one notable difference that, again, served to underline their dependence on the king's goodwill.[111] By commanding a *lit de justice*, the king and the ministry had asserted and retained control of the ceremony of return. There was no triumphal procession of parlementaires through the streets of Paris. Illuminations and public applause were postponed until after the *lit de justice* had been used as a setting to confirm that the parlementaires returned on the king's terms.[112] The closest to a triumphal return ceremony was the *messe rouge* celebrated on the later date of 21 November to

> acclamations, in fact all that real and sincere testimony that not only the Parlement, but each of its members has individually received from the Public, either at the red mass, in the halls and courtyards of the Palais and in the streets.[113]

The following month, the princes of the blood and peers were invited by the parlement to discuss the legislation passed on 12 November. The session was attended by about 130 voting members, including the parlement's bugbear – the duc d'Aiguillon – and the king's two brothers. The latter's attendance was proof of the difference in attitude to the parlement between Louis XV and Louis XVI, since the young princes had not attended such sessions in their grandfather's reign. Indeed, the new king showed a willingness to countenance debate which seemed quite novel. The chargé d'affaires at the British Embassy wrote that 'the King does not conceive the least Jealousy of these Proceedings. On the contrary, He is very gracious to the [leading parlementary agitator] Prince of Conti with whom he had lately very long secret conversations.'[114] While Monsieur took the unpopular line of speaking strongly in favour of submission to the king's will,[115] Louis XVI apparently did not agree that this was appropriate, saying to him after the meeting 'please, dear brother, do not be so anxious about my authority. I will take care of it myself'.[116] Monsieur's rhetoric was striking: he was at pains to emphasise that he did not speak as a prince of the blood but as a gentleman with the country's best interests at heart. The other princes of the blood on the day spoke in favour of remonstrances. The prince de Conti's suggestion that, rather than appointing the usual committee to draw up a document, all members of the assembly should be allowed to submit written remarks, carried the day by 120 votes to 10. The duc d'Aiguillon, exercising the peerage rights the parlement had sought to deny him in 1770, backed Monsieur's motion for obedience.

9 Monument to the Glory of Louis XVI and of France presented by abbé Lubersac, Noirlac and de Brive.

Conclusion

What, then, was the significance of the *lit de justice* ceremony in 1774? While the historiography of the exile of the parlement has been revisited and revised, as we saw in the Chapter 2, that of the recall is thin by comparison – with the idea that it was a mistake, revelatory of the king's personal weakness, still having some currency. Looking at ceremony during these months reveals careful consideration of the matter and the gradual unfolding of a plan to recall the parlement at an appropriate and propitious time. Clearly, the recall of the parlement was a pivotal event in the early reign of Louis XVI, deeply woven into the rich political tapestry of that year. It ended the major political dispute of Louis XV's reign, a dispute that had the potential to continue to poison the authority of his successor.

The street rituals of the summer of 1774 show a high level of engagement with the major political questions of the day. People burned and hung effigies of ministers, they gathered to drink and sing in the shadow of the Palais de Justice. The *poissardes* of Les Halles sang topical songs of congratulations to the parlementaires, revealing a vibrant political culture in wider society nonetheless intimately connected to the grand ceremonial set-pieces.

For the first time, the *lit de justice* of 12 November 1774 has been examined here as a ritual in its own right. The flexibility of the ritual has been noted and, above all, the intentional introduction of novel forms to emphasise political points has been highlighted. The king's occupation of the *grand'chambre* in the absence of the parlementaires was deeply symbolic, as was their summoning to his presence and the requirement that they sit without distinction of rank or office until informed of their 'new' positions. This was a ritual fiction since, after all, they resumed the offices they had held in 1771 later in the ceremony and, we may assume, they entered the Palais de Justice reasonably certain that they would. This physical enactment, in miniature, of their recall from exile and reinstatement in office was arguably a more effective assertion of authority than royal bluster. It also points to the strength of conviction on the governmental side: this sort of planning smacks of decision, not capitulation.

However, this *lit de justice* did not resolve the difficulties inherent in ritual interactions between the king and his parlement, nor should we expect one ceremony to have accomplished that gargantuan task at a stroke. The *lit de justice* was a highly unusual ceremony since it was part of a continuum of relations between government and parlement.

Its format was stable, but its outcome was contingent and unpredictable since it depended on the reactions of the parlement to the specific content of the law in question. The *lit de justice* could be, and often was, carried out without its main issue being closed. Hence, it would be easy to categorise the more celebratory *lits de justice*, such as those marking the majority of a king or the reinstatement of the parlement, as 'successful' ceremonies, while those that dealt unsuccessfully with complex policy issues could be deemed 'failures'. However, this sort of utilitarian characterisation of ceremonies is simply not appropriate since their work was in the infinitely less quantifiable realm of staging the relationships that formed the bedrock of the *ancien régime*. Though kings and their ministers perhaps seemed to confirm the utilitarian approach by at times conducting their legislative business for some years without recourse to a *lit de justice* – eleven years for Louis XVI, twenty-four years in the case of Louis XV and over forty years for Louis XIV – the ceremony always reappeared. Even Louis XIV contemplated convening a *lit de justice* on the topic of *Unigenitus* in the last days of his reign.[117] It was not a necessary part of relations between king and parlement but it was, it would seem, integral to them.

Contemporaries found these highly ritualised meetings significant and expected them as part of their political landscape. The permissions and silences of the *lit de justice*, as well as of the deputations that often met with the monarch, did not accommodate the representative concerns of the parlement, nor were they adequate to the needs of government.[118] By the late 1780s, this had become clear to the vast majority of politically aware French people who began to call for the convocation of the Estates General. The government's summoning of the Assembly of Notables in 1787 and 1788 was a response to this deeply felt need, though this did not mean an end to political ritual since both the Assembly of Notables and the Estates General were framed by their own specific ceremonies and, of course, the invention of new political rituals was thought necessary throughout the revolution and beyond.

Notes

1 There is no mention of the ritual aspects in J.H. Shennan, *The Parlement of Paris*, Second Edition (Stroud, 1998), 319 *passim*; in Jean Egret, *Louis XV et l'opposition parlementaire, 1715–1774* (Paris, 1970), 225; or in Bailey Stone, *The Parlement of Paris, 1774–1789* (Chapel Hill, 1981), 35–38, when dealing with the *lit de justice* of 12 November 1774, or any other *lit de justice*.

John Rogister, *Louis XV and the Parlement of Paris, 1737–1755* (Cambridge, 1995), chapter one, touches on some ritual aspects, though there is no analysis of the *lit de justice* as a ceremonial form. David A. Bell, *Lawyers and Citizens: The making of a political elite in old regime France* (Oxford, 1994), notes ceremonial aspects of everyday behaviour at the parlement but does not deal with the *lit de justice* as such. Olivier Chaline, *Godart de Belbeuf: le parlement, le roi et les normands* (Paris, 1996), pays attention to ceremony at the parlement in Rouen throughout, though of course there are no *lits de justice*.

2 Julian Swann, *Politics and the Parlement of Paris, 1754–1774* (Cambridge, 1995), 368; see also William Doyle, 'The parlements of France and the breakdown of the old régime, 1771–1778', *French Historical Studies*, 6:4 (Fall 1970), 440.

3 See John Hardman, *The Life of Louis XVI* (New Haven, 2016), chapter two; Jean-Christian Petitfils, *Louis XVI* (Paris, 2005), chapter 6 'le roi manipulé'; Evelyn Lever, *Les Dernières Noces de la monarchie: Louis XVI* (Paris, 2005), chapter V. Munro Price adds the nuance that this was 'respectful brainwashing': 'Politics: Louis XVI', in *The Oxford Short History of France: Old Regime France* (Oxford, 2002), 230. These analyses all draw on the account provided by the abbé Véri, a confidant of Maurepas who was disposed to paint him in a powerful light and whose version of events is rarely challenged. Compare Joël Félix, *Louis XVI et Marie-Antoinette: un couple en politique* (Paris, 2016), 112 *passim*.

4 Jean Louis Giraud de Soulavie, *Mémoires historiques et politiques sur le règne de Louis XVI* (Paris, 1801), volume 2, 203. Alfred Cobban adds '[i]f we ask why reform had to give place to revolution, the explanation … must primarily be … the personality of the ruler' in *A History of Modern France, volume I* (London, 1957), 112. But see also Félix, *Louis XVI et Marie-Antoinette*, 115.

5 Munro Price, 'Politics', 37; John Hardman and Munro Price in *Louis XVI and the Comte de Vergennes: correspondence 1774–1787* (Oxford, 1998). According to Hardman, this is nine-tenths of the king's surviving correspondence, *French Politics 1774–1789: From the accession of Louis XVI to the fall of the Bastille* (London, 1995), 184. How might historians' pen portraits of Louis XVI in 1774 differ if his thoughts on other matters had survived?

6 Viscount Stormount to the Earl of Rochford, 22 June 1774. NASPF, SP 78/292.

7 The exact legal status of registration was unclear. On this 'confusion of powers', see Albert Hamscher, *The Parlement of Paris after the Fronde, 1653–1673* (London, 1976), 84.

8 For examples from the mid-seventeenth century, see Shennan, *The Parlement of Paris*, 250 passim.

9 Ibid., 4. On the parlement as an emotional community, see my 'We disobey by serving you well': the *lit de justice* in the eighteenth century' in *Rituals of Power*, Anna Kalinowska (editor) (forthcoming).

10 *Gazette de Leyde*, Numéro XLVI, 10 juin 1774, Suite des nouvelles de Paris du 3 juin. Maupeou was not given the opportunity to defend his reforms in Council, see *Mémoire de Maupeou à Louis XVI* printed in Jules Flammermont, *Le Chancelier Maupeou et les parlements* (Paris, 1883), 599–646.

11 Viscount Stormont to the Earl of Rochford, 25 May 1774. NASPF, SP 78/292.

12 Ibid.

13 Doyle, 'The parlements of Paris', 437; Émile Raunié, *Chansonnier historique du dix-huitième siècle* (Paris, 1883), volume 8, 259.

14 The king summoned a deputation of parlementaires to Versailles. Rogister, *Louis XV*, 247.

15 Studies of the *lit de justice* as a ceremony have barely addressed the eighteenth century, with the second half of the century even less remarked upon. See Sarah Hanley, *The* Lit de Justice *of the Kings of France: Constitutional ideology in legend, ritual and discourse* (Princeton, 1983); critical commentary from: E.A.R. Brown and Richard C. Famiglietti, *The Lit de Justice: Semantics, ceremonial, and the parlement of Paris, 1300–1600* (Sigmaringen, 1994); Mack P. Holt, 'The king in parlement: the problem of the *lit de justice* in sixteenth-century france', *The Historical Journal*, 21 (1988), 507–23; and R.J. Knecht, 'Francis I and the "lit de justice": a 'legend' defended', *French History*, 7 (1993), 53–83. Shennan, *The Parlement of Paris* remains the key general history of the parlement, well complemented for the second half of the eighteenth century by Julian Swann, *Politics and the Parlement of Paris under Louis XV, 1754–1774* (Cambridge, 1995), and Stone, *The Parlement of Paris*. These monographs are political and institutional in focus. See also Julian Swann, 'Repenser les parlements au XVIIIe siècle: du concept de "l'opposition parlementaire" à celui de "culture juridique des conflits politiques", in *Le Monde parlementaire au XVIIIe siècle: l'invention d'un discours politique*, Alain J. Lemaître (editor) (Rennes, 2010), 17–37. I am not aware of studies of the *lit de justice* as a ceremony in this period.

16 See John J. Hurt, *Louis XIV and the Parlements: The assertion of royal authority* (Manchester, 2002), particularly chapters one and two. On the content and role of remonstrances, see Rogister, *Louis XV*, 12.

17 Michel Antoine, *Louis XV* (Paris, 1989), 931.

18 Julian Swann, 'Robe, sword and aristocratic reaction revisited. The French nobility and political crisis (1748–1789)' in *Der europäische Adel in Ancien Régime: von der Krise der ständische Monarchien bis zur Revolution (1600–1789)*, Ronald Asch (editor) (Cologne, 2001), 151.

19 See footnote 1 above, and particularly the work of David Bell.

20 John Rogister also points to the dominance of Flammermont as a difficulty in the historiography of the parlement, *Louis XV*, xviii.

21 By the eighteenth century, *lits de justice* were synonymous with the parlement in Paris. In earlier centuries, *lits de justice* were also held in other parlements. See Henri Bastard d'Estang, *Les Parlements de France*, volume 1 (Paris, 1857), 194 *passim*.

22 This sort of elevated canopied chair had also been used at royal entry ceremonies. Lawrence M. Bryant, *The King and the City in the Parisian Royal Entry Ceremony: Politics, ritual and art in the renaissance* (Geneva, 1986), 100.

23 Rogister, *Louis XV*, 13, quoting a speech by Drouyn de Vandeuil on 9 March 1767.

24 Bastard d'Estang, *Les Parlements de France*, volume 1, 610.

25 Ibid., 170; Chaline, *Godart de Belbeuf*, 51–52.

26 Bastard d'Estang, *Les Parlements de France*, volume 1, 608.

27 Bell notes in passing in *Lawyers and Citizens*, 54, 198. See also André Grellet-Dumazeau, *L'Affaire du bonnet et les mémoires de Saint-Simon* (Paris, 1913), 52, which reports the fury sparked by retention of his hat by *premier président* Novion while addressing the dukes and peers when it had been removed to speak to the princes of the blood and the *présidents à mortier*. One peer responded in kind: 'Le duc d'Uzès perdit patience, enfonça son chapeau et opina couvert avec un air de menace'.

28 Bell, *Lawyers and Citizens*, 60–61.

29 Swann, 'Robe, sword', touches on relevant points. See also discussion of the status of the princes of the blood in the preceding chapter.

30 This probably explains the absence of the otherwise conscientious duc de Penthièvre from *lits de justice* and casts an interesting light on his nomination to chair a bureau of the Assembly of Notables.

31 See Antoine, *Louis XV*, 693, *passim*. For an unusual reading, see John D. Woodbridge, *Revolt in Pre-revolutionary France: The prince de Conti's conspiracy against Louis XV, 1755–57* (Baltimore, 1995).

32 See Rogister, *Louis XV*, 16, for a diagram of seating arrangements in the *grand'chambre*.

33 See my 'We disobey by serving you well'.

34 *Journal de Monsieur le président d'Ormesson de Noiseau*, AN 144 AP 120, volume 4, f 493–94.

35 See Hardman, *French Politics*, 31–44, for the appointments of 1774.

36 Hardman, *Louis XVI*, 35. Lever, *Louis XVI*, 86–87. Petitfils, *Louis XVI*, 182. Félix, *Louis XVI*, 122. All reproduce Véri's account on which a note of caution is appropriate since, as the confidant of Maurepas, he should not be taken to be entirely objective.

37 Jean-Frédéric de Phélypeaux, comte de Maurepas (1701–81). Minister for the marine under Louis XV, he was exiled from court from 1749 until his

return as adviser to the young king in 1774. Hardman, *French Politics*, 31–32.

38 D'Aiguillon resigned rather than be dismissed. Hardman, *Louis XVI*, 31. On du Muy, see Hardman, *French Politics*, 33–34.

39 Resident ambassadors were uncomfortable with the idea of an interim minister since they did not quite know what status to accord him and whether to conduct serious business with him. Vergennes was in Paris and holding meetings in his new capacity by the end of July. Ambassador Stormont was convinced that Maurepas had no influence in the appointment of de Muy and Vergennes. NASPF SP 78/292 (7 June, 22 June, 26 July and 27 July 1774).

40 Jean Egret, *Louis XV et l'opposition parlementaire, 1715–1774* (Paris, 1970), 223.

41 Price, 'Politics', 229; Rogister, *Louis XV*, 30–31.

42 Simeon Prosper Hardy, *Mes Loisirs ou journal d'événements tel qu'ils parviennent à ma connaissance*, BNF Ms Fr 6681, f 402.

43 *Nouvelles à la main de Penthièvre*, BM MS 2397, 24 août 1774. Given the timing of the events to be described, they must be taken as public actions of approval of royal policy rather than protests, though gestures of protest and disapproval were not uncommon. This suggests perhaps a longer and more complex political learning curve for protesters in Paris. See Micah Alpaugh, *Non-violence and the French Revolution: Political demonstrations in Paris, 1787–1795* (Cambridge, 2015), 46.

44 *Nouvelles à la main de Penthièvre*, BM MS 2397, 24 août 1774.

45 Ibid., 28 août 1774.

46 *Journal historique du rétablissement de la Magistrature: pour servir de suite à celui de la révolution opérée dans la Constitution de la Monarchie Françoise, par M de Maupeou, Chancelier de France* (London, 1775), volume 6, 170.

47 Maupeou's sallow complexion earned him the nickname 'little Seville orange' (petit bigarrade) from Louis XV.

48 *Journal historique*, volume 6, 172.

49 'Lettres De M. R** à M. M** Concernant Ce Qui S'est Passé D'intéressant à La Cour Depuis La Maladie Et La Mort De Louis XV. Jusqu'au Rétablissement Du Parlement De Paris', in *Mélanges publiés par la Société des Bibliophiles Français* (Paris, 1826), 87.

50 Michèle Fogel's interesting study, *Les Cérémonies de l'information dans la France du XVIe siècle au XVIIIe siècle* (Paris, 1989). See also the discussion of the entry into Reims in chapter four.

51 See David A. Bell, 'The "public sphere", the state and the world of law in eighteenth century France', *French Historical Studies*, 17:4 (Autumn 1992), 912–34.

52 Hardy, *Mes Loisirs*, f 410.

53 'Lettres De M. R** à M. M**', 88.

54 Jean-Charles-Pierre Lenoir (1732–1807), a magistrate, took office as lieutenant general in August 1774, replacing Antoine de Sartine, who had joined the royal ministry.
55 *Journal historique*, volume 6, 177.
56 Ibid., 175.
57 'Lettres De M. R** à M. M**', 87.
58 *Journal historique*, volume 6, 186.
59 Hardy, *Mes Loisirs*, f 410; *Journal historique*, volume 6, 174.
60 *Journal historique*, volume 6, 179, 189. Conti's patronage links with the parlement are set out in Julian Swann, 'Parlement, politics and the *parti janséniste:* the *grand conseil* affair, 1755–56', *French History*, 6:4 (1992), 455–57.
61 Nor was it universal. Condorcet, for one, lamented the return of the old parlement 'avec son insolence, ses prétensions et ses préjugés'. *Correspondance Inédite de Condorcet et de Turgot, 1770–1779* (Paris, 1883), Lettre CLII, 201.
62 Ormesson, *Journal*; AN 144 AP 120, volume 3, 1 juillet, f 1071.
63 *Journal historique*, volume 6, 248–49.
64 Ibid., 181.
65 It has proved impossible to find as detailed a description of the decoration of Notre Dame as was produced in the *Description du Mausolée érigé dans l'abbé royal de Saint Denis…* seen in the previous chapter. The descriptions in this chapter rely on engravings of the decorations: Louis-Simon Lempereur's etching, after Challe, of *Plan and elevation of false façade erected on Notre-Dame for the funeral of Louis XV* and an anonymous etching of *Catafalque of Louis XV,* both published in Richard P. Wunder, 'Charles Michel-Ange Challe: a study of his life and work', *Apollo* (January 1968), 22–39.
66 Hardy, *Mes Loisirs*, f 437.
67 Ibid., f 414.
68 Wunder, 'Challe', 29.
69 For Louis XIV, the same catafalque seems to have been used at Saint Denis and at Notre Dame. Rousset de Missy, *Supplément*, Tome IV, 415.
70 *Renaultés, arrêts, etc., enregistrements d'édits, déclarations, et lettres patents du parlement de Paris, concernant les affaires publiques, ou les particuliers de distinction, des différens événemens qui y ont donné lieu, avec la description des différents prestations de serment, réceptions et installations; des cérémonies publiques, et des séances du Roy, princes du sang et ducs au Parlement 1765–1788, par Regnault huissier au Parlement*, BMV, MS G120.
71 See Chapter 2.
72 *Journal historique*, volume 6, 188.
73 Hardy, *Mes Loisirs*, f 414.
74 Rogister, *Louis XV*, 4.
75 Regnault, *Recueil*, BMV, MS G120.

76 *Récit abrégé de ce qui a précédé et suivi le lit de justice*, AN K 700 no 1 bis. In 1754, letters of recall for the exiled parlement were delayed for a month before they were dispatched, according to Rogister, *Louis XV*, 237–39.

77 *Journal historique*, volume 6, 252.

78 Ibid., 295.

79 *Récit abrégé.*

80 *Extrait des registres de Parlement de samedi douze novembre mil cent soixante-quatorze, du matin*, AN K 700 n°1 ter.

81 *Nouvelles à la main de Penthièvre*, BM, MS 2293, le 23 8bre – le 11 9bre 1774.

82 Antoine de Séguier, *procureur du roi*, in his speech at the *lit de justice* of 12 November 1774. *Procès-verbal de ce qui s'est passé au lit de justice tenu par le Roi, le 12 novembre 1774*, AN K 700 n° 1.

83 Hardy, *Mes Loisirs*, f 448.

84 This account derives from *Procès-verbal de ce qui s'est passé au lit de justice tenu par le Roi, le 12 novembre 1774.*

85 *Extrait des registres du parlement*, AN K 700 n° 1 ter.

86 Ibid.

87 I can find no record of a similar incident, but see Knecht, 'Francis I and the *lit de justice*', particularly 67.

88 Durand Echeverria, *The Maupeou Revolution: A study in the history of libertarianism: France 1770–1774* (Baton Rouge and London, 1985), 33.

89 *Récit abrégé.*

90 Pierre Joseph Victor de Besenval, *Mémoires de Monsieur de Besenval, écrits par lui-même* (Paris, 1805), volume 2, 199.

91 See Rogister, *Louis XV*, 240. But he did not proclaim it at a *lit de justice.*

92 *Lettres de cachet* to exiled parlements of Besançon seem to have been issued to individuals, see Julian Swann, 'Parlements and political crisis in France under Louis XV: the Besançon affair, 1757–1761', *The Historical Journal*, 37:4 (1994), 808. In February 1757, in relation to those parlementaires who had resigned their offices and been exiled, Louis XV was heard to remark 'qu'il avait puni des *particuliers* pour des raisons à lui personnelles, qu'il n'admettait pas que le Parlement intercédât pour des personnes qui ne faisaient pas partie de la compagnie, qui avaient donné volontairement leurs démissions', cited in Émile Campardon, *Madame de Pompadour et la cour de Louis XV* (Paris, 1867), 249.

93 *Récit abrégé.*

94 *Procès-verbal.*

95 Ibid.

96 This remark savours more of the sentimental rhetoric of mutual love between the people and the king which was widespread at the beginning of the new reign than of a potentially revolutionary nod to an elective monarchy. See Chapter 4 for a discussion of the rhetoric of sentiment and virtue.

97 *Procès-verbal.*

98 Ibid.

99 Besenval, *Mémoires*, volume 2, 201, 203.

100 Elie Carcassone has argued that repeated maxims should not be read as always having the same meaning over decades, that the parlementaires did not have a set ideological stance on their own constitutional position between 1750–1770. *Montesquieu et le problème de la constitution française* (Paris, 1926), volume 1, 294. This differs from later interpretations, such as Dale Van Kley's *The Damiens Affair and the Unravelling of the Ancien Régime, 1750–1770* (Princeton, 1984).

101 Except for the duc de Chartres, who made 'bitter reproaches' ['des reproches amers'] to Miromesnil when he circulated to collect opinions on the edict re-establishing the Grand Conseil: 'he added that he had been exiled twice rather than recognise the new tribunal, & he would do it twenty times if necessary' ['il a ajouté qu'il s'étoit fait exilé deux fois, plutôt que de reconnoître le nouveau tribunal, & qu'il se seroit exiler vingt, s'il étoit nécessaire']. *Journal historique*, volume 6, 310.

102 Ibid., 309; *Procès-verbal.*

103 *Récit abrégé.*

104 *Journal historique*, 191, 237. The *Journal historique* takes a dim view of d'Aligre throughout.

105 *Nouvelles à la main de Penthièvre*, BM, MS 2397. Similar celebrations in 1754, see Rogister, *Louis XV*, 241–42, 245. Horace Walpole suggested that, in Paris alone, 100,000 people experienced exile and redundancy, quoted in Peter Burley, 'Louis XVI and a new monarchy: An institutional and political study of France, 1768–78', unpublished PhD thesis (University of London, 1981), 136. This figure seems high, but it is indubitable that the parlementaires' exile would have had direct and severe economic repercussions.

106 *Journal historique*, volume 6, 311. Unfortunately the text of the song is not recorded.

107 Archives Municipal du Havre, AA.34.

108 *Journal historique*, volume 6, 315. On festivities in Bordeaux, see William Doyle, *The Parlement of Bordeaux and the End of the Old Regime, 1771–1790* (Oxford, 1974), 163.

109 Richard Wittman, *Architecture, Print Culture, and the Public Sphere in Eighteenth Century France* (London, 2007), 167–172.

110 Wittman, *Architecture, Print Culture, and the Public Sphere*, 169. Wittman suggests the various projects were not intended for construction and that this phenomenon, of writing about architecture with a political message, was widespread under Louis XVI (see 173 and illustration overleaf).

111 On the returns from exile of the parlement of Grenoble in 1764, 1775 and 1788, see Clarisse Coulomb, *Les Pères de la patrie*, 359, 399–400, 427,

502–03. Rogister does not provide any detail on celebrations to mark the return of the Paris Parlement in 1754, in *Louis XV*.

112 Marcel Marion, 'Grèves et rentrées judiciares au XVIIIe siècle. Le grand exil du Parlement de Besançon', *Revue des questions historiques* (1913), 71.

113 Regnault, *Recueil*, BMV, MS G 122, f 19–20.

114 NASPF SP 78/294, Horace St Paul to Earl of Rochford, 14 December 1774.

115 The comte d'Artois said nothing, though he was usually characterised as the more pro-parlementary brother and could have taken the opportunity to agree with motions by his relations, the duc d'Orléans and the prince de Conti.

116 NASPF SP 78/294, Horace St Paul to Earl of Rochford, 14 December 1774.

117 Hurt, *Louis XIV and the Parlements*, 126.

118 Swann, *Politics*, 367. Munro Price underlines how unfortunate it was for the reign that Maurepas had no interest in constitutional reform, in 'Politics', 229.

4

'Le roi se fait sacré': preparing the coronation, 1774–75

Introduction

Following the great ceremony of the *lit de justice* in November, the next ritual epoch in the court calendar was the end of mourning for Louis XV, on 15 December, the coming of Christmas and the commencement of carnival season. Now allowed to wear full colours and all cloths, a spirit of innovation was abroad, mirroring the widespread sentiment that the new reign marked a new beginning.

Louis-Philippe, comte de Ségur,[1] recounts how, during the first carnival season of the new reign, he and a group of others came into conflict with older courtiers over their 'plan to revive the clothing, costumes and games of Francis I, Henri III and Henri IV'.[2] The group, drawn from both sexes and of good court stock, won the support of the queen and the king's brothers. Rehearsals began for a set of quadrilles to be danced in these costumes. It was the king's brothers, according to Ségur, who chose the era of Henri IV – the founder of the Bourbon dynasty and their most popular ancestor – as their model. The Swedish ambassador thought the costumes were based on Henri III, and Ségur's own mingling of a century's worth of Valois with the first Bourbon further blurs the lines of reference.[3] The initial presentation of the dances met with such success that it was decided that all men invited to the queen's ball should wear the costume. On 24 January 1775, ninety people were seen dressed in this manner at the ball at Versailles and, on 30 January, the king himself danced the whole night in such an outfit. It was thought possible that it would become a sort of national dress until the king declared he did not wish to decree changes to customary apparel and that the costume should cease to be worn on Shrove Tuesday, the end of carnival.[4] The intendant of the *menus plaisirs* complained about the cost of providing the new outfits and the splendid décor for the carnival balls, though neither the king nor his controller general, Anne-Robert Turgot, baulked at the bill for more than 100,000 livres, deeming it reasonable for entertaining the entire court for the winter.[5] The significance of the events reported by Ségur should not be over-estimated. In the end this revival amounted to a set of new clothes, though one seen by this group of young courtiers themselves as emblematic of 'all that was best suited to a chivalric, gallant court of warriors'.[6] It tells us something about how they viewed themselves and the new reign: innovative in the best traditions.

In light of this anecdote, Louis XVI's decision to proceed with the full coronation in the usual style at Reims does not seem out of touch. In the case of the English coronation, Roy Strong has argued that though the basic liturgical text or *ordo* was defined by the end of the thirteenth century:

> [f]rom the very outset it proved amazingly flexible and accommodating, not only as to what was performed in the Abbey but equally to whatever accrued around it, for … the Coronation had expanded into a multiple event involving all sorts and conditions of people.[7]

While it may be unavoidable that a once-in-a-reign ceremony should seem somewhat unfamiliar when performed after nearly sixty years, the events of the time show that Strong's interpretation also holds true for the French coronation of 1775, with a high level of engagement and interest in this supposedly antiquated ritual. Through a close, contextualised reading of the ceremonies, the next three chapters will show that, in fact, the coronation provides some of the best examples of grandiose and less glamourous rituals together forming part of a meaningful whole with each individual ceremonial moment having its own history and meaning. The coronation was not simply the moment when the king was crowned but also the setting for several other ceremonies with diverse origins and purposes: entry into Reims, Vespers in the cathedral, a cavalcade, the ransoming of the Holy Ampulla and the administration of the royal touch for scrofula. To call the coronation itself a single ceremony is, moreover, something of a misnomer since it comprised a sequence of rites of various derivations. It was an intensely complex form whose overall shape is difficult to describe accurately: Marina Valensise calls it a polyhedron in constant movement.[8] Its many-faceted nature is emphasised in the discussion of the coronation day that follows in the next chapter.

This chapter provides an exploration of the decision to proceed with the coronation together with the preparations made by the officers of the *menus plaisirs*, that part of the king's household staff responsible for 'lesser pleasures' which nonetheless organised major events such as royal funerals and coronations. It will set the coronation in context, giving the details of the king's journey to Reims, including his ceremonial entry procession. The subsequent chapter will deal with the coronation day and, thanks to research in the little exploited archives of Reims, Chapter 6 will give an unusual complementary view, highlighting the role of the people of Reims at the heart of coronation ceremonial, including the historiographically controversial ceremony of touching for scrofula.

The enduring symbolic power of the coronation ceremony is amply demonstrated by the vigorous venom with which deputy Rühl, sent to Reims in 1793 after the execution of Louis XVI to destroy the artefacts of royalty, approached his task. Having smashed the Holy Ampulla, Rühl reported to his colleagues at the National Convention in Paris:

> This immense and glorious people will never again see the insidious farce of the coronation of a fortunate thief, everything associated with the coronation, everything which fed the devotion of the people towards its oppressors, by making them believe that heaven had chosen more favoured mortals to put them in chains, should be obliterated.[9]

The power of royalty persisted in 1793, disturbing and attractive enough to evoke destructive urges in its opponents. Rühl's strong need to destroy relics of monarchy and symbolically release the people from the thrall of royalty convincingly undermines the notion of the 1775 coronation as the faded culmination of an underlying historical process.[10] As Mona Ozouf noted on a related topic, 'description … is tied up with political success or failure… no festival fulfilled the remoter consequences expected of it, or even kept its immediate promises.'[11] This was to be the last great coronation at Reims of the *ancien regime*, but no one who was there in 1775 knew this to be the case.

Preparations for the coronation

Preparations for the coronation were in hand almost from the moment of Louis XVI's accession to the throne. The decision on the coronation was one of the first of Louis XVI's reign. Denis Papillon de la Ferté, intendant of the *menus plaisirs*, had begun his research on historical precedents as soon as the old king died and, by 23 May 1774, had handed a memorandum on the matter to the duc de Duras, first gentleman of the bedchamber, for the king's attention.[12] This was returned to him on 3 June with the 'bon du roi', an indication that he was proceeding along the right lines and should continue his investigations. By the beginning of July, though deep in the throes of organising the funeral catafalque ceremony discussed in Chapter 2, the intendant had produced further detailed work on the matter and was ready to send his junior officers to Reims to begin taking measurements. On their return, the intendant converted their measurements into concrete proposals to take to the king, including the frugal suggestion that the king's wardrobe and the *menus plaisirs* should consult in order to identify materials already in their possession that could be re-used.

From 8–15 August 1774, a high-level team of royal officials made an inspection visit to Reims. Papillon de la Ferté accompanied the duc de Duras, the most senior official with responsibility for the organisation of the coronation, to the town where they were joined by Fontanieu, the intendant of the king's wardrobe, the controller general of the king's household and the marquis de Dreux, the grand master of ceremonies, as well as the chief artisans of the *menus plaisirs*. It was agreed that the archbishopric, where the royal couple would stay, needed as much work as the cathedral to prepare it for the ceremonies.

All of these preparations took place prior to the nomination of Anne-Robert Turgot, longstanding member of the royal bureaucracy and well-known *philosophe*, to the post of controller general at the end of August 1774.[13] Turgot's intervention in the coronation preparations is sometimes regarded as a microcosm of the clash of enervated *ancien régime* values with the vigorous new growth of rationalism.[14] The fact that tradition won out on this occasion has been taken as an accurate indicator of the obsolescence of the monarchy, though this reading of events is based on an at best partial understanding of the mechanics of ceremonial preparations and a total misreading of the association between the king's household and his ministers.

The conscientious Papillon de la Ferté made it his business to draft a comprehensive note on spending for the coronation for the duc de Duras to discuss with the new minister as soon as the nomination was known. This note included details of the decisions already taken by Dreux, the grand master of ceremonies, and by the duc de Duras, one of the most senior officials of the royal household as well as one of the most distinguished nobles in the land. Turgot's suggestion to the king on 11 September that the coronation be moved to Paris should be seen as

10 Print of Louis XVI as King of France and Navarre, with an allegory of his coronation, by Pierre Adrien LeBeau, 1774 (courtesy of Waddesdon Image Library, Bodleian Imaging Services).

a footnote to the massive preparations already in train, rather than the defining moment of ceremonial considerations. The decision to hold the coronation at Reims had been taken three months before Turgot's nomination as controller general. A significant amount of work and energy had been expended on the ritual before he took office. The ceremony was not the province of ministerial competence but under the aegis of the royal household. Turgot's proposal would not, therefore, have been seen as one for very serious consideration, coming as it did so far after the fact of decision. With preparations so far advanced, it was not a question of equally weighing the pros and cons of holding the ceremony either in Reims or in Paris, with a clear decision made to reject the 'enlightened' idea of holding the events in Paris in favour of an 'old-fashioned' idea of crowning at Reims.[15] Turgot, quite properly in view of his office, framed his proposal entirely in terms of the projected expense and the potential for savings, though these were not costed in his memorandum. While seeking economy, Turgot accepted that the ceremony would take place,[16] and did not describe any element of it as old fashioned or outmoded.[17] Though historians have pointed to these discussions around the coronation to prove a high level of what Duindam called the erosion of baroque ceremonialism 'by utilitarianism and enlightenment',[18] the facts here disprove rather than support the case.

Turgot's concern about expense was not novel and, as we shall see below, it was shared by the king.[19] The intendant of the *menus plaisirs*, Papillon de la Ferté, kept a keen eye on the cost of all the events he was asked to produce and the *sacre* was no exception. He denied himself the privilege of claiming possession of all the wood- and ironwork after the ceremony, which had netted his predecessor, Le Fèvre, the pleasing sum of 300,000 livres at the 1722 coronation.[20] Already, by the end of October, his staff were in Reims producing exact plans of the construction work to be undertaken so that this could be costed in advance. The possibility of re-using materials already in stock was examined in detail as well as the potential to rent, rather than buy, materials in Reims. On 1 December, the duc de Duras had in his hands a complete plan for the ceremony together with projected costings. Papillon de la Ferté, using the ceremony as conducted in 1722 as a template, envisaged a total spend of 630,023 livres 12 sols 4 deniers, which together with requests for additional decoration from the duc de Duras in the amount of 123,070 livres, brought the total expense to the round figure of 760,000 livres. These extra elements were for public edification, for the decoration of the exterior of the archbishopric as well as the temporary bridge to be constructed between that building and the cathedral, and to provide public platforms inside the royal banqueting hall. Turgot was pleasantly surprised that the total was not higher, having expected at least 800,000 livres, and suggested that the saving permitted the production of commemorative engravings.[21] Papillon de la Ferté, who had thought he had secured a saving of 2–300,000 livres by persuading the duc de Duras not to print a new handbook for the *sacre*, was dumbstruck by this suggestion from the parsimonious controller general.[22] The full plan was presented to the king for his approval on 5 December: he seconded the duc de Duras' request for additional public decoration. The king's close adviser, the comte de Maurepas, one of few who had witnessed the previous coronation, was pleased with the plan. Papillon de la Ferté, after six months' work, now had a complete blueprint for the coronation and adjunct ceremonies. It remained to execute it and, from the beginning of February, there were regular shipments of materials from Versailles and Paris to Reims by land and by water.[23] These were misrepresented by the disapproving Mathieu Pidansat de Mairobert in *L'Espion anglois* as unnecessary expenditure (on transport) rather than thrifty reuse.[24] The complexity of the age is well illustrated by the fact that this prolific and often scathing *nouvelliste* held the post of king's secretary from the early 1760s and worked for both the rakish duc de Chartres, later Philippe Égalité, and for his father-in-law, the pious duc de Penthièvre. In spite of the sad circumstances of Mairobert's suicide in 1779, he received religious burial thanks to Louis XVI's direct intervention with the parish priest.[25]

On 22 May, the royal family inspected and approved the gold and silver dining service, the church ornaments and, importantly, the costumes which were to be used for the coronation. At the duc de Duras' suggestion, a two-day exhibition of the coronation ornaments including the coronation coach was held at the Hôtel des Menus Plaisirs in Paris in the week of 26 May. It was hugely popular with 'an incredible crowd of people of all ranks'.[26] Pidansat de Mairobert wrote that it was attended in indescribable numbers: the artefacts on display were of a richness and beauty to astonish even connoisseurs.[27] The regalia were then packed and sent to Reims. A pamphlet circulated with details of all the treasures deployed at the ceremony.[28] The intendant moved to Reims on 5 June to supervise final preparations. His arrival was an occasion of wonder. Though involved in the preparations from the earliest days, he was stunned by the grandeur and elegance of the work done. He had the highest praise for the decoration, deeming it 'the most perfect thing the Menus have ever done'.[29]

The meaning of coronation in 1775

Stepping back for a moment from the graft and glitz of ceremonial staging, it behoves us to ponder the meaning of the coronation in 1775. The reality of instant dynastic accession in the eighteenth century prompts the question of the ceremony's purpose. The widespread association of coronation with the beginning of a reign cannot be maintained as historically valid since power had long antedated crowning.[30] Louis XVI's entry into kingship was heralded by the duc de Chartres, one of the most senior nobles outside his immediate family, addressing him as king when announcing the death of his grandfather.[31] In ceremonial terms, it has been suggested that the Renaissance funeral superseded the coronation as the cries of 'vive le roi!' at the graveside implied that recognition of the new king stemmed from that instant.[32] The moment of dynastic accession had already passed at that point, however. Though the idea of elective kingship bubbled to the surface in the troubled 1570s and 1580s,[33] in practical terms of the exercise of power, dynasticism trumped coronation from the earliest days of French monarchy.[34]

Nevertheless, the coronation, known most frequently in French as the *sacre* or consecration, retained an unimpeachable status as a rite of public recognition and of power. The linguistic emphasis on consecration is surely a hint at the *sacre* ceremony's special relationship to the complex powers associated with kingship; the other ceremonies which formed part of the larger coronation event should also be taken into account in considering the significance of the coronation. By 1775, the ceremony, a composite of several rites, incorporated aspects of chivalry and elements of the mythology of French kingship, such as the Holy Ampulla and the role of the peers, alongside religious forms. There are so many more layers than the simple performance of a Catholic ceremony to consolidate relations with the Church and they make it difficult to agree with arguments for a mainly ecclesiastical vision of the ceremonies.

The complexity of the ceremonies mirrors the composite construction that was the Bourbon monarchy. The monarchy was a secular administrative edifice resting on fundamental laws shared with the parlements and others. It was a successful dynastic enterprise which had entrenched the notion of the priority of Bourbon blood through insistence on distinctions of rank based on sanguine proximity to the ruling monarch, regularly enacted in various ceremonies. The Bourbon monarchy also was surrounded with intense religious ritual. The sacred aspect of the monarch could not be captured by the secular handover model of the *avènement.* This description of the diverse qualities of the Bourbon monarchy argues against seeing it as exclusively sacral or administrative and against the assumption that these were incompatible opposites. Rather the monarchy should be seen as an elaborate whole with several fundamental, though seemingly contradictory, characteristics. The rational (administrative) and the irrational (sacred) came together in the role and person of the king. This notion of sacredness may seem a bad fit with the late eighteenth century, but it persisted as a powerful motif. Part of the king's power continued to reside in an irrational aspect which was by no means limited to its Catholicity, a sort of social magic associated with kingship and, indeed, ceremonies.[35] Those who questioned the purpose of the event were blinded by their functionalist view of power and, perhaps, somewhat repelled by the demonstration of the attraction of the irrational.[36] Consideration of the manifold ceremonies enacted at the coronation, together with reflection on the irrational aspects of power, lead this study in quite a different direction from that of historians whose prime consideration in the study of ceremony has been to elucidate its relationship to public law.

From the moment of his accession, Louis XVI was closely associated with ideas of virtue, 'the hope of my country! Adored young king! / Your reign is the time to reconsider our morals'.[37] An engraving entitled *The guarantors of public happiness* praised the young couple: 'your reign is the reign of the virtues'.[38] Speeches at the *lit de justice* of 12 November 1774, quoted in Chapter 3, dwelt on his virtues.[39] These notions of personal virtue were one theme of the popular sentimental discourse which, as we shall see, was the language widely used by those attending the coronation to describe it.[40] Sensibility was ubiquitous in eighteenth-century life and, as a corollary of this omnipresence, it was also highly debated and indeterminate, meaning many different things to different people.[41] Historians and literature scholars identify the sentimental strand most prominently in the theatre (both on stage and in the audience) and novels (again on the page and in the readers' behaviour) but also in paintings, medicine and even court proceedings.[42] What united all these was the definite moral element that ran alongside aesthetic, philosophical or scientific threads. Sentiment required reaction: one read a text, watched a play, contemplated a painting, and gave the appropriate outward signs of moral impact, sharing it with others. Without the outward sign, there is no *sensibilité.* The visual and gestural rhetoric of sentimentalism was well disseminated in France by 1775, the date of the coronation, having enthralled a large part of the public at least since the publication of

Rousseau's *La Nouvelle Héloïse* in 1761. A clear association was made between physical manifestation of emotion, authenticity of feeling and personal virtue. To be recognised as expressing genuine emotion was the highest praise in this discourse. Irrepressible gestures were the prime marker of the sensitive soul. Sensitivity was interpreted as closely related to virtue: the sensitive were virtuous and vice versa.

We might expect to encounter sentimental tears at the clandestine lovers' meetings or in the edifying family tableaux which were so popular in novels, plays and paintings of the period. They are unexpected in court ritual. From Rousseau's polemics to the sociology of Norbert Elias, there has been a marked tendency to see an irreconcilable opposition between the sort of conduct expected in court circles and such behaviour. In this analysis, the king's court is a desert in which the pure flower of sentiment cannot survive. Yet, as we shall see in the following chapter, contemporary commentators experienced and described the ceremony of the coronation in terms clearly derived from the sentimental discourse, and prized the coronation not only for the consecration of their virtuous king but also for the display of their own virtue in response. This is not to say that this ceremony was inherently more moving than previous iterations, but rather to recognise that its performance and reception were both contingent products of their time.

We can reconcile the enthusiastic weeping on the coronation day with norms of courtly behaviour in the 1770s by paying due attention to a shared culture of noble values, of widespread 'participation in nobility' even by those who were not, and would never be, noble.[43] Even if the idea of separating society neatly into three orders seem untenable at this stage, and indeed provoked outrage in 1788–89, identifying with the nobility makes sense in a society largely organised around corporate identities and in which individuals had many overlapping allegiances depending on context. The 'quality model' which adapted characteristic noble behaviour or virtues to the usage of the middling sort, and which asserted delicacy of feeling as a primary trait, was undoubtedly widespread and popular.[44] It was common to say that it was becoming impossible to tell a duchess from a dairymaid: the truth of this may have been more than skin-deep. Over the course of the eighteenth century, two commoners a day chose to join the nobility, that is, between eight and ten thousand men and their families between the death of Louis XIV and the opening of the Estates General.[45] Noble culture prized display of status, not only in clothing and coaches but also in behaviour. Noble manners were aped by aspirants and by those who wished to have a veneer of nobility even without hope of officially entering this class, or, an infinitely distant prospect for most, being presented at court. The influence of nobility spread far beyond the confines of Versailles, as did practices of 'living nobly'; the values of noble culture were disseminated further than any survey of title-holding would indicate. Though sentimentalism was universalising, predicated on the idea of a shared human propensity for certain feelings in certain situations, there is no reason to suppose that the implied flat hierarchy was meant to reduce everyone to membership of *le peuple.* It was a levelling up rather than down. The theatre-going and novel-reading public remained a minority of the population of Paris and predominantly noble, or noble-aspirational.[46] In May 1769, Madame de Riccoboni wrote to the English actor David Garrick that current playwrights avoided comedy because it was *ignoble* to smile or laugh in public, and therefore writers sought to make their audiences cry.[47] Around the same time, Voltaire wrote that 'it would be a great impertinence today to undertake to make the public laugh, when they claim they want only comedies of tears'.[48] Certainly writers were tapping into the current vogue for sentimentality: they were also observing more venerable niceties of social conduct. Displays of *sensibilité*, though they raised some eyebrows, were more permissible within the noble ethos than knee-slapping laughter. This ethos was influential on manners throughout society, not merely at court, or, indeed, at court ceremonies. In a society where the court was the ultimate horizon of vaulting ambition,[49] it was natural that noble manners carried a premium. However, it was certainly not the case that such social influences were unidirectional. Neither noble manners nor the court had ever been immune to fashion: legendary Versailles was founded on the wholesale lifting of ideas from cutting edge Vaux-le-Vicomte, the palatial abode of the fabulously wealthy, but soon dispossessed, *robin* Nicolas Fouquet.[50]

Public crying, crying at the theatre, was not new in the 1770s though it was given a new impetus and new meaning by the highly publicised private practices associated with the writings of Marivaux, Richardson, Rousseau and others. The comedies of the eighteenth century were *comédies larmoyantes* giving way from the mid century to the new *genre sérieux*, the *drame bourgeois* pioneered by Denis Diderot.[51] These were no less tear-jerking than the *comédies larmoyantes*, as tableaux of virtue in distress served as way-markers along the route to the vilain's conversion. It was not the permissibilty but rather the acceptablity and categorisation of tears that exercised writers and dramatists at this time.[52] Their rival theories smacked more of competition in a hierarchy of quality than any attempt to banish crying: Charles Collé, *lecteur* to the duc de Chartres and author of the popular play *La Partie de chasse de Henri IV*, scorned the tears shed at Nivelle de La Chausée's plays of the earlier century, which he classfied as overwhelmingly female, while displaying pride at the manly sobs elicited by his own work.[53] Tears were not in themselves rejected but rather certain sorts of tears – excessive, childish, female, medically dubious, convulsive tears in reaction to inappropriate stimuli. The ability to feel and to control that feeling was the mark of a civilised man. This self-mastery fits entirely with the image of the graceful *honnête homme* who had the correct response to every social situation: tears and, increasingly occasionally, smiles.[54]

Even at the Opera, audiences began not only to listen but also to weep. In 1774, *Iphigénie en Aulide* and *Orphée et Eurydice* by the distinguished German composer Christoph Willibald Gluck made conquest of Parisian audiences, including Jean-Jacques Rousseau who congratulated Gluck on achieving the impossible task of making French suitable for music. The younger commentator Louis-Sébastien Mercier admitted that through Gluck he now knew 'the charms of music … I have at last felt myself shedding tears as I never have before in this place of enchantment'.[55] Gluck had been brought to France through the offices of his former pupil, the queen, Marie Antoinette. Here, demonstrating the mutual exchange of ideas, *la cour* clearly influenced tastes in *la ville*: by 1786, it was felt that the *ville* generally endorsed the theatrical judgement of *la cour*, rather than vice versa.[56]

These threads of sentiment, public conduct and theatre-going came together vividly on the occasion of the coronation of Louis XVI. At a time when '[t]he elites of French society were already primed to swoon and sob', in 1774–75, tears remained a crucial medium of social communication, one which was hotly debated but certainly not in decline.[57] If ways of thinking and feeling in the theatre had infiltrated attitudes to, for example, legal cases,[58] then there is no bar to suggesting that this could also be true about royal ceremonies, bearing in mind Edward Muir's suggestion that the work of ritual is primarily in this realm of emotion evocation.[59] Theatre audiences were thought to be small;[60] those for royal ceremonies even smaller. However, as we have already seen in chapters on the funeral and *lit de justice*, the audience for any given ceremony extended well beyond the invitation list. This applies to the coronation ceremony, the choreography of which included the admission of crowds at a crucial juncture, and to its allied outdoors ceremonies and minor ritual moments. From the formal entry to the city of Reims and the administration of the royal touch for scrofula to the king's informal strolls among his people in the evenings, the coronation events presented a series of moments of contact between the king and the people ripe with sentimental theatrical possibilities. But what did people see at the coronation that made them weep?

The 1760s and 1770s enjoyed public celebrations of virtue. In 1766, Madame de Genlis, in the earliest days of her career, helped bring to public attention the village festival of Salency in Picardy at which – and, it was claimed, since time immemorial – a young girl of the village was awarded with a rose in recognition of her outstanding goodness. Orthodox religion played some part in the festival – it was legendarily founded by a saint, featured a mass and the priest had an organising role – but, interestingly, even in her post-revolutionary guise, de Genlis omitted these elements from her description of the celebration, emphasising its rural and communitarian character and placing local officials in the main responsible roles (the *bailli* and the *intendant*).[61] Similar festivals began to appear throughout northern France under noble sponsorship and it rapidly became a popular theme for stage, enacting the tableau of rural virtue in the very heart of Paris before those effervescently *sensible* theatre audiences. In March 1774, *La Rosière de Salency* by the marquis de Pézay, with music by Grétry, was playing at the Théâtre des Italiens.[62] Such was its popularity that William Everdell has characterised it as a '*rosières* movement'.[63] When the Salency festival later became the object of a court case between the *seigneur* and the villagers, its legal defenders dwelt on its secular virtues, and won.[64] The case was one of the first heard by the parlement after its return to work in December 1774. The vindication of the villagers, with the assistance of the new king,[65] was perfectly in tune with the mood of the times. This simple ceremony attracted noble attention because it encapsulated several topical themes:[66] the love of nature, the celebration of innocence and virtue, the festive opportunity for amateur theatricals in the shape of versifying, posing and music making and, importantly, the demonstration of liberality towards the less well off – *bienfaisance*. As Maza suggests, its appeal lay in its malleability.[67] It was closely allied to the attractions of a polymorphous concept of virtue that was endlessly various in its application: the virtue of a village maiden was celebrated through the entirely distinct virtue of the nobility allied to the different qualities of the clergy.[68] None of these was identical to the virtue of a king, yet all were eminently worthy of celebration. The festivals' popularity arose out of their ability to accommodate seemingly contradictory yet equally prized beliefs and social practices: the simplicity of village democracy and the innocence of village youth could, in the 1770s, be celebrated by stagey aristocratic posturing to the delight and benefit of all concerned.[69] Though there was a clear disparity in wealth, power and agency here, the festival was understood as a display of social harmony. The wide spectrum of ideological stances available to the French élite, the as yet unfocused yet fervently felt wish for social improvement, was refracted through this and similar events, including the debate on *bienfaisance*. The *rosières* phenomenon remained popular and took on some qualities of a panacea: in 1787, in an essay competition on the promotion of patriotism, it was suggested that prizes for virtue should be founded in every town in France.[70] The idea of improving the virtue of the many by actively rewarding the virtue of the few was undeniably powerful and attractive.

The notion of a virtuous king, however, was decidedly more complex. It was agreed that a king *should* be virtuous but, following the reigns of the bellicose Louis XIV and the amorous Louis XV, was it possible that a king *could* be virtuous? And, if so, what did that mean? Statues of Louis XV enshrined his public qualities as peacemaker, father of the nation and even political reformer.[71] The young Louis XVI came to the throne with a solid reputation for chaste (perhaps too chaste) personal behaviour and, while this was a welcome change from his grandfather, there was clearly more to being a virtuous king than sexual continence. Among the sobriquets mooted for the new monarch was Louis *le bienfaisant*; the décor for his entry into Reims was dominated by an arch not of triumph but of *bienfaisance*.[72] The idea was not new: Louis XVI's childhood lessons had propounded this model as had his maternal grandfather, Stanislaus Leszczynski, erstwhile king of Poland and author of the well-received *Oeuvres du philosophe bienfaisant*.[73] A proposed inscription for a statue of Louis XV erected in Reims in 1764 read 'Within our walls a beneficent king / came and swore to be our father' though the reference to the king as *bienfaisant* was later dropped.[74] On the deaths of his father, the dauphin, and his grandfather in 1765 and 1766, a young Louis-Auguste heard the real and ambitiously imputed virtues of these two men extolled, with *bienfaisance* taking pride of place.[75] There was clearly a strong current of feeling aspiring to the association of kingship with *bienfaisance*. Louis XVI was the first monarch repeatedly apostrophised as *bienfaisant* since the term had previously been applied to two men with monarchical potential but no actual kingdom or power. *Bienfaisance*, from its very origins in the writings of Abbé de Saint-Pierre in 1725, had always been understood as the practical impact of a person in the world literally doing good and defined always in opposition to doing ill.[76] In this it was akin to *sensibilité* since, without outward show and contact with others, it was meaningless. *Sensibilité* and *bienfaisance* alike both sprang from pressing concerns about virtue and its place in the world. A shift in the meaning of *bienfaisance* occurred around the same time as the emergence of sensibility, in the decade 1755–65, when a new generation of writers and thinkers took Abbé de Saint-Pierre's idea and essentially stripped it of its orthodox religious content. In this new reading, *bienfaisance* proceeded from the most natural of emotions – natural being a value-laden term and one of high praise – the love of other humans, which found its expression in doing good for others in a practical manner and without thought for personal gain.[77] Many of the popular sentimental paintings of Greuze were illustrations of *bienfaisance* in action;[78] the familiar sick- or deathbed tableaux depicted touching domestic scenes but also showcased theorists' preference for home assistance over the institutionalisation of the poor.

11 'Humanité et bienfaisance du roi' (after Debucourt).

Given his power to legislate, to command great projects and to dispense wealth, the king was potentially the ideal-type of *bienfaiteur*.[79] Apostrophising the king as a *bienfaiteur* was not a simply a piece of aspirational royal image-making, understandable as that would be in the context of the new reign, but also a political exercise in co-optation by optimistic élites, as we shall see in our description of the coronation entry into Reims. This co-optation raises questions about the complex mechanics of defining kingship in the period and indicates that this was not a top-down, or centre-periphery, exercise. The king and his administration might convey their preferred images from Versailles, while, *at the same time*, other parts of the administration and the public projected their preferred images onto the king, and the resultant mingling is evident at the coronation. If 'kingly virtue became an expression of the king's fundamental humanity',[80] to be seen as virtuous in 1774 the king should demonstrate human and humane qualities. An engraving of 1774 associates the king in the earliest days of his reign with giving.[81] This is very far removed from the public image promoted for Louis XIV and suggests that Louis XVI needed to be a very different sort of king to his august ancestor. The kingly virtue of Louis XVI was conceived in a way very specific to his time. In 1775, his *bienfaits* were seen in terms of his great public acts to date: the selection of ministers, the renunciation of the *joyeux avènement* tax, the recall of the parlements. The day after the coronation on which both the royal touch for scrofula and the pardoning of prisoners took place was described as '*la journée de la bienfaisance*'.[82] Insisting on his *bienfaisance* might also have been a future-oriented strategy: repeatedly informing the king that he does good, in order to ensure that he will do good. In the 1780s, as philanthropic societies emerged throughout France, images of the king as *bienfaiteur* appeared.[83] These depictions of small-scale personal interventions by the king may err on the side of traditional charity as opposed to *bienfaisance* as such, being punctual acts of alms-giving rather than organised assistance. The best known is Philibert-Louis Debucourt's *Louis XVI's humane actions in February 1784*, followed by the *Just actions of Louis XVI* (1784) and *Louis XVI distributing aid to the poor* (1786).[84] The former painting was reproduced as an engraving by Guyot dedicated to the duc de Charost in his capacity as president of a philanthropic society with the new title 'Louis XVI's humane and charitable action', reproduced in Figure 11. The text appended to Guyot's mangled reproduction of Debucourt's image recounts both the king's immediate personal giving and his more formal arrangement of longer-term support for the worthy family in question, thus encompassing both more traditional alms-giving and strategic *bienfaisance*, encompassing both patterns of giving in order to demonstrate the king's compassion. Underlining these charitable preoccupations among the wealthy, we should not forget, was a very real ongoing subsistence crisis among the poorest due to rising population, rising prices, stagnant wages and harsh weather.

The king travels to Reims

The days of royal presence in Reims for the coronation were structured around several key rituals: the royal entry in the city, vespers on the eve of the coronation, the coronation itself, a cavalcade through the city, the ceremony of the royal touch for scrofula. These events were all part of the three Bourbon coronations held at Reims before 1789 but they did not always occur in the same order or manner.[85] Louis XIII was crowned before he reached his majority so he received the sacrament of confirmation at Reims prior to the *sacre*.[86] Louis XIV's time in Reims was evenly divided into time before and time after the *sacre* so that the major post-coronation events had to take place on successive days.[87] Louis XV and Louis XVI both spent more time in Reims as crowned king than as uncrowned.[88] While Louis XVI had no formal appointments on the day after the *sacre*, Louis XIV and Louis XV rode in cavalcade through the town to the church of Saint Rémi where they would, some days later, perform the ceremony of the royal touch.[89] These two visits were telescoped into one for Louis XVI who combined the cavalcade with the royal touch.[90] Louis XV's visits to a range of churches, convents and religious orders were not continued by his grandson who attended only the cathedral and the abbey of Saint-Rémi, with the church of Saint-Nicaise visited by his wife. The ceremony of the royal touch was the last public event in Reims for both Louis XIV and Louis XV.[91] Louis XIII conducted the ceremony at nearby Corbeny, the usual resting place of the relics of Saint-Marcoul, though it was arranged on subsequent occasions that these relics be moved into Reims for the coronation. Louis XVI participated in the municipal Corpus Christi procession between the royal touch and his departure.[92] Both Louis XIV and Louis XV were busier with formal attendance at churches and visits than their successor who took more opportunities to mingle with the people.

While Louis XIII and Louis XIV set out from Paris for their coronations,[93] and it had been the major stop en route for Louis XV who stayed overnight at the Tuileries, the city played no role in Louis XVI's journey to Reims. Louis XV made a veritable progress through the Île de France, from Versailles to the Tuileries in Paris to La Villette, Dammartin, Villiers-Coterêts, Soissons and, via Brênes, finally to Fîmes, with formal receptions along the way and lodging and entertainment provided by the high nobility.[94] Louis XVI went from Versailles to the royal palace at Compiègne and spent one night at Fîmes. There he stayed in *la maison dite heurtevin* as had his predecessors, 'a very mediocre house' opined the duc de Croÿ.[95] This choice of route might appear dictated by fear following the disturbances of the Flour War, though a letter of 31 May attributed to Louis XVI suggests economy was the main motivation:

> The cost of my coronation must be further reduced, if possible … I will stay only a few days at Compiègne and the sums allocated for different expenses should be used to pay part of the expenditure necessary for the protection and relief that I owe to those of my subjects who have been victims of sedition [during the Flour War].[96]

In the day immediately preceding the ceremony, the road to Reims resembled nothing so much as a busy shopping street.[97] The duc de Croÿ describes a complex set of transport arrangements put in place to facilitate those journeying from Paris to Reims, planned around the allocation of hundreds of post-horses. The precision with which this system was run presupposed the roads remaining clear of other traffic, particularly the kind of slow-moving processions that a royal progress would have occasioned.[98] Louis XVI set out from Versailles on 5 June, the same day as Papillon de la Ferté and the duc de Duras arrived at Reims to finalise arrangements. After a brief stop to visit his aunt, Madame Louise, at the Carmelite convent in Saint Denis, he was welcomed to Compiègne at ten o'clock at night by the local governor, the duc de Gesvres, accompanied by local military and municipal officers and by the Condé cavalry regiment, as the bells of the town pealed.[99] He stayed there until 8 June then spent one night at Fîmes and arrived at Reims with his brothers on 9 June. Louis XIII, by way of contrast, had spent a leisurely three weeks journeying from Paris to Reims and back.

Even before Louis XVI arrived at Reims, the presence of various dignitaries meant the city was alive with ritual moments. The duc de Bourbon, a prince of the blood who was also governor of Champagne, was welcomed on his arrival on the evening of 7 June with cannon-fire and a parade of armed bourgeoisie. Mesdames Clothilde and Élisabeth, the king's younger sisters, were greeted at the Porte de Vesle by municipal officers and the sound of gunfire on 8 June. The queen and the comtesse de Provence arrived incognito around one in the morning of 9 June. At the same time, the town was filling with courtiers and nobles who passed the time inspecting the cathedral, the decoration and the temporary royal residence at the archiepiscopal palace – where they deplored the small size of the rooms – as well as paying calls and dining.[100]

While Louis XIV had not enjoyed a formal entry procession into the city of Reims, 'because he did not wish for one',[101] a grand ceremony was held for both Louis XV and Louis XVI,[102] reviving a briefly disused ceremony rather than simply aping the usage of Louis XIV's time. Around one o'clock on the afternoon of 9 June 1775, a mounted parade departed from the Hôtel de Ville. Municipal officers, dressed in black embroidered with golden fleurs-de-lys, were preceded by ranks of uniformed archers, eight sergeants wielding staffs and Monsieur Cocquebert,[103] the *lieutenant des habitants*, bearing an unsheathed sword. With two trumpet players at the head of the procession, they made their way outside the town to await the king's arrival with the duc de Bourbon, governor of Champagne, the marquis d'Ecquevilly, lieutenant general of the province, the intendant

12 The carriage used at Louis XVI's coronation in Reims, June 1775, decorated by Aubert and Prieur.

Rouillé d'Orfeuil and the marquis d'Ambly, the king's captain in Reims. A crowd gathered in the surrounding fields.

At quarter past four, the king, accompanied by his household troops and officers, arrived and transferred to his golden ceremonial coach before greeting the local party.[104] The first cries of 'vive le roi!' went up as the carriage halted to enable the governor, lieutenant general and intendant to present the municipal officers to the monarch. The officers of the Hôtel de Ville all knelt as Cocquebert offered a brief harangue on the theme of public rejoicing at the king's arrival. Cocquebert was joined by the king's local captain, d'Ambly, in presenting the king with the keys to the city.

Receipt of the keys signalled that the time had come for the king to enter the city. Church bells rang and artillery fired from the ramparts of Reims as the massive procession advanced through the Porte de Vesle and wound its way past the magnificent decorations erected for this entry ceremony.[105] Alongside ornaments praising the kind of attributes usually associated with these events, such as piety and faithfulness, were images and verses on contemporary topics which were unabashed in their composition and included references to, for example, the contrast between the new king's continence and his grandfather's philandering. The entry display therefore evoked both transcendent values and contemporary concerns in context-specific ways.[106] It not only feted the king but aimed to impress upon him the wit and sheer merit of the élite of Reims. The recall of the Paris parlement was repeatedly celebrated. Some stock images of kingship were deployed but the décor for this ceremony, organised from Reims, not Versailles, was by no means clichéd. The Reimois took the ritual opportunity offered to them to make clear political points in a display meant not just for the king's eyes, but which remained in the streets for days before and after the king had passed. An explicatory pamphlet was published in Reims on 18 May, and presumably distributed in the days before the *sacre*, to inform the public of the intended messages.[107] The purpose of the decorations was to share the sentiments of the people of Reims: their 'tender and respectful devotion' was intended for the king and their 'delight … and joy' to be shared with lesser visitors.[108] Through ceremony, the municipal officials of Reims spoke to the king indicating their endorsement of his conduct and government to date, and to the public, instructing them in current affairs and providing a lexicon of references regarding the king's achievements and qualities. There is a striking difference in tone between the décor for this entry in 1775 and the iconography of that of Louis XV in 1722. The

1722 entry programme referred to the 'return of the golden age', a statement which could be read as political though embedded in a decorative scheme predicated on the innocence of the young king (then aged 12), depicted by cupids, figures of truth and the evocation of sunny plenitude and natural prosperity.[109] In an image which subsequently acquired ironic significance, but which had no such intent at the time, at Louis XV's entry into Reims a statue of Mars, god of War, was shown being replaced with one of Peace by a crowd of cupids, laurels substituted for oak leaves and flowers.[110]

The décor in 1775 was overseen by the intendant of Châlons-en-Champagne, Gaspard Louis Rouillé d'Orfeuil.[111] Though as intendant he was a royal appointee, he enjoyed considerable independence of action in his area of authority and the choice of decorative motifs was not subject to approval from Versailles.[112] D'Orfeuil, in the post of intendant from 1761, had also orchestrated the province's reception of the dauphine Marie Antoinette on her bridal journey from Vienna to Versailles.[113] The only organisational link to Versailles for the coronation was the involvement of the first painter to the comte d'Artois, Doyen, in providing sketches for work which was then carried out by local artists Clermont and Gauthier.[114] Like so many men of his position and education, Rouillé d'Orfeuil was a man of letters, publishing anonymously in 1771 his utopian vision of social relations in *L'Ami des français* followed in 1773 by *L'Alambic des lois* and *L'Alambic moral.* He was immersed in and an exponent of the contemporary discourse of virtue and sentiment, a fact reflected in the pedagogical content of the display. This commitment to the public good had a practical impact on his conduct of business. In April 1775, during preparations for the coronation, his subordinate at Reims, the sub-delegate Polonceau, sent him a copy of his printed *Avis sur les corvées*, which threatened any laggards in the performance of unpaid labour with exemplary punishment. Rouillé's reply could not have been more disapproving: given the high bread prices, he said, Polonceau should be treating the populace more gently than usual rather than threatening them. He besought Polonceau to withdraw the pamphlet from circulation immediately, before it could do too much damage.[115] Indeed, had Polonceau reflected on his superior's record in office, he might have thought twice before writing: one of Rouillé's first acts on arriving in Châlons had been the abolition of corporal punishment for recalcitrant *corvéables*.[116] Rouillé wrote to his former colleague, now minister, Turgot in April 1775 arguing that a reform of the *corvée* was the most urgent act needed for the relief of the ordinary people, and he continued throughout his period as intendant to search for ways to alleviate the burden of the *corvée*.[117] *Bienfaisance* was part of policy for many intendants, not merely a fashionable trope.[118] Rouillé's close collaborators on the coronation entry were the *vidame*, or, roughly, vicar of Reims, Bergeat, and the abbé Deloche, both canons of the cathedral who had been nominated by the city councillors to direct the work.[119] The participation of two religious officers did not noticeably skew the message of the entry decorations towards any ecclesiastical or religious import since literary and classical allusions dominated alongside notions of secular virtue.

Two 10-foot high statues on 15-foot high pedestals, one of religion and the other of justice, were the first station along the path of the entry procession. They were intended by the organisers to represent the king's personal virtues.[120] The figure of religion held a crown in her left hand which rested on the bible and presented an olive branch with her right hand, in token of the sacred oils to be used in the *sacre*. The figure of justice looked with satisfaction at the perfectly balanced scales she held. The accompanying verses emphasised the king's actions to re-establish balance in law, a nod to the recall of the parlement the preceding November.[121]

The pedestal devoted to religion was prominently embellished on one side with the figure of Circe confounded, her wand and cup abandoned, thanks to the king's youthful wisdom in resisting temptation.[122] A clearer reference to the change of tone since Louis XV's passing was scarcely possible. Another face of the pedestal evoked the new king's dislike of flattery and flatterers, shown by a cypress whose perfume prevents insects from landing. The figure of justice was matched with depictions of king's birth showing the return of the constellation Virgo to the skies with the sun shining on fruitful fields, evoking the very positive associations for the Paris parlement of king's birth in August 1754.[123] The *Explication* stated outright 'the recall of the Parlement is one of the good deeds that makes our MONARCH so dear to the nation'.[124] The sun appeared again on another face of the pedestal combined with the figures of the zodiac in order, depicting the king's attachment to the laws of his kingdom while, on the third face, a sundial receiving light after a stormy day was another evocation of the recall of the Paris parlement, echoing Antoine de Séguier's speech at the *lit de justice* of 12 November in which he referred to the 'happy days' after the storm of exile.[125]

Louis XVI is here personally associated with the sun in a manner more familiar for Louis XIV, though such emblems were often more about the monarchy than the individual monarch.[126] It will be remembered that these images were selected in Reims, not by royal officials from Versailles. To be sure, they drew on an established, shared vocabulary of images associated with royalty, but they were neither restricted nor dictated to in their final choice. The entry decorations are indicative of how the monarchy was seen outside of Versailles, of a dialogue between people and king, and of an imagined conversation between the élite of Reims and their upper-class visitors, in which officials took this opportunity to signal their approval of the new king and, more surprisingly, open disapproval of the old king. There are multiple imagined audiences, multiple publics, for the decorations: primarily, of course, the king, but also the high nobility accompanying him, other high-status visitors, the high society of Reims (whose admiration the intendant and his colleagues doubtless courted) and the people of Reims. The entry decoration is very much in the control of the Reimois, not of the court officials: here we see the fluid and shared nature of meaning in this ceremony – meaning is not something simply emitted from the centre.[127] The specificity of the messages in the decoration also attests to a personalised idea of the monarch: these messages are for Louis XVI, who is differentiated repeatedly from Louis XV. The king is not a distant, generic figure: he is a recognisable individual.

Further along the route into the city, the narrow Porte de Paris had been demolished and replaced with an iron-work structure further embellished with temporary pillars and a pediment displaying images of Numa Pompillius, priest-king of Rome, receiving celestial blessings, a convenient shorthand for both the powers of the Holy Ampulla and the holy orders conferred on the king at his *sacre*.[128] At the foot of this structure, the spirit of happiness revealed to the people of France a medallion featuring the queen, the first and only reference to Marie-Antoinette,[129] who was watching the procession from the house of Sieur Andrieux on rue Vesle. The contribution of the king's close adviser the comte de Maurepas were celebrated in an image showing a tree heavy with fruit trained against an aged wall.[130] The procession continued on past two altars erected on rue Neuve, one to pity and the other to faithfulness,[131] before arriving at a triumphal arch dedicated to *bienfaisance*, 'this virtue so precious to kings and to humanity',[132] whose chief decoration was a pair of verses in Latin and French. These praised Louis XVI as the heir of the Bourbons, distinguished by his personal attachment to *bienfaisance*, and urged him to follow his heart in emulating his august predecessors. The verses included an intriguing brief guide to the Bourbon dynasty, in

Latin, praising Henri IV's paternal tenderness, Louis XIII's justice and piety, Louis XIV's 'lofty soul and spirit' and, rather noncomittally, Louis XV's non-specific 'warlike and pacific virtues'.[133] The spirit of *bienfaisance* was figured presenting a crown, with the gloss that this depicted the triumph of the beneficent new monarch which was evident even 'in his acts of authority'.[134] *Bienfaisance* was therefore neither an attribute of weakness nor an exclusively private quality.

Facing the arch, a façade, 60 feet across by 30 feet high, had been erected depicting the commercial interests of the town including figures denoting viticulture, weaving, vigilance and navigation. This building was designed both to obscure some unsightly older constructions and, together with the arch of beneficence, to reshape the top of the street into an attractive square for the duration of the celebrations.[135] The scale of these decorations, together with their vigorous promotion in print, attests to the energy with which they were executed in 1775.[136] The overwhelming message of the king's entry was one of endorsement: of the king and of his rule to date. This much is not surprising. The unexpected feature, perhaps, is the forthrightness with which the Reimois engaged in current political issues, including the issues that might be seen as private to the king – the philandering of his grandfather and his political decisions around ministerial appointments and the parlement.

This square marked the end of the king's entry procession, concluding in front of the cathedral. In the cathedral square, the municipal décor gave way to the work of the *menus plaisirs*. As had occurred at Saint Denis and Notre Dame for the funerals of Louis XV, a false façade in the neo-classical style had been erected in front of the cathedral. Here it served the practical purpose of providing a passageway from the archiepiscopal palace to the cathedral. Both bridge and façade were painted to resemble white marble with doric columns and pediments.

The interior of the cathedral itself had been refashioned for the ceremony.[137] The entire nave, as far as the entrance to the choir, now had barriers between the pillars behind which were four tiers of seating. The pillars were hung with tapestries from the royal stores and additional chandeliers had been hung to improve the lighting. A row of purple and gold Corinthian columns had been erected to enclose the space around the choir and the sanctuary, which now contained a number of galleries, again in white marble effect, to seat the higher ranking guests. At the entrance to the choir, raised on a platform, was the throne under a canopy supported by four columns, hung with purple satin embroidered with golden fleurs-de-lys. At the junction of the transept and the nave, two particularly large and magnificent galleries of seating were allocated to the queen and her ladies and to the foreign ambassadors. At the rear of the choir was seating for the orchestra of 100 musicians. The whole choir was further decorated with royal tapestries and cherubic groups bearing additional lights, necessary in view of the early hour of commencement of ceremonies.

As his household troops manoeuvred to the sound of trumpets and drums, and the cathedral bells chimed, the king descended from his carriage and, after hearing a *Te Deum* to mark his arrival, he formally received groups of Reimois worthies at the archiepiscopal palace. Each group had a prepared address and some offered gifts to the king. The cathedral chapter presented a basket of bread, an ironically inexpensive symbol of their worldly goods in view of their persistent lobbying of Papillon de la Ferté for richer vestments and decoration for the cathedral for the coronation, to be kept by them after the ceremony. The municipal officers, who had met with the royal couple at Versailles on 26 May,[138] brought sixteen dozen bottles of wine, half red, half sparkling white, and three baskets of local produce. Representatives of the local university, the local *présidial* court and the officers of the *élection* also harangued the king. The same groups were then presented to the queen, concluding formal engagements for the first day.

Conclusion

Many months of preparations bore fruit on the day of the king's entry into Reims. The first festivities of the coronation were well conducted and well received. The occasion of the king's entry into the town in June 1775 was seized on with enthusiasm by local officers who produced an impressive spectacle. They did not mechanistically repeat ancient gestures nor did they merely reproduce stock references in the decorative elements of the entry ceremony. Topical contemporary images were deployed in an unfolding narrative which reviewed the king's personal qualities, the facts of his life (birth, marriage) and his brief career as king. The coronation was not simply organised and ordered from Versailles but also incited active participation in Reims. Following elaborate preparations, in Versailles and in Reims, and the public enactment of grandiose entry ceremonies, the stage was now set for the coronation itself, which is described in the next chapter.

Notes

1 Louis-Philippe comte de Ségur (1753–1830), diplomat, author.

2 *Le comte Louis-Philippe de Ségur, Souvenirs et anecdotes sur le règne de Louis XVI*, avec une préface de M le marquis de Ségur (Paris, n.d), 47. On the popularity of fancy-dress, see Aileen Ribeiro, *Dress in Eighteenth Century Europe, 1715–1781* (London, 1984), chapter seven. The nobles' uniforms for the Estates General of 1789 were also described as *à la Henri IV.*

3 Comte de Creutz, *La Suède et les lumières: lettres de France d'un Ambassadeur à son Roi (1771–1783), Correspondance établie, présentée et annotée par Marianne Molander Beyer* (Paris, 2006), 143.

4 *Correspondance secrète, politique et littéraire ou Mémoires pour servir à l'histoire des cours, des sociétés et de la littérature de France, depuis la mort de Louis XV* (London, 1787), 196. France was an exporter of luxury dress and Versailles one of its main showcases.

5 Denis Papillon de la Ferté, *L'Administration des menus plaisirs* (Paris, 1887), 378–80.

6 Ségur, *Souvenirs et anecdotes*, 47. As Madame de Genlis commented '[l]'histoire des modes n'est pas si frivole qu'on le croit; elle est en partie celle des moeurs', quoted in Ribeiro, *Dress in Eighteenth Century Europe*, 186.

7 Roy Strong, *Coronation: From the eighth to the twenty-first century* (London, 2006), 158.

8 Marina Valensise, 'Le sacre du roi: stratégie symbolique et doctrine politique de la monarchie française', *Annales ESC*, 41 (1986) 543.

9 Quoted in Michel Le Moël, *Le Sacre des rois de France* (Paris, 1983), 14.

10 Jeffrey Merrick, 'The coronation of Louis XVI: the waning of royal ritual', *Proceedings of the Eighth Annual Meeting of the Western Society for French History* (1981), 191–204; Chantal Grell, 'The *sacre* of Louis XVI: the end of a myth' in *Monarchy and Religion: The transformation of royal culture in eighteenth century Europe*, Michael Schaich (editor) (Oxford, 2007), 345–66; but see also Valensise, 'Le sacre du roi', and Jens Ivo Engels, 'Beyond sacral monarchy: a new look at the image of the early modern French monarchy', *French History*, 15:2 (2001), 139–58. John McManners, 'Authority in church and state: reflections on the coronation of Louis XVI' in *Christian Authority: Essays in honour of Henry Chadwick* (Oxford, 1988), 278–95, takes the coronation as the starting point for a reflection on the political roles of the French clergy in the second half of the eighteenth century, by no means depicting them as irrelevant due to the irresistible rise of unbelief. On the growth of work on the place of religion in the Enlightenment, see Simon Grote, 'Review essay: religion and enlightenment', *Journal of the History of Ideas*, 75:1 (January 2014), 137–60.

11 Mona Ozouf, *Festivals and the French Revolution*, translated by Alan Sheridan (Cambridge, Mass, 1988), 14.

12 Papillon de la Ferté, *L'Administration*, 365 *passim*. See also *Dans L'Atelier des Menus Plaisirs du Roi: spectacles, fêtes et cérémonies aux XVIIe et XVIIIe siècles* (Paris, 2010); Pierre Jugie and Jérôme de la Gorce (editors), *Les Menus plaisirs du roi (XVIIe–XVIIIe siècles)* (Paris, 2013).

13 Malcolm Hill, *Statesman of the Enlightenment* (London, 1999) is the most recent biography of Turgot.

14 See Gustave Schelle, *Oeuvres de Turgot et documents le concernant* (Paris, 1922), volume 4, 119 for the text of Turgot's memorandum to the king. Schelle comments '[l]es intérêts particuliers et le respect des traditions l'emportèrent sur les conseils de Turgot' (120). Richard A. Jackson locates the decision to proceed in line with precedent and at Reims in September rather than May Jackson, *Vive le Roi! A history of the French Coronation from Charles V to Charles X* (Chapel Hill and London, 1984) 215–16. Hill merely notes Turgot's suggestion to move the ceremony for reasons of economy, 132. John Hardman, *The Life of Louis XVI* (New Haven, 2016), 88–90, discusses the coronation briefly with the focus firmly on Turgot.

15 Mathieu-François Pidansat de Mairobert, *L'Espion anglois, ou correspondance secrète entre milord All'Eye et milord Alle'Ar* (1779), tome 1, 321 *passim*.

16 Schelle, *Turgot*, volume 4, 119. He did not seek to advise the king to dispense with the ceremony as has been suggested. See Merrick, 'The coronation of Louis XVI', 194; Jackson, *Vive le Roi*, 219; Grell, 'The *sacre* of Louis XVI', 347–48.

17 Condorcet wrote to Turgot on 23 September 1774 '[n]e croyez vous pas que, de toutes les dépenses inutiles, la plus inutile comme la plus ridicule serait celle du sacre? Trajan n'a point été sacré.' There were those in Turgot's circle who saw the *sacre* as ridiculous, this does not necessarily mean that Turgot did. He did not respond to Condorcet in kind. *Correspondance Inédite de Condorcet et de Turgot, 1770–1779* (Paris, 1883), lettre CLI, 201. Grell quotes this letter to Turgot to demonstrate his scepticism but does not produce documentation from Turgot himself, 'The *sacre* of Louis XVI', 348.

18 Jeroen Duindam, 'Ceremony at Court: reflections on an elusive subject', *Francia*, 26 (1999), 131. Duindam's comment is a general one, not specific to the coronation.

19 Papillon de la Ferté wrote a memo for each new controller general setting out the administration and finances of the department, and regularly updated them. *L'Administration*, 25–26.

20 Papillon de la Ferté, *L'Administration*, 375.

21 The final total was calculated by Papillon de la Ferté as 835,828 livres 12 sols 10 derniers including all garments for the royal party, gifts, transport, construction and decoration in the cathedral and the archbishopric. *L'Administration*, 400. Disputes about who should pay the costs of the city

of Reims continued for years afterwards, see the printed *Ordonnance de M l'Intendant de Champagne concernant les frais du sacre de Louis XVI du 15 août 1778*, Archives Municipales de Reims (AMR), Fonds Anciens C 732 liasse 21.

22 Papillon de la Ferté, *L'Administration*, 374.

23 *État des effets employés au Sacre de Louis XVI*, AN O[1] 3250.

24 Pidansat de Mairobert, *L'Espion anglois*, volume 1, 326.

25 Jeffrey Merrick, 'Le suicide de Pidansat de Mairobert', *Dix-huitième siècle*, 35 (2003), 331.

26 Papillon de la Ferté, *L'Administration*, 382.

27 Pidansat de Mairobert, *Mémoires secrets pour servir à l'histoire de la république des lettres en France, depuis MDCCLXII jusqu'à nos jours* (London, 1780–89), Volume 8, 47.

28 *Richesses Tirées du Trésor de l'abbaye de St Denis, du gardemeuble de la couronne et de différens artistes de Paris pour servir au sacre de l'auguste monarque de France le roi Louis XVI*, AMR, Fonds Anciens C 732 liasse 21.

29 *L'Administration*, 382.

30 See Constant Leber, *Des Cérémonies du sacre* (Reims, 1825), 171–72. Marc Bloch, *Les Rois thaumaturges: étude sur le caractère surnaturel attribué à la puissance royale particulièrement en France et en Angleterre* (Paris, 1983), 218.

31 See Chapter 1.

32 Jackson, *Vive le Roi*, 9.

33 On this see Jackson, *Vive le Roi*, chapter eight.

34 See also Georges Péré's interesting discussion, *Le Sacre et le couronnement des rois de France dans leurs rapports avec les lois fondamentales* (Paris, 1921).

35 See also Chapter 1. The bookseller Hardy and his friends avidly followed the news of Louis XV's deathbed but would not be berated into participation in prayers for his health. There was more to adherence to monarchy than Catholic ritual.

36 Edward Shils, 'The meaning of coronation', in *Center and Periphery: Essays in macrosociology* (Chicago, 1975) 136.

37 Claude-Joseph Dorat, 'Hymne à la bienfaisance', *Journal Encyclopédique* (Bouillon, 1774), volume 2, part ii, 320.

38 *Les Garants de la félicité publique*, engraving, Collection of the Palace of Versailles, INV.Grav 864.

39 See Chapter 3 and AN K 700 n° 1, *Procès-verbal de ce qui s'est passé au lit de justice tenu par le Roi, le 12 novembre 1774.*

40 See Marisa Linton, *The Politics of Virtue in Enlightenment France* (Basingstoke, 2001), and David J. Denby's emphasis on the self-consciousness of this discourse throughout his *Sentimental Narrative and the Social Order in France, 1760–1820* (Cambridge, 1994).

41 Ann Lewis, *Sensibility, Reading and Illustration: Spectacles and Signs in Graffigny, Marivaux and Rousseau* (London, 2009), 256.

42 Emma Barker, *Greuze and the Painting of Sentiment* (Cambridge, 2005); Anne C. Vila, *Enlightenment and Pathology: Sensibility in literature and medicine in Enlightenment France* (Baltimore and London, 1998), 2; Sarah Maza, *Private Lives and Public Affairs: The causes célèbres of Prerevolutionary France* (Berkeley, 1993); James Johnson, *Listening in Paris: A cultural history* (Berkeley, 1995).

43 The phrase is Colin Lucas's, in 'Nobles, bourgeois, and the origins of the French Revolution', *Past and Present*, 60 (August 1973), 104. Michael Kwass, 'Big hair: a wig history of consumption in eighteenth century France', *The American Historical Review*, 111:3 (June 2006), 631–59.

44 David Garrioch, *Neighbourhood and Community in Paris, 1740–1790* (Cambridge, 1986), 76–77.

45 William Doyle, *Aristocracy and its Enemies in the Age of Absolutism* (Oxford, 2009), 12.

46 There is strong evidence of greater theatrical attendance of humbler sorts in the 1770s and 1780s. Louis-Sébastien Mercier attested that workmen were among the regulars at the Comédie Française in 1773. In his campaigning writings, he advocated greater inclusion of *le peuple* 'but exclusion of *le vile populace* which is far beneath what I call the people', in *Du théâtre, ou nouvel essai sur l'art dramatique*, (Paris, 1773), 202 n, quoted in John Lough, *Paris Theatre Audiences in the Seventeenth and Eighteenth Centuries* (London, 1957/1965), 221.

47 Quoted in Lough, *Paris Theatre Audiences*, 230. My emphasis.

48 Writing on 25 April 1770. Quoted in Anne Vincent-Buffault, *The History of Tears: Sensibility and sentimentality in France* (Basingstoke, 1991), 65.

49 Antoine Lilti, *Le Monde des salons: sociabilité et mondanité à Paris au XVIIIe siècle* (Paris, 2005), 174.

50 Claire Goldstein, *Vaux and Versailles: The appropriations, erasures and accidents that made modern France* (Philadelphia, 2007); Ronald G. Asch, 'The court: prison or showcase of noble life?' in *Nobilities in Transition, 1550–1700: Courtiers and rebels in Britain and Europe* (London, 2003).

51 See Sarah Maza, *The Myth of the French Bourgeoisie: An essay on social imaginary 1750–1850* (Cambridge Mass, and London, 2003), 66–67.

52 Vincent-Buffault, *The History of Tears*, chapter three.

53 *Mercure de France*, août 1768, 174, *passim*. Collé notes his authorship of these uncomplimentary *Réflexions sur le genre larmoyante* in his *Journal et mémoires de Charles Collé: sur les hommes de lettres… du règne de Louis XV, 1748–1772*, edited by Honoré Bonhomme (Paris, 1868), volume III, août 1768, 199. See also Vincent-Buffault, *The History of Tears*, 76.

54 As Colin Jones argues in *The Smile Revolution in Eighteenth Century Paris* (Oxford, 2015).

55 Johnson, *Listening in Paris*, 60.
56 Gluck's triumph was not, of course, uncontroversial as the later 'War' of Gluckists and Piccinists attested. See Johnson, *Listening in Paris*, 62 *passim*. Lough, *Paris Theatre Audiences*, 232.
57 Johnson, *Listening in Paris*, 65. On the persistent popularity of sentimental plays throughout the Revolution, see Cecilia Feilla, *The Sentimental Theater of the French Revolution* (Farnham, 2013).
58 As Sarah Maza suggests in *Private Lives and Public Affairs*.
59 Edward Muir, *Ritual in Early Modern Europe* (Cambridge, 2005), 2.
60 'The public, the reading public, is composed of forty or fifty people, if the book is serious, and four or five hundred, if it is pleasant, and about eleven or twelve hundred if it is a play. There are always more than five hundred thousand people in Paris who never hear a word about all of that' wrote Voltaire in 1765, quoted in Lough, *Paris Theatre Audiences*, 211.
61 Stéphanie-Félicité Du Crest, comtesse de Genlis, *Mémoires inédits de Madame la comtesse de Genlis, sur le dix-huitième siècle et la Révolution française, depuis 1756 jusqu'à nos jours* (Paris, 1825), volume 1, 246 *passim*.
62 *Journal Encyclopédique*, juin 1774.
63 William Everdell, 'The *rosieres* movement, 1766–1789: a clerical precursor of the revolutionary cults', *French Historical Studies*, 9:1 (Spring 1975), 23–36.
64 See Sarah Maza, 'The Rose-Girl of Salency: Pre-revolutionary representations of virtue', *Eighteenth Century Studies*, 22:3 (Spring 1989), 395–412, and Maza, *Private Lives*, chapter two, Marisa Linton, *The Politics of Virtue*, 189 *passim*.
65 According to Everdell, 'The *rosières* movement', 27.
66 Everdell, 'The *rosières* movement', 31. I agree with Everdell on the reason for its attractiveness, if not precisely on the thematic content.
67 Maza, 'The Rose-Girl of Salency', 403 n 37.
68 On the power of the idea of virtue in eighteenth-century France, see Linton, *The Politics of Virtue*, introduction.
69 Though of course there is little or no testimony from the villagers on their experience.
70 Linton, *The Politics of Virtue*, 191.
71 Daniel Rabreau, 'Statues of Louis XV: illustrating the monarch's character in public squares whilst renewing urban art', in *Reading the Royal Monument in Eighteenth Century Europe*, Charlotte Chastel-Rousseau (editor) (Farnham, 2011), 39.
72 *Explication des emblêmes inventés et mis en vers par M Bergeat, vidame de Reims, & M l'abbé Deloche, tous deux Chanoines de l'Église Métropolitaine, pour la décoration des Édifices, Arc de Triomphe & autres monumens érigés par les soins Messieurs du Conseil de la Ville, lors du cérémonie du Sacre de Sa Majesté* (Reims, 1775), BNF Rondel Collection, Ra4 618 (1), 11.

73 *Oeuvres du philosophe bienfaisant* (Paris, 1763), 3 volumes.

74 'Ce monument prouve à la terre/Qu'il fut fidèle à son serment' was suggested. This was amended to the more pompous '[D]e l'amour des Français éternal monument/Instruisez à jamais la terre/Que Louis dans ces murs jura d'être leur père/Et fut fidèle à son serment'. Gérard Jacob-Klob, *Description historique de la ville de Reims* (Reims, 1825), 123.

75 Linton, *The Politics of Virtue*, 134.

76 Catherine Duprat, *'Pour L'Amour de l'humanité' Le temps des philanthropes: La philanthropie parisienne des Lumières à la monarchie de Juillet* (Paris, 1993), volume 1, xv–xvi.

77 Duprat, *'Pour L'Amour de l'humanité'*, xvii. Colin Jones, *Charity and* Bienfaisance*: The treatment of the poor in the Montpellier region 1740–1815* (Cambridge, 1982), 2 *passim*.

78 Emma Barker, 'From charity to *bienfaisance*: picturing good deeds in late eighteenth-century France', *Journal for Eighteenth Century Studies*, 33:3 (September 2010), 285–311.

79 Duprat, *'Pour L'Amour de l'humanité'*, xxxi; Linton, *The Politics of Virtue*, 132.

80 Linton, *The Politics of Virtue*, 194.

81 See Print of Louis XVI as king of France and Navarre, Figure 9.

82 Pierre Jean Baptiste Nogaret, *Anecdotes du règne de Louis XVI, 1774–1776* (Paris, 1776), 87.

83 See Duprat, *'Pour L'Amour de l'humanité'* and Barker, 'From charity to *bienfaisance*'.

84 *Le Trait d'humanité de Louis XVI en février 1784*, *Trait de justice de Louis XVI* (1784), *Louis XVI distribuant des secours aux pauvres* (1786). All in the Collection of the Palace of Versailles.

85 The following is based on a close reading of Jean Rousset de Missey, *Supplément au Corps Universel diplomatiqe du droit des gens etc* (Amsterdam/The Hague, 1739) and Thomas Jean Pichon, 'Journal historique de ce qui s'est passé' in *Sacre et couronnment de Louis XVI* (Paris, 1775).

86 'Les cérémonies du sacre et couronnement du très chrétien roi de France et de Navarre Louis XIII par le cardinal de Joyeuse, à Rheims, le dimanche 17 Octobre 1610', Rousset de Missey, *Supplément*, 207.

87 See 'Cérémonie du sacre et couronnement du roi Louis XIV à Rheims le 7 juin 1654', Rousset de Missey, *Supplément*, 212–21.

88 See 'Rélation de la cérémonie du Sacre & Couronnement du roi Louis XV faite en l'Eglise Metropolitaine de Reims, le dimanche 25 Octobre 1722', Rousset de Missey, *Supplément*, 221–35, and Pichon, 'Journal historique'.

89 Rousset de Missey, *Supplément*, 220, 230.

90 Pichon, 'Journal historique', 73 *passim*. See Chapter 6 for a discussion of the royal touch ceremony.

91 Rousset de Missey, *Supplément*, 220–21, 233.
92 Pichon, 'Journal historique', 80–81.
93 Rousset de Missey, *Supplément*, 207, 212.
94 *Journal du voyage du roi à Rheims, contenant ce qui s'est passé de plus remarquable à la cérémonie de son sacre.. avec la description des fêtes données à SM et quelques remarques historiques de M l'abbé de Vayrac sur les lieux qui ont été honoré de la présence du Roi (16 october au 12 Novembre)* (La Hague, 1723), 2 volumes.
95 Emmanuel de Croÿ, *Journal inédite du duc de Croÿ* (Paris, 1906), volume 3, 169; Pichon, 'Journal historique', 5.
96 Quoted in Armand François d'Allonville, *Mémoires secrétes de 1770 à 1830* (Paris, 1838–45), volume 1, 58. See also Cynthia A. Bouton, *The Flour War: Gender, class, and community in late Ancien Régime french society* (University Park, 1993) and Steven L. Kaplan, *Bread, Politics and Political Economy in the reign of Louis XV*, 2 volumes (The Hague, 1976).
97 Pidansat de Mairobert, *Mémoires secrets*, volume 8, 75.
98 Six to eight hundred post-horses were available at each major staging post. The duc was obliged to wait for a day at Soissons until his allotted travel time, along with the marchéaux de Richelieu, de Contades and de Noailles. They relaxed at a local *auberge*. Croÿ, *Journal*, volume 3, 168–69.
99 *Relation de la cérémonie du sacre et couronnement du roi faite en l'église métropolitan de Rheims le dimanche 11e jour de juin 1775*, BNF Ra4 612.
100 Croÿ, *Journal*, volume 3, 174.
101 He slept at Reims for one night before being officially welcomed by the municipality at the town gates. There was no grand decoration in his honour. Rousset de Missey, *Supplément*, 212.
102 For Louis XV, see *Explications des emblèmes heroiques inventées par M le Chevalier D*** pour la décoration des Arcs de Triomphe érigez aux Portes de Reims lors de la Cérémonie du Sacre de Louis XV*, BMV MS G 276.
103 The distinguished nature of the post of *lieutenant des habitants* is proven by the other offices held by Cocquebert: *écuyer, président, trésorier de France au bureau des finances de Champagne*. Pichon, 'Journal historique', 8.
104 *Ordres du grand écuyer pour le sacre de Louis XVI*, AN K 1714 no 21 (3).
105 Pichon, 'Journal historique', 7–11, for an account of the king's entry into the city.
106 Michael Wintroub, *A Savage Mirror: Power, identity, and knowledge in early modern France* (Stanford, 2006), 7.
107 *Explication des emblêmes inventés et mis en vers par M Bergeat, vidame de Reims, & M l'abbé Deloche* (Reims, 1775), BNF Ra4 618 (1).
108 *Explication*, 4.
109 Nicolas Menin, *Le Sacre de Louis XV* (Paris, 1723), 411 *passim*.
110 Menin, *Le Sacre de Louis XV*, 426.
111 Ibid., 22. Paul Ardascheff, *Les Intendants de province sous Louis XVI* (Paris,

1909), 455. Étienne Prévost de Lavaud, *Les Théories de l'intendant Rouillé d'Orfeuil* (Paris, 1909).

112 *Les Intendants de province*, xi.

113 'A la Porte Sainte-Croix', *Mémoires de la Société d'agriculture, commerce, sciences et arts du département de la Marne* (Châlons-sur-Marne, 1909), 368–93.

114 *Explication*, 22; Marc Sandoz, *Gabriel François Doyen, 1726–1806* (Paris, 1975), 17, 74.

115 Cited in Ardascheff, *Les Intendants*, 183.

116 Ibid., 295.

117 Ibid., 304.

118 Ibid., chapter IV: 'les intendants et la "bienfaisance éclairée"'.

119 Pichon, 'Journal historique', 10. *Explication.*

120 The following description is from the *Explication.* Pichon, 'Journal historique', 10–16, reproduces the content of that pamphlet.

121 *Explication*, 5.

122 Ibid., 7.

123 Ibid., 7–8, and as discussed in the chapter above on the *lit de justice.*

124 Ibid.

125 *Procès-verbal de ce qui s'est passé au lit de justice tenu par le Roi, le 12 novembre 1774*, AN K 700 n° 1.

126 Sydney Anglo, *Images of Tudor Kingship* (Guildford, 1992), 5. Louis XV and Louis XVI retained the device of their predecessor, both the sun image and the motto 'nec pluribus impar'.

127 Similarly, see Wintroub, *A Savage Mirror*, for an enthralling account of an entry ceremony in Rennes in 1554.

128 *Explication*, 9.

129 Ibid. On her role at the coronation, see the following chapter.

130 Ibid., 11.

131 The altar to pity paired the king with his father as two souls most likely to feel and act on pity. *Explication*, 17, 20.

132 Ibid., 11.

133 *Explication*, 15.

134 *Explication*, 12.

135 Ibid., 16–17.

136 Bryant, *The King and the City*, 218.

137 Pichon, 'Journal historique', 23 *passim.*

138 *Gazette de France*, Lundi 29 mai 1775.

5

'Vive le roi!': the coronation of Louis XVI, 11 June 1775

Introduction

The coronation began early on the morning of Trinity Sunday, 11 June. Rather than simply focusing on the moment of consecration, the event will here be considered as a sequence of rites, as indeed it is described by Thomas-Jean Pichon in his official guide.[1] Pichon was historiographer to Monsieur, the king's brother. Called the 'general' of the *anti-Encyclopédistes*, his writings shed an interesting light on the coronation itself since the tracts he penned included *Les Droits respectifs de l'État et de l'Église rappelés à leurs principes* (The respective rights of the State and the Church recalled in their principles). His central claim in this was that previous writers had been biased on the topic, and that he therefore would simply consult reason in order to reach a sound conclusion, because 'healthy philosophy is not characterised by enthusiasms'.[2] Pichon here can be taken as representative of a reforming religious strand of contemporary thought which did not reject 'philosophy' but rather deployed all the rhetorical tools of reason, nature and naturally arising intuitively correct social arrangements to contest more radical thinkers' claims to exclusive rights to the term.[3] This approach was vigorous at this time, supportive of the new reign with great hopes invested in the new monarch, having felt their hopes eclipsed by the death of the dauphin in 1766.

The official book of the coronation was composed of several elements bound together in one volume entitled *Le Sacre et couronnement de Louis XVI, roi de France et de Navarre*. In keeping with the spirit of the age, and under Pichon's editoral guidance, Nicolas Gobet, secretary of the comte d'Artois's council, produced two essays of historical research on the coronation and the monarchy, firmly grounded in notions of French national progress – in particular the interesting history of the Franks – and minimising religious aspects.[4] Pairs of engravings by Charles Emmanuel Patas followed: several *tableaux* depicted key moments of the ceremony each with a matching allegorical picture and explanatory text. This section was modelled very closely on, not to say directly copied from, the volume produced for the coronation of Louis XV by Antoine Danchet.[5] This was followed by an illustrated guide to the detail of coronation costume and, finally, Pichon's own main contribution, the *Journal du sacre et du couronnement de Louis XVI*, on which we draw here, and which Louis XVI personally amended prior to its publication later in the year. This portmanteau volume was published, or as the publisher has it, presented to the Nation,[6] soon after the coronation. There were several other printed guides available on the day itself.

Coronation proceedings were due to begin at six o'clock and, from four in the morning, people were taking their seats. Entry to the cathedral was by ticket only. Scion of a family of Grenoble parlementaires, Laurent de Franquières travelled to Reims to see the *sacre*. Despite a family connection to the maréchal de Clermont-Tonnerre, who was at the king's side throughout the coronation, he was unable to enter the cathedral because all the tickets had already been allocated. Franquières was one of many disappointed since there were only 500 seats available in the cathedral for non-courtiers.[7] Writing to his family, he estimated that he was one of 30,000 people gathered in the cathedral square, while Jean-François Marmontel, historiographer to the king, claimed there were 50,000.[8] While these estimates perhaps are likely somewhat inflated, they convey well the sense of the size and press of the crowds. Seating in the cathedral was based on office rather than individual status and order in such matters was assisted by a printed *Ordre de la marche et des cérémonies* distributed by the *menus plaisirs*. There was a bench for the members of the Order of the Holy Spirit, for example, and the duc de Croÿ ensured he arrived early to get a good place on it. Even the court ladies, in full formal garb, were in place by half past five.

The interior of the cathedral had been completely remodelled to accommodate the ceremony. Galleries were erected between the massive pillars and were filled with finely dressed onlookers in a raised amphitheatre which overlooked the proceedings on the floor of the cathedral. From the engravings circulated at the time, it is difficult to deduce that the ceremony took place in a cathedral.

13 Decoration for the coronation of Louis XVI.

In *Décoration du sacre de Louis XVI, roi de France et de Navarre, à Rheims, le XI juin 1775 sous les ordres de M le Maréchal de Duras*, shown in Figure 13, there are no signs of the religious purpose of the edifice, no crucifixes, no sacred images. The only discernable altar is minute and covered in any case with a cloth of fleurs-de-lys, cloaking its religious purpose in royal colours. The only hint of the true nature of the building is the vaulted ceiling and the rose window spied towards the right-hand corner of the picture; otherwise the addition of many chandeliers merely serves to enhance the secular appearance. The prelates' vestments blend in with the multitude of elaborate get-ups on display. The heroic scale used in the image serves to emphasise the numerous audience, the individual figure of the king must be sought among the many. Besides those in the galleries, there were many also seated, closer to the king, on chairs on the floor of the cathedral though, if the image reflects some of the reality, some of these people chose to stand up, presumably to get a better view, adding to the air of informality and movement. This arrangement, of a lively parterre close to the action combined with raised tiers of further spectators recalls nothing so much as a theatre, certainly not a cathedral, as the duc de Croÿ commented at the time.[9]

14 Coronation of Louis XV, 1722.

Rather than a frivolously fashionable attempt to erect a theatre inside the cathedral, however, it seems that these arrangements were very similar to those made for the coronation of Louis XV which had also featured galleries built between the columns and seating on the main floor of the cathedral. The difference lies in perception and depiction. Croÿ feared that what he perceived as innovations would undermine the religious tone of the event. Engravings in 1775 took a perspective that obscured or minimised the religious import of the image: in images from 1722, such as the one shown in Figure 14, crucifixes and clergy featured more prominently. Nonetheless, the representation of both occasions conveys a strong sense of theatricality and display, and of a space remade for a special purpose. In a move similar to the royal occupation of the Grand Chambre at the Palais de Justice, seen in Chapter 3, the cathedral was no longer strictly the preserve of the religious, but became a new kind of space, a ceremonial space dominated by majesty and mysticism.

At six o'clock, the canons of the cathedral took their places in the choir and began to sing the office of prime. They continued to sing the full divine office during the ceremonies, marking the canonical hours of terce and sexte, complementing the office of vespers observed the previous evening. At the same time, the cardinal-archbishop of Reims, de la Roche-Aymon, and his assisting clergy donned their vestments in the sacristy and entered the cathedral processionally to take their seats on the altar. Three religious from Saint Denis were on hand to watch over the treasures they had brought to the ceremony: the crown of Charlemagne, the 6-foot high sceptre decorated with gold and pearls, the hand of justice ('a hand of ivory, or rather of unicorn horn'), the sword of Charlemagne, the ruby and diamond brooch to pin the royal mantle, the ruby and gold spurs and the gilded, engraved book of the *sacre*.[10] The three senior marshals of France destined to carry the crown, sceptre and hand of justice (de Contades, de Broglie and de Nicolaï) were seated directly behind the five ecclesiastical peers who, dressed in cloth-of-gold mitres and copes, were seated on a bench covered in purple and gold.[11] The king's ministers, councillors of state, masters of requests and secretaries were in place. Turgot was there, seated among the councillors of state, separately from the other ministers Bertin, de Vrillière, Sartine and Vergennes.

The queen, together with the king's female relatives and her ladies, entered the cathedral via the arcaded bridge from the archiepiscopal palace and was conducted to her galleried seating. The absence of any special procession or ceremony at this time confirmed her minor role. No queen of France had been crowned on the same day as her husband since 1365, neither was the queen included in the many illustrations in Pichon's guide which offered detailed depictions of those directly involved. Facing the women in an identical structure were the papal nuncio, the ambassadors of the Holy Roman Empire, Spain, Naples, Sardinia, Portugal, Sweden, Venice, the Netherlands and Malta as well as other foreign dignitaries and envoys, including a representative from Tripoli. The British ambassador had purposely, and with his government's consent, absented himself so as not to have to give way to either the nuncio or the Spanish ambassador, the comte d'Aranda, whose preferment was possible as an 'ambassadeur de famille'.[12]

At seven o'clock, the six lay peers, dressed in purple, gold and ermine, wearing golden crowns mounted on purple satin bonnets, entered the cathedral. These roles were taken by the contemporary princes of the blood, as befitted a ceremony which celebrated at this point in the monarchy's history the triumph of Bourbon dynasticism. For the purposes of the ceremony they were known by extinct titles of lay peers whose participation in the ceremony was a key part of the mythology of French royalty, evoking notions of continuity and antiquity. The lands from which these ancient peerages derived their titles had all been absorbed in the royal domain or redesignated as *apanages*, thus in a very concrete way illustrating the alteration in power within France since the medieval origin of this part of the rite.[13] Pride of place went to the king's brother, next in line to the throne, Monsieur, the comte de Provence. His seat was distinguished from that of the others by a higher footrest. He was accompanied by the youngest of the three royal brothers, the comte d'Artois, and fathers and sons, the ducs d'Orléans and de Chartres, and the prince de Condé and the duc de Bourbon.

Seeking the king

The first act of the coronation proper began with the lay and ecclesiastical peers convening around the chair of the archbishop of Reims in order to deputise the archbishops of Laon and Beauvais to seek the king. The grand master of ceremonies led the chanting canons and the two archbishops accompanied by choirboys carrying candles and holy water in a procession which exited the cathedral, leaving the congregation waiting, in order to enact the rite of the sleeping king. The meaning of this ritual is mysterious, yet, since it provides several clues to the broader meaning of the coronation in 1775, it will be treated here in some detail.

Inside the archiepiscopal palace, the procession stopped at the king's chamber door and the cantor knocked.[14] The duc de Bouillon, grand chamberlain, and the archbishop of Laon exchanged the ritual words from either side of the closed door ('What do you seek?' 'The king.' 'The king sleeps.') On the third iteration, Laon changed his response to 'Louis XVI who God has given us for king' the door was opened and the bishops entered to find the king reclining on a bed of state. The room was decorated with matching furniture made for Francis I: the bed, four armchairs, eighteen stools, table covering, canopy and screen were in red embroidered with scenes from the life of Moses in gold.[15] The king wore garments specific to the ritual he was about to undergo: a scarlet camisole and shirt, both with openings to allow anointing of his body. Having offered him holy water and recited a prayer, the two bishops raised him from the bed.

Though Pichon is content merely to describe the rite and offers no explanation of its origins or meaning,[16] historians have exerted themselves to unravel the meaning of the king's sleep.[17] Since Louis XVI came to the throne as an adult, it is impossible to adopt the explanation that sleep was a metaphor for the king's extreme youth, as has been suggested for other coronations.[18] Given that Louis XVI had exercised royal power in the year since his accession, it is equally difficult to rely on the more theoretical exegesis derived from the principle of undying monarchy, equating the king's sleep to his non-consecrated status. This in turn relates to analyses of the king's two bodies which seek the incarnation of the verities of public law in the physical conduct of ritual;[19] Jackson argues that these rituals reflect the rise and fall of absolutism.[20]

As for origins, the first usage of this rite can be dated precisely to the coronation of Louis XIII on 17 October 1610, at which the ritual dialogue was performed through a closed door.[21] The essential structure of the king being sought and formally brought to the church for his coronation appears to have much older antecedents. There is mention of Pope Innocent II seeking the king in such a manner at the coronation of Louis VII in 1131.[22] The template for coronations, 'formulaire des sacres', commanded by the same king in 1179 states that the king should enter the cathedral with archbishops, bishops and barons but does not set out any particular ceremony for seeking the king. Subsequent records mention or omit the fact of raising the king from a bed with no apparent pattern.[23] The unaccountable vagaries of ceremonial records are clear here. It seems most likely that the practice of raising the king from a bed and conducting him to church continued even when it was not deemed worthy of separate note by those recording events. The formal coronation template endorsed by Charles V in 1365 firmly commands that the king should be found on an ornate bed and then conducted to the church. Accounts of subsequent ceremonies – for example, of Charles VIII in 1484 and of Francis I in 1514 – confirms that this stricture was observed.[24]

The confirmation of the long inclusion of a bed in this rite does not immediately assist in the unravelling of the myth of the king's sleep, however. The earliest records make no mention of closed doors or of ritualised dialogue on the topic of a slumbering monarch. Indeed, the

15 The king's first coronation outfit, from Thomas Pichon, *Sacre et Couronnement de Louis XVI*. Engravings by Charles Emmanuel Patas.

suggested template for the coronation of Louis XIII in 1610 omits both of these features, following the usage for the ceremony of his predecessor Henri IV by which the designated peers, having entered his room in procession, greeted the king with prayers, raised him from his bed and returned to the church with him.[25] Although it seems incontrovertible that the king was positioned on a bed for many iterations of this ceremony, the bed should not necessarily be associated with sleep, as we know from the *lit de justice* that beds could and did have more formal connotations in the French monarchical context, as well as in ceremonies of knighthood. The earliest records make no mention of the king sleeping on the bed nor is there any indication of specialised dialogue, though absence is of course not necessarily proof of non-performance.

The first positive record of an exchange across the threshold is from the coronation of Charles IX on 15 May 1561 when the king was said to be at rest rather than asleep.[26] A procession including all twelve lay and ecclesiastical peers knocked at the closed door of the king's chamber and asked 'where is our new king, who God has sent to reign over us?'. The grand chamberlain replied from behind the closed door that he was within. The peers inquired 'What is he doing?' with the chamberlain responding that he was resting. The peers commanded the chamberlain to rouse him so that they might do him reverence and a moment later the door was opened by the grand chamberlain who said that the king was awake. Charles was found reclining and the cardinal greeted him with a short speech, beseeching him to come to the church which had been prepared for his coronation. The peers then returned to the church *without the king*, and sent two bishops back to bring him to the church.[27] Ritual dialogue at the king's door was thus introduced in 1561 but it was not until 1610 that it became part of the seeking of the king and bringing him to church. These questions and answers are not mentioned in records for the coronation of Henri III in 1571 nor for that of Henri IV in 1594, where the king was sought and brought to church in a more straightforward manner.[28]

At the ceremonially crucial coronation of Louis XIII in 1610, the bishops requested to see 'Louis XIII, son of Henry the Great' and were told he was sleeping. It was their request to meet 'Louis XIII, who God has given us for king' which opened the door.[29] For historians applying the classic 'two bodies' theories, the ritual appears to mean that the king, the physical Louis son of Henry, was sleeping, his power in abeyance, while that abstract, enduringly potent legal entity, the King, stood ready for coronation.[30] The application of these theories, developed so brilliantly by Ernst Kantorowicz, is not unproblematic in the French context, as discussed in the Introduction.[31] English royal rites, Kantorowicz's point of departure, do not include anything resembling the rite of the sleeping king. The granting of the king's title, calling for Louis XIII at each iteration and not merely 'Louis fils d'Henri', is more redolent of the young king throwing off temporal tutelage than of abstract political theory. He is no longer a son but a King, a power in his own right and, indeed, God's chosen ruler.

The sleeping king was already King. In 1715, Hyacinthe Rigaud was commissioned to paint a portrait of the 5-year old Louis XV in full coronation regalia.[32] This first official portrait of the new king asserted the fullness of his kingship, showing him in robes with the crown and hand of justice on a side table, just as they appear in Rigaud's portraits of Louis XIV (1701) and the adult Louis XV (1730). Significantly, it was painted seven years *before* Louis XV was crowned king. An earlier painting by Henri Testlin is tellingly titled *Louis XIV en 1648, seulement âgé de dix ans mais déjà roi de France.* His coronation took place five years later. Louis XVI was depicted as king in an engraving of 1774 (Figure 10) reproduced in Chapter 4 of this book. His brother, Louis XVIII, who was never formally crowned, appeared in several portraits in full regalia: one by François Gérard even appears to show him sitting on a throne. Alexis Simon Belle's portrait of Louis XV's son at age 1 shows the infant dauphin sitting on ermine, possibly on a throne, with one chubby hand wrapped around a crown. Glosses on the coronation from the seventeenth and eighteenth century unabashedly confirmed that the coronation did not make the king, who was said to be king, or perhaps King, by virtue of his birth. As early as the 1620s, Jean Bodin stated emphatically that 'the king does not cease to be king without crowning or consecration, which are not in the least the essence of sovereignty' and, in 1722, Nicolas Menin, a keen afficinado of royal ritual, added 'we recognise the rights of our monarch independent of all ceremony'.[33] These paintings announced the power and status of the sitter, and by extension, the solidity and grandeur of his kingdom. They were political statements as much as works of art, recognised as an important element of the ambassadorial equipment necessary to properly represent the interests of France.[34] Such statements proved necessary and useful through the Bourbon period which, it is often forgotten under the smooth veneer of absolutist myth, regularly experienced the perilous proximity of dynastic instability. The assertion of instant succession was vital to Bourbon success from the first moment of Henri IV's kingship. Assurance of the continuity of the line through the birth of an heir was seen as confirmation of heaven's blessing on the dynasty, as at the birth of Louis XIV who was also named Dieudonné, God-given. Even the more obscure and overtly religious elements of coronation ritual demonstrated the belief that the king was God's elect prior to coronation rather than because of it. The Holy Ampulla, according to legend, miraculously appeared to facilitate the baptism of Clovis, before either his baptism or his consecration as king. God's favour permitted religious rites to take place and did not depend on them. The function of the coronation was not to endow the king with kingship but, as discussed above, to harness irrational powers to an already powerful monarch. The ritual of the sleeping king, which appeared in this form for the first time at the coronation of Louis XIII, enacted the triumph of Bourbon dynasticism not of absolutism.

As early as 1403, immediate dynastic succession was enshrined in law. The political realities of the late sixteenth century, when the mortality of kings repeatedly had direct and catastrophic effects on the polity, served not only to popularise but also to cement the application of legal maxims such as 'le mort saisit le vif' and 'le roi ne meurt jamais'.[35] Having fought his way to the throne and brought peace to a blood-stained kingdom, the official response to the assassination of Henri IV in 1610 was to strive to preserve that hard-won stability.[36] This would not be achieved by emphasising the weakness an 8 year-old king but rather by emphasising his immediate legitimacy and authority as successor in spite of his minor status. The accession of Louis XIII in such alarming circumstances prompted high levels of ritual inventiveness, evident in both the novelty of the inaugural *lit de justice*[37] and the ceremony of the sleeping king which, in 1610 and thereafter, emphasised the young heir's identity as king in his own right and as the elect of God. In both cases an existing ceremonial form was turned to a new purpose. Thanks to good record-keeping and dynastic stability, this became the new ritual template for coronations and thus was enacted by Louis XIV, Louis XV and finally Louis XVI at his coronation in 1775. Arguably, by the late eighteenth century, the meaning of the ritual had become indistinct for contemporaries, so unquestioned was the idea of dynastic succession. Following the upheavals of the Revolution, there was no analogous ceremony during the imperial coronation of Napoleon in 1804.[38] When it reappeared at the *sacre* of Charles X in 1825, it was stripped of references to the king sleeping. Only one question and answer was required before the door opened: 'What do you seek?' 'Charles X, who God has given us for king'. The king rose unaided from an armchair and proceeded to the cathedral in procession.[39] The rite had come full circle, back to the traditional form of seeking the king.

On the morning of 11 June 1775 – Louis XVI having risen from his bed with the assistance of the bishops – a much larger procession, now incorporating the diverse elements at work in the *sacre*, formed and wound its way back to the church.[40] Various detachments of the king's guards, the king-at-arms and heralds, members of the Order of the Holy Spirit, officers of the household and the keeper of the seals, Miromesnil, all marched to the sound of oboes, drums and trumpets. On arrival at the cathedral, at about half past seven in the morning, wearing a coronation robe measuring 8.5 metres long and weighing over 80 kilos,[41] the king was seated in an armchair under a canopy on the altar. The time had come for the next ritual stage: the arrival of the Holy Ampulla.

Swearing and consecration

The Holy Ampulla was a key element of French royal mythology. According to legend, the container descended from heaven containing the oil for the baptism of Clovis and, reputedly, had been used at every coronation since.[42] Such was its symbolic importance that an entirely separate ritual for its transport from the church of Saint-Rémi to the cathedral was enacted about half past six that morning. On arrival at the cathedral, the grand prior of Saint-Rémi handed the Ampulla to the cardinal-archbishop in exchange for a promise of its immediate return and was seated, with the *chevaliers* and *barons de la Sainte Ampoulle*, among the grandees in the choir. The cardinal-archbishop deposited the Ampulla on the altar as an antiphon was sung in its honour.

This rite accomplished, and the holiest artefact of the royal mythology in place, it was time for the king to swear his solemn oaths. The king remained seated in his armchair, with his hat on, while the bishops of Laon and Beauvais asked him to promise to protect the rights of the church and of each bishop.[43] This request was more gallican and political in tone than Catholic and spiritual, invoking the political relationship of monarchy and church through references to 'the canonical privileges, rights and jurisdictions' rather than any more abstract notions of religious unity. In return for the king's positive response, a promise to the bishops rather than an oath to any deity,[44] the bishops raised him from his chair to face the congregation. This was the moment when the consent of the assembly was sought for the new king. The duc de Croÿ was puzzled by the performance of this act in 1775: he expected the bishops to ask the

16 The king's second coronation outfit, from Pichon, *Sacre et couronnement de Louis XVI*. Engraving by Charles Emmanuel Patas.

assembly to accept the king and consent to be indicated by a respectful silence. The bishops informed him that they had been instructed to raise the king but not to say anything: 'so that's the truth: the famous question is no longer posed'.[45] While the bishops' request is documented in previous coronations, it seems likely that the vocal acclamation of the king by the congregation at this point of the ceremony was something of a myth, perhaps developed over the long sixteenth century in tandem with theories of elective kingship derived from antique Frankish antecedents. There is little evidence for the performance of such gestures in early modern coronations before that of Henri II in 1574.[46] In any case, as we shall see, noisy acclamation of the king did take place in 1775 at a later point in the ceremony.

Louis XVI resumed his seat and, with his hand on the Bible, swore an oath to the kingdom, oaths as head of the Orders of the Holy Spirit and of Saint Louis and an oath against duelling. The content of the oaths largely regarded military and chivalric matters, while the king's commitments to the church were made in the form of a personal promise. It has been argued that this promise had the force of an oath, though the difference in wording and in gesture makes it difficult to see this as an act of oath-taking.[47] The promise to the clergy was in response to a request ('we ask you …' 'I promise') whereas the oaths, unprompted, were recited with hands on the Bible and included the vocabulary of swearing ('I confirm by oath', 'I swear'). Pichon's *Journal historique* of the *sacre* places this moment under the heading 'the king's promises and oaths' referring to the 'promise' to the clergy and the other 'oaths'.[48]

The oath to the kingdom was a venerable text, dating in parts perhaps from the thirteenth century,[49] and including the famous phrase on fighting heresy condemned by the Church. This came fourth in a list of undertakings including general commitments to pursue justice and peace and to prevent people of all ranks from commiting 'thievery and iniquities of whatever sort'.[50] Heresy was neither the subject of an oath in its own right nor the main thrust of the oath in which it was included, a point not usually considered by historians who detect personal conservatism, not to say chauvinism, in Louis XVI's enunciation of this oath.[51] The oath on the Order of the Holy Spirit was first taken by Louis XIV at his coronation and the anti-duelling oath first taken by Louis XV at his coronation where he pledged to uphold his grandfather's edicts once he reached his majority.[52] As the first coronation after the foundation of the Order of Saint Louis in 1693, Louis XV's was the first at which the oath on the Order of Saint Louis was taken. Three of the four oaths taken by Louis XVI were therefore of relatively recent vintage. Given the pervasive traces of chivalric ritual throughout the coronation, it seems rather appropriate that new oaths on quasi-chivalric orders were added. Overall, the incorporation of evermore oaths on different matters is perfectly consonant with the sensibility at work in this ceremony: little, if anything, was ever discarded and much was added, creating a complex and sometimes dissonant whole.[53]

While this took place, the necessary accoutrements of the consecration were placed on the altar: three crowns, including the great crown of Charlemagne, the sword of Charlemagne, the sceptre, hand of justice, spurs and ceremonial book from Saint Denis as well as special garments for the king's investiture with holy orders. The ritual dressing of the king in the chivalric accessories of his predecessors was performed before the altar by the cardinal-archbishop, the duc de Bouillon, as grand chamberlain, and Monsieur, as lead lay peer. Though automatically inducted into the chivalric orders by virtue of his birth rank, this was the first ritual in which the king was endowed with knighthood. It was also the first time in the ceremony that the king removed his hat, which he had retained throughout the promise and oath-taking. This chivalric aspect is one to which few commentators at the time, or since, have been sensitive.[54] The king, bareheaded and seated in an armchair, accepted the freshly blessed sword of Charlemagne, holding the unsheathed sword aloft with the point towards the ceiling. It was held in that position for the rest of the ceremony by the 88 year-old maréchal de Clermont-Tonnerre, in the office of constable,[55] symbolic of the protection and penalties of royal authority but also of the presence of the king.[56] This gesture, performed at the moment of knighthood rather than of consecration, reminds us of the strong quasi-religious, chivalric layer of meaning in the coronation.

Once the king had been knighted, the moment of consecration arrived as the grand prior of Saint Rémi passed the Ampulla, and a golden needle for extracting the precious oil, to the cardinal-archbishop. The king prostrated himself before the altar on purple velvet cushions while the bishops and choir intoned verses and prayers. Such prostration was a normal part of the ordination the king was about to receive as well as a preparation for consecration. The cardinal-archbishop resumed his seat and, with the king kneeling before him, anointed him on the crown of the head, on the stomach, on both shoulders and between them, and on both elbows, making the sign of the cross and saying on each occasion 'I consecrate you king, with this blessed oil, in the name of the Father, and of the Son, and of the Holy Spirit' to which the assisting clergy responded 'amen'. The grand chamberlain then robed the king in purple and gold vestments symbolic of the offices of sub-deacon, deacon and priest. A final unction was performed on the palm of each hand and the archbishop placed a pair of gloves on the king's hands. A ring was put on his finger and the sceptre and hand of justice were taken from the altar and placed in the kneeling king's hands. The *sacre* was complete: Louis XVI girded as a knight, anointed as a king and invested as a priest.

Miromesnil, the keeper of the seals, now came forward and called the lay and then ecclesiastical peers for the ritual of crowning. The cardinal-archbishop held the crown of Charlemagne over the king's head while the other peers stretched their hands out in support. The crown was placed on the king's head by the cardinal-archbishop alone, followed by more blessings and prayers.[57] Such was the ceremony of *couronnement*, its brevity in contrast to the elaborate nature of the combined knighting-consecration ceremony, perhaps a good explanation for the general usage of *sacre* to describe the rite rather than *couronnement*.

The great crown of Charlemagne was quietly changed for a lighter diamond-studded crown as a procession formed to conduct the king to his throne.[58] The heralds-at-arms led the way and the lay and ecclesiastical peers took positions on either side of the throne as the king, preceded by the sword-bearing constable and surrounded by his guards and members of his household, was guided by the cardinal-archbishop towards the raised throne. Even before the archbishop gave the traditional triple cry – 'French hearts could not longer wait'[59] – shouts of 'vive le Roi!' had been echoing around the cathedral for some time as the excited congregation could no longer contain itself. The usually self-contained duc de Croÿ found the moment 'sublime': everyone was out of their seats, crying and clapping.[60] Against this hubbub, as the king was seated, the cardinal-archbishop recited several prayers, removed his mitre, bowed low and called out three times 'vivat rex in aeternum'. The doors were flung open to allow the people to enter, small birds were released inside the cathedral, music swelled from the orchestra. Gunfire, cannonfire and church-bells were heard outside. The traditional shouts of 'vive le roi!' were joined by more modish tears and hand-clapping, creating a period of such overwhelming, exuberant din that the congregation could not hear the service continue, which it did with a *Te Deum*.[61] The commotion redoubled as the king's brothers and the peers embraced him.

This was the moment when ceremonialism embraced and became entwined with the fashionable current of sentimental gesture and language. Even the rather staid duc de Croÿ describes it as an outpouring of

17 The king's third coronation outfit, from Pichon, *Sacre et couronnement de Louis XVI*. Engraving by Charles Emmanuel Patas.

emotion which none could contain. This was perfectly in tune with the spirit of an age which, inspired by writers including Rousseau, sought out occasions to be moved to tears as a proof of the authenticity of their emotions.[62] The patrician Croÿ, the *historiographe du roi* Jean-François Marmontel and Remois writer Louis Jean Lévesque de Pouilly[63] share this sentimental vocabulary to remarkable extent: 'I well know that I have never felt such a wave of enthusiasm', 'an inexpressible wave of tenderness seized the whole assembly, and tears flowed … we were besotted', 'tears of emotion flowed from every eye'.[64] Not only was there unity of feeling among the congregation, this extended to the royal actors of the ceremony and, particularly for Pouilly, the purity of this shared feeling transformed the *sacre* into a school for virtue.[65] Heralds-at-arms moved around the choir and nave distributing commemorative medals in gold and silver featuring the king in profile on the obverse and an allegorical image of his consecration on the reverse, a tangible yet symbolic representation of the king's largesse to his people. These valuable mementos were, remarks Pouilly, ignored as the people preferred to remain where they could see their king rather than collect the medals: 'the love of their prince had become their sole passion, and this passion brought forth almost unknown virtues'.[66]

This wave of public crying was entirely normal social behaviour. What interests us here is the motive for these tears in the moment, and the ways in which they were subsequently described: in other words, broadly, how they were understood at the time and how they were used immediately afterwards. They were sparked by the moment of enthronement, a moment at which the ceremony was designed to achieve a peak of stimulation through the use of sound and movement after a long period of solemnity and near silence. The ceremonial format was clearly very effective in focusing emotional energy and triggering responses, even in those who did not expect to react in such a manner, such as the duc de Croÿ. The experience of the moment of enthronement was one of ebullient and irresistible emotion. There is of course a difference between the fleeting experience of this moment and its subsequent recording. The set-piece of enthronement combined dynastic and domestic elements in a manner reminiscent of sentimental theatre and literature, notably the king's interactions with his brothers and cousins, and with the queen. Writings about the ceremony presented the moment of enthronement as a series of *tableaux* – procession from the altar, seating the king, the ritual embrace by the peers – which fitted perfectly with sentimentalist practice.

The Austrian Ambassador, Florimond Claude de Mercy-Argenteau,[67] harnessed this effusion of elevating emotion to signal to Empress Maria Theresa a pivotal role for the queen, her daughter. Marie Antoinette was very much a spectator at the ceremony, following the failure of the ambassador's campaign to have her crowned alongside the king.[68] Mercy-Argenteau constructs his whole narrative of the coronation around the queen's tears and includes details that the queen herself omits from her rather bland letter to her mother on the *sacre*.[69] The image of a sensitive queen had been praised from the earliest days of the reign, as Dorat wrote in 1774, 'and I would die happy, picturing a sensitive queen, and a citizen king'.[70] At the moments of the coronation and enthronement, wrote Mercy, echoing the sentimental lexicon we have just noted,

> the queen, seized by emotion, shed an abundance of tears; she was even obliged to withdraw from her seat, and when she reappeared a few moments later, then the whole church rang with cries, hand-clapping and indescribable demonstrations. Everyone was weeping; it was noticed that the king raised his head to look at the queen and that the monarch's face was painted with an unmistakeable air of contentment. The queen's sensibility made such an impression on the king that for the rest of that day his attitude to his spouse was one of indescribable adoration. At every instant he spoke to his courtiers of the queen's tears, and he ceaselessly returned to this chapter, showing a satisfaction and gaiety that few had seen in him until that day.[71]

Thus, and rather improbably, the focus of the ceremony, even for the king, becomes the queen. Mercy-Argenteau's lobbying to have the queen crowned alongside the king having failed, he found another way to instrumentalise the coronation to boost the queen's influence on the king, at least in his reports to Vienna. Bolstering his reputed indirect influence on the king could only improve his standing with the empress.

The king remained enthroned as the service continued with a mass with music. He descended only at the moment of the offertory when four knights of the Order of the Holy Spirit, making triple bows as they approached the throne, presented him with a golden chalice of wine, a silver loaf of bread and a golden one, and a red velvet purse containing thirteen pieces of gold matching the *jettons* distributed earlier.[72] Accompanied by the peers, heralds-at-arms and ceremonial staff, the king followed these knights in procession to the altar where he knelt to present the offerings to the cardinal-archbishop. He returned to the throne but descended again at the end of the mass for communion. Divested of his crown, sceptre and hand of justice, he entered a small tent to the side of the altar and made his confession. Emerging, he knelt before the altar to receive communion in both kinds, thanks to his ordination. The communion cloth was held by Monsieur and the comte d'Artois assisted by the bishop of Senlis and one of the king's almoners. He resumed the crown of Charlemagne for his prayers after communion: this was replaced with the lighter diamond crown for the grand procession back to the archiepiscopal palace. The crown of Charlemagne was placed on a velvet cushion and carried before the king as his guards and household led the parade of musicians, heralds, knights of the Order of the Holy Spirit, pages and the constable carrying the naked sword of Charlemagne. The king, in his royal robes and holding the sceptre and hand of justice, was accompanied by the peers with the cardinal-archbishop and Monsieur, as senior ecclesiastical and lay peers, on his right and left hand. His splendidly uniformed bodyguards closed the procession through the nave and along the arcaded bridge to the archi-episcopal palace. The large crowd in the cathedral square cheered their passage, 'another moment of splendour'.[73]

After the coronation

It was now around half eleven in the morning. On arrival at his quarters, the king removed the coronation garments. The royal gloves and shirt were sent to be burnt since they had had contact with the holy unction and could not be re-used for base activities. The king took some time to examine the treasures of Saint Denis, along with the duc de Croÿ and others. At half past one, the crowned and consecrated king hosted the *festin royal*, the royal feast for the peers, ambassadors, local dignitaries and clergy with the lay and ecclesiastical peers remaining in their coronation garments throughout. Feasting was here, as always, a display of power through the public demonstration of hospitality and, atavistically, the ability to command vast quantities of high quality fare, most of it meat. While the vast personnel of royalty were all in action – carrying napkins, tasting food, standing ready – this demonstration of power was something of an illusion since the central matter of concern, the food itself, was paid for by the city of Reims.[74] The king entered the hall in procession, holding his sceptre and hand of justice which were then displayed prominently at his table as was the great crown of Charlemagne. Seated under a velvet dais decorated with golden fleurs-de-lys, Louis dined with his brothers at a table on a platform raised above the other diners. The doughty 88 year-old Clermont-Tonnerre, still in his adopted role as constable of France, stood before the king throughout the meal bearing the sword of Charlemagne with point aloft. The lay and ecclesiastical peers, the hostages of the Sainte Ampoule, and the marshalls of France who had carried the royal *honneurs* were seated at the other tables. Service was performed with the highest level of pomp by the king's household, dishes brought in parade escorted by heralds, *maîtres d'hôtel* and fanfares for each course. As was customary, this event was open to public viewing with platforms provided for spectators who included the queen and her ladies since the meal was a male-only event. The lesser tables were served by the municipal officers of Reims assisted by 130 bourgeois notables. These same men later served a meal for sixty at the Hôtel de Ville for the constable, as Clermont-Tonnerre was finally allowed to sit down, the hostages of the Sainte Ampoule, courtiers and locals: there was yet another feast later in the day at the Hôtel de Ville for 200 at which the municipal officers hosted their counterparts from Chalons and Troyes, and the notables who had served at the *festin*. Feasting was clearly not an exclusive practice of the court, nor were the feasters exclusively courtly.

That evening, Reims was resplendent with illuminations in celebration of the coronation.[75] Those at the archbishopric were perhaps the most beautiful, showing images of Versailles, while the illuminations at the intendant's residence displayed images of the Trianon.[76] This was not the only royal presence on the streets of Reims that night as the king himself ventured out and mingled with the people. This direct contact with the people offered further proof of his virtuous disposition, according to views expressed at the time of his accession:

> Oh, let your subjects approach you freely
> To offer their glances, which turn towards you,
> The touching tokens of a king's bounty,
> To show their ecstasy, or to bring you their tears.
> At the height of vain honours,
> the soul still sighs, seeking true pleasure,
> wishing for a purer and enduring happiness.
> There is only one, my son, that is inexhaustible:
> banish all fear, and inspire love.
> Be guarded by it alone, rejoice in its delight;
> Let a happy crowd, true foundation of might,
> Be the new luxury reserved for your court![77]

The excursion is the subject of a fascinating diversity of accounts, all of which harness aspects of the fashionable sentimental rhetoric of the day in praise of the king and queen.

The queen's role inevitably dominates the account given by the imperial ambassador, Mercy-Argenteau, writing to the empress Maria-Theresa. He credits the queen with suggesting the outing and paints it as a personal triumph for her. Surprisingly, considering the empress's regular admonitions to cultivate her relationship with the king, Marie Antoinette makes no mention of the outing in her letters. About seven in the evening, according to the ambassador, the royal couple strolled arm-in-arm along the wooden gallery between the archiepiscopal palace and the cathedral. Though the gallery was crowded, the king gave orders to allow all to remain. The king and queen, with a discreet guard, spent an hour among the multitude who cheered 'vive le roi et la reine', according to the ambassador. 'The public were truly besotted, above all with the gracious and affable air that was remarked on the queen's countenance.'[78] The ambassador's over-emphasis of the queen's role, his questionable assertion that all eyes were on her rather then on the king, betrays his exertions in crafting his account for his audience and his own benefit. Nonetheless, he is not alone in striking a note of effusive emotion in his description.

The more theatrical account by Marmontel depicts the king, hearing that the people are assembled, acting on an irresistible impulse to spend more time among them. Accompanied only by the queen, the king walks through the crowd, speaking with them, listening to them, even allowing them to touch him, dispensing proofs of his love for his people. The feeling is mutual: the king's presence is an automatic guarantee of dignified behaviour, 'the people, of their own accord, formed two lines'.[79] Adding more notes of sentimental merit, another narrator, the Reimois Pouilly, tells of the king slipping away from his courtiers after the long coronation day when he hears his people calling, 'it makes his heart tremble'. In this version, his attendants search for him and he is found in a touching tableau surrounded by his adoring people. The courtiers fear he is fatigued, the king replies that what he sees and hears restores his energy. Eventually, the king and people separate reluctantly.[80] For Pouilly, who does not mention the queen in this scene, this is a family romance, the reunion of loving children with a long-lost father, the young king compared to Henri IV.[81]

While Mercy-Argenteau wrote as an ambassador seeking to burnish his credentials, Marmontel was in Reims in his role as *historiographe de France* and, already a well-known public author, sought to capture this major event for public consumption.[82] Pouilly, as a local worthy, understandably indulged in florid advocacy on behalf of Reims as the site for the coronation, though this does not fully explain the fervour of his emotional engagement with the events. Though the diverse motivations of these writers shape their portrayal of this event, there is a common core of sentimental rhetoric to all three accounts. The encounter of the king and his people is described in terms of reciprocal sentimental arousal, love, physical and emotional contact. Though tears, the customary substrate of sentimental encounters, were reserved for the coronation ceremony, the fervent feeling depicted here is equally strong. Stripped of ceremonial apparatus, there is nonetheless a ritualistic tone to this consecration of the king by feeling as he is recognised by the people through the power of their emotion.[83]

Conclusion

The coronation ceremony was an amalgam of several traditions: among them the chivalric, the mythological, the Catholic. Rather than the hollow performance of an antiquated rite, the coronation was the focus of an outpouring of emotion in a very contemporary fashion and appreciated as such at the time. This '[p]ublic expression of intense feeling, rather than causing embarrassment was a badge of generous sincerity and of social connectedness' and as such argues for the compelling and uniting nature of the experience of the coronation.[84] We shall see in the following chapter how another ritual connected to the coronation combined elements of local tradition, popular recollection and religion, that it was, as Roy Strong has suggested about the English coronation, 'a multiple event involving all sorts and conditions of people'.[85]

While sentimental plays and paintings idealised the domestic interior, and this has generally been seen as the counterpart of the public realm of political debate, these scenes of enthusiasm were undeniably public and populated. Rather than the *tête-à-tête* or small family group, the coronation was the occasion of mass emotion in which sentimental responses were exhibited on a large scale. As such, the coronation seems a *sui generis* moment in the history of sentimentalism and ceremony. It sheds new light on the potential for positive engagement with the monarchy at this late juncture in the eighteenth century. The classic sources for historians of the coronation have been sceptics, sterling representatives of the 'traditional' sort of public sphere, male writers whose works have been printed: the abbé Véri, the *publiciste* Pidansat de Mairobert, neither of whom attended the event. Véri, who was forthright about his lack of interest in the ceremony, suggested that the expression of emotion was simply business as usual for such an event and essentially meaningless,[86] which, evidently, it was to him. His main concern was the expense, a point on which his friend Turgot might have reassured him, and in this he was echoed by Mairobert in the *Mémoires sécretes*, who described the printed account of the coronation as 'this very long hotch-potch of childish customs'.[87] Mairobert's complaint that building works for the coronation were carried out by *corvées* rings hollow since he refers to major building works at Soissons, a city which the king did not visit, and we have noted the *intendant*'s concern with the *corvée* above.[88] Mairobert's anxiety for peasants forced to carry out municipal works instead of cultivating their crops is laudable, another fashionable topic which he seeks unsuccessfully to hang on the coronation. The shared concern about finance, in which they were joined by the king, conveys what was being said in some politically minded circles at the time, not necessarily the dominant feeling, and, of course, it does not invalidate differing points of view.

These moments of emotion also raise questions for our understanding of royal ritual. While ritual is generally perceived as a sequence of intentional gestures within a fairly fixed ceremonial framework,[89] here we have examples of gestures which were not planned, which interrupted an important ceremony, and which were universally admired. These apparently transgressive tears served as a seal of approval on the ceremony, proof of its effectiveness in uniting the king with his people.[90] Participants' records of the event have demonstrated the suffusion of the ceremony with sentiment, the triumph of the irrational both in the moment of ceremonial climax and in encounters between the monarch and his people.

Though the king was now consecrated and crowned, he remained in Reims for several days to accomplish other ceremonies connected with the coronation. In the next chapter, we will examine another event with an eye particularly to the strong role played by the people of Reims and from further afield, not royal officials, in organising and enacting them. This will demonstrate that the coronation was not merely a royal 'show' performed in 1775 in the spirit of pale mimicry of past glories.

Notes

1 Thomas-Jean Pichon (1731–1812) was a doctor of theology, a canon of the Cathedral of Mans and historiographer to the king's brother, the comte de Provence. His collaborator on the coronation handbook was his colleague

Nicolas Gobet, *gardes des archives de Monsieur*. Pichon was a writer of *anti-philosphe* tracts. See Antoine Laporte, *Bibliographie clérico-galante. Ouvrages galants ou singuliers sur l'amour, les femmes, le mariage, le théâtre, etc. écrits par les abbés, prêtres, chanoines, religieux, religieuses, évêques, archevêques, cardinaux et papes par l'Apôtre bibliographe* (Paris, 1879), 141.

2 Thomas-Jean Pichon, *Les Droits respectifs de l'État et de l'Église rappelés à leurs principes* (Avignon and Paris, 1766), xii.

3 Darrin M. McMahon, *Enemies of the Enlightenment: The French Counter-Enlightenment and the making of modernity* (Oxford, 2001).

4 A similar volume published for Louis XV's coronation in 1722 drew on biblical antecedents and strongly linked unction to religion, claiming that French king Clovis was the first Christian king, see Nicolas Menin, *Traité historique et chronologique du sacre et couronnement des rois et des reynes de France* (Paris, 1723).

5 Antoine Danchet, *Le Sacre de Louis XV* (Paris, 1722).

6 *Le Sacre de Louis XVI*, 'Avertissement', v.

7 Pidansat de Mairobert attests to the many who wished to attend in *Mémoires secrets pour servir à l'histoire de la république des lettres en France, depuis MDCCLXII jusqu'à nos jours* (London, 1780–89), volume 8, 57.

8 Anatole de Gallier, 'Laurent Aymon de Franquières, le sacre de Louis XVI à Rheims', *Revue de Champagne et de Brie* (1880), VIII, 101; Jean-François Marmontel, *Correspondance, Tome I (1744–1780)*, Texte établi, annoté et présenté, par John Renwick (Clermont-Ferrand, 1974), 303.

9 Emmanuel de Croÿ, *Journal Inédit Du Duc De Croÿ, 1718–1784* (Paris, 1906), volume 3, 171.

10 This last was most likely the coronation *ordo* – the 'liturgical sequence of prayers and blessings by which various actions are given sacramental significance, in particular by invoking divine sanction, blessings and the descent of the gifts of the Holy Spirit …' though without any directions as to their performance. Definition from Roy Strong, *Coronation: From the eighth to the twenty-first century* (London, 2006), 23.

11 See Danielle Gaborit-Chopin, *Regalia: les instruments du sacre des rois de France, les 'honneurs de Charlemagne'* (Paris, 1987).

12 Viscount Stormont to Lord Rochford, Most Private letter, 8 February 1775. NASPF 78/295/108.

13 Marina Valensise, 'Le sacre du roi: strategie symbolique et doctrine politique de la monarchie', *Annales ESC*, 41:3 (1986), 559.

14 Triple knocks on closed doors were features of both ecclesiastical and quasi-religious guild rites, see Constant Leber, *Des Cérémonies du sacre*, Reims (1825), 156 *passim.*

15 *Richesses Tirées du Trésor de l'abbaye de St Denis, du gardemeuble de la couronne et de différens artistes de Paris pour servir au sacre de l'auguste monarque de France le roi Louis XVI, AMR, Fonds Anciens C 732 liasse 21*, 3.

16 Pichon, *Le Sacre de Louis XVI*, 97–98; *Journal historique du sacre*, 31. Nicholas Menin does not offer any more insight in his *Le Sacre de Louis XV* (Paris, 1723).

17 Leber, *Des Cérémonies du sacre*; Richard A. Jackson, *Vive le Roi! A history of the French coronation from Charles V to Charles X* (Chapel Hill, 1984), chapter 9, and, 'The sleeping king', *Bibliothèque d'Humanisme et de la Renaissance*, 31:3 (1969), 525–51; Alain Boureau, 'Ritualité politique et modernité monarchique', *L'État ou le roi: les fondations de la modernité monarchique en France (XIVe-XVIIe siècles) textes réunis par Neithard Bulst, Robert Descimon et Alain Guerreau* (Paris, 1996), 9–25.

18 Jackson, *Vive le Roi!*, 143; Leber, *Des Cérémonies*, 165, 171.

19 Ralph E. Giesey, *Cérémonial et puissance souveraine* (Paris, 1987), 42 *passim*.

20 Jackson, *Vive le Roi!*, his chapter on the sleeping king appears in part three entitled 'Striving towards absolutism'.

21 Denys Godefroy, *Le Cérémonial de France* (Paris, 1649), volume 1, 407–08.

22 Charles Bévy, *Histoire des inaugurations des rois, empereurs, et autres souverains de l'univers, depuis leur origine jusqu'à présent* (Paris, 1776), 192.

23 Godefroy, *Le Cérémonial*, 2, 13, 26.

24 Godefroy, *Le Cérémonial*, 32, 194, 246.

25 Ibid., p 57.

26 Bévy confuses his sources and connects this narrative to the coronation of Henry II. Bévy, *Histoire*, 408. Leber, *Des Cérémonies*, 162. Charles IX's coronation took place barely eighteen months after that of his brother Francis II in September 1559. The paucity of records makes it sadly impossible to know the manner in which the king was sought on that occasion.

27 Godefroy, *Le Cérémonial*, 312.

28 Ibid., 325, 356. *L'Ordre des ceremonies du sacre et couronnement du Tres-Chrestien Roy de France et de Navarre Henry quatriesme du nom* (Lyon, 1594), 21.

29 Godefroy, *Le Cérémonial*, 408.

30 Though it seems somewhat contradictory to crown the undying King, it is the invocation of that abstract figure, and not reference to the physical person, that is said to open the door. Jackson, 'The sleeping king', 541–42.

31 Ernst Kantorowicz, *The King's Two Bodies: A study in medieval political theology* (Princeton, 1957); Bernard Jussen, '*The King's Two Bodies* today', *Representations*, 106:1 (2009), 102–17. Fanny Consandey, *La Reine de France, symbole et pouvoir, XVe–XVIIIe siècles* (Paris, 2000), 9–10.

32 Stephan Perreau, *Hyacinthe Rigaud, 1659–1743: le peintre des rois* (Montpellier, 2004), 105–06.

33 Jean Bodin, *Six livres de la république*, Book 1, chapter ix, 203. Menin, *Sacre de Louis XV*, 168.

34 Sarah Medlam, 'Callet's portrait of Louis XVI: a picture frame as diplomatic tool', *Furniture History*, 43 (2007), 143–54.

35 Jackson, *Vive le Roi*, 143; Leber, *Des Cérémonies du sacre*, 172.

36 Michel Cassan, 'L'annonce de la mort d'Henri IV dans le royaume', in *Les Funérailles princières en Europe, XVe–XVIIIe siècle*, volume 3, Juliusz Chorścicki, Mark Hengerer and Gérard Sabatier (editors) (Rennes, 2015).

37 On which see Sarah Hanley, *The* Lit de Justice *of the Kings of France: Constitutional ideology, in legend, ritual and discourse* (Princeton, 1983), chapter x; Katherine Crawford, *Perilous Performances: Gender and regency in Early Modern France* (London, 2004), chapter 3.

38 *Cérémonies et Fêtes du sacre et couronnement de leurs majestés impériales Napoléon 1er et son auguste épouse* (Paris, n.d.),

39 Charles Joseph Christophe Siret, *Précis historique du sacre de S. M. Charles X, contenant les détails de cette auguste cérémonie, avec des notes et l'état du logement fait à Reims à cette occasion* (Reims, 1826), 65–66; Jackson, 'The sleeping king', 550.

40 Pichon, *Journal Historique*, 101–06.

41 Hervé Pointeau, 'Le roi et la reine de France en majesté', *Fastes de cour et cérémonies royales: le costume de cour en Europe sous la direction scientifique de Pierre Arizzoli-Clémentel et Pascale Gorguet Ballesteros* (Paris, 2009), 113.

42 Henri IV did not have access to it for his coronation at Chartres as Reims was in the hands of the League. The oil given by the Virgin Mary to Saint Martin of Tours was used instead. Théodore Godefroy, *Cérémonial de France* (Paris, 1619), 611. See also Jackson, *Vive le Roi*, 46, and Michael J. Enright's interesting discussion of oil rituals as 'believable miracles' in Frankish culture in *Iona, Tara and Soissons: The origin of the royal anointing ritual* (Berlin, 1985), 139 *passim*.

43 Pichon, *Journal historique*, 40.

44 Ibid., 41.

45 Croÿ, *Journal*, volume 3, 183.

46 Jackson, *Vive le Roi*, 116 passim.

47 See Marcel David, *Le Serment du sacre du IXe au XVe siècle* (Strasbourg, 1951). Jean de Viguerie, 'Les serments du sacre des rois de France à l'époque moderne, et plus spécialement le "serment du royaume"', in *Le Sacre des rois: actes du colloque international d'histoire sur les sacres et couronnements royaux (Reims 1975)* (Paris, 1983), 206, shares my analysis.

48 Pichon, *Journal historique*, 41.

49 Jackson, *Vive le Roi*, 58. See also Jackson, *Ordines coronationis Franciae* (Philadelphia, 2002), volume 2, 291 *passim*.

50 Pichon, *Journal historique*, 41.

51 See, most recently, Ambrogio A. Caiani, *Louis XVI and the French Revolution* (Cambridge, 2012), 216.

52 The text specifically listed edicts of Louis XIV from 1651, 1669 and 1679. On reaching his majority in 1723, Louis XV promulgated his own edict on the matter. Stuart Carroll notes resurgences in duelling during Louis XIII's reign,

in 1611–14, 1621–26, 1631–33, and during the Frondes which may explain the emphasis on these oaths at the coronation of Louis XIV. Stuart Carroll, 'The peace in the feud in sixteenth and seventeenth century France', *Past and Present*, 178 (February 2003), 111, 114.

53 But see Jackson, *Vive le Roi*, 60, for a somewhat contrary view.

54 Strong, *Coronation*, 58; Leber, *Des Cérémonies du sacre*, 158.

55 The office of constable of France was abolished in 1627. The most senior *maréchal de France* took the role for the coronation ceremony.

56 Edward Shils, 'The meaning of coronation', in *Center and Periphery: Essays in macrosociology* (Chicago, 1975), 142. Strong traces the bearing of unsheathed swords in English coronation ceremonies to the vogue for Arthurian romances in the twelfth century, romances which originated in France, *Coronation*, 58.

57 The right of the archbishop of Reims to place the crown on the king's head alone was recognised in a bull issued in 1089 by Pope Urban II, cited in Marc Bloch, *Les Rois thaumaturges: étude sur le caractère surnaturel attribué à la puissance royale particulièrement en France et en Angleterre* (Paris, 1983), first published in 1924, 228.

58 This newly made crown, 9 inches tall, featured the famous Sancy diamond. It was made by the royal jeweller Aubert at the Louvre. *Richesses*, 7.

59 Croÿ, *Journal*, volume 3, 187.

60 Ibid.

61 Ibid.

62 As Linton's study makes clear, the language of virtue was not new but was put to new uses including in the discourse of sensibility and sentiment. See Marisa Linton, *The Politics of Virtue in Enlightenment France* (Basingstoke, 2001), 21, 22 and Chapter 4 above.

63 Also known as Jean Simon, Louis Jean was the son of a more famous father with the same name who wrote *Théorie des sentimens agréables* (Paris, 1749), and was linked in friendship and philosophy to Voltaire and Lord Bolingbroke. The family resided in Reims, and father and son were members of the local *présidial* court.

64 Croÿ, *Journal*, volume 3, 187; Marmontel, *Correspondance*, 302; Louis Jean Lévesque de Pouilly, 'Précis historique de ce qui s'est passé depuis l'arrivée du roi à Rheims, jusqu'au jour de son départ', in *Journal Encyclopédie*, volume 5, part 3, August 1775 (Bouillon, 1775), 517.

65 Linton notes the contemporary idea that ordinary people were most capable of virtue since they less exposed to the corrupting influence of wealth and status in *Politics of Virtue*, 79.

66 Pouilly, 'Précis', 518.

67 (1727–94), ambassador to Paris since 1766, and deeply involved in the reversal of alliances, he maintained a secret correspondence with the Empress on the subject of her daughter in which he continually sought to bolster his

favour with the Empress by demonstrating his influence on Marie Antoinette and, in turn, her influence on her husband.

68 When consulted by Mercy-Argenteau, Maria-Theresa rejected the notion out of hand. It was never formally proposed to Louis XVI.

69 Marie-Antoinette to Maria-Theresa, 22 June 1775: Alfred von Arneth and Mathieu Auguste Geoffroy, *Correspondance secrète entre Marie-Thérèese et le Comte de Mercy-Argenteau, avec les lettres de Marie-Therese et de Marie-Antoinette* (Paris, 1874), volume 2, 342–43.

70 Claude-Joseph Dorat, 'Le nouveau regne, ode à la nation,' *Journal Encyclopédique* (Bouillon, 1774), volume 5, part II. Dorat (1734–80) was a prolific writer in various genres and the author of two well-known novels, *Les Sacrifices de l'amour* (1771) and *Les Malheurs de l'inconstance* (1772).

71 Mercy-Argenteau to Marie-Theresa, 23 June 1775: Arneth and Geoffroy, *Correspondance secrète*, volume 2, 346–47.

72 They are listed as one silver loaf and one vermoulu made by Auguste, *Richesses*, 8.

73 Croÿ, *Journal*, volume 3, 188.

74 Pichon, *Journal historique*, 62.

75 Illuminations took place in Paris at the end of June on the day of the *Te Deum* at Notre Dame to celebrate the coronation. Pidansat de Mairobert, *Mémoires secrets*, volume 8, 95.

76 De Gallier, 'Laurent Aymon de Franquières', 101.

77 Dorat, 'Le nouveau règne, hymne à la nation', 307.

78 Mercy-Argenteau to Maria-Theresa, 23 June 1775. Arneth and Geoffroy, *Correspondance secrète*, volume 2, 347.

79 Marmontel, *Correspondance*, 303, published as *Lettre de M Marmontel à M *** sur la cérémonie du sacre de Louis XVI* (Paris, 1775). Also reported by Pidansat de Mairobert, *Mémoires secrets*, volume 8, 84.

80 Pouilly, 'Précis', 519.

81 On this, see Lynn Hunt, *The Family Romance of the French Revolution* (Berkeley, 1993).

82 Jean-François Marmontel was elected to the *Académie* in 1763 and appointed *historiographe de France* in 1772.

83 Emma Barker, *Greuze and the Painting of Sentiment* (Cambridge, 2005) 15–16.

84 Reddy, William, *The Navigation of Feeling: Framework for a history of emotions* (Cambridge, 2001) 164. See also Barker on sentimental art and social solidarity, *Greuze*, 11.

85 Strong, *Coronation*, 158.

86 Véri, *Journal de l'abbé de Véri*, 304.

87 Pidansat de Mairobert, *Mémoires secrets*, volume 8, 60. For the intendant's progressive views on the *corvée*, see chapter 4.

88 *Mémoires secrets*, volume 8, 38–39. The Porte de Vesle, or Porte aux Ferrons,

in Reims was demolished in advance of the *sacre* in 1775 but the king allocated money for this operation, according to Gérard Jacob-Kolb, *Description historique de la ville de Reims* (Reims, 1825), 10.

89 Michael J. Braddick, 'Introduction: the politics of gesture', *The Politics of Gesture: Historical perspectives, Past and Present: supplement* 4, (2009), 10 *passim*.

90 Ibid., 10.

6

'Le roi te touche': the coronation and the king's healing touch

Introduction: the days after the coronation

The day after the coronation, 12 June, began with the king hearing mass in the chapel of the archiepiscopal palace. He then received the compliments of the ladies of the court, fittingly since neither the *sacre* nor the *festin royal* had permitted female participation. A further, and rather different, female presence made itself known as forty fishwives and resellers, *poissardes et revendeuses*, of Reims arrived to pay their respects.[1] They presented the king with a wicker basket containing an allegorical piece of sugarcraft and embroidery, showing him holding the hand of the female figure of truth trampling envy, lies and jealousy underfoot and inscribed with the legend 'the true happiness of the French, long live Louis XVI'. Their spokeswoman, la femme Tabary, addressed the king in similarly sweet terms saying that if he went on as he had begun they would all soon be as bathed in happiness as fish are in water. The queen received an equally flattering visit and address, as did the king's brothers. The grandees granted small gifts of money to the women so that, after expenses, they had twenty-two livres each as well as free entry to the theatre that night to enjoy with twelve bottles of wine donated by the queen. The women's enthusiasm for the experience may be judged by the fact that later that summer they spent ten days travelling to Versailles with the intention of presenting the king with another bouquet for his nameday on 25 August. Since they had not been invited, and indeed there was no tradition of their *corps* attending the king on that day which was already crammed full of compliments, they were not admitted. The comte d'Artois received them and showed them his newborn son, the duc d'Angoulême.

On 13 June, the king was absorbed in the solemn rituals of the Order of Holy Spirit, along with about forty of the highest lay and ecclesiastical lords of the land.[2] These rituals were prepared on 12 June by the first assemblies of the Order for some years. Louis XVI was received as grand master of the Order in a ceremony in the cathedral and several new members were inducted. From a day with the highest, the king then turned to a day with the lowest of his subjects. This chapter will examine 'the day of charity', '*la journée de la bienfaisance*', when the king dispensed the royal healing touch for scrofula on the same day as grace was granted to prisoners.[3]

The main aim of this chapter is to look at the coronation 'from below', while acknowledging all the problems that attend such a perspective, particularly in terms of sources. The ceremonies under examination are shown to have deep roots and significant participation beyond the scope of anything commanded by the ceremonial officers of Versailles. We have previously touched on street ceremonies when looking at responses to the dismissal of Chancellor Maupeou and Abbé Terray.[4] Those were punctual replies to political events which took the form of particular ritual forms adapted for specific occasions. In a sense, one could burn an effigy in response to many different political events; meaning is conveyed by the naming of that effigy. Hermann Weber, referring to members of the intellectual élite, has written about the uncertainty, even unease, felt by contemporaries struggling to understand the meaning of the coronation.[5] In this chapter, we will deal with a unique ceremony which was inseparable from the great royal set-piece we have just examined. What distinguishes this ceremony is the level of involvement of the people outside officialdom and the high degree of commitment shown to participation in these rituals. As such, this rite serves as testimony to the attachment to the institutions, and irrational powers, of royalty in 1775. This chapter will serve as a further illustration of the monarchy's propensity to claim, and attempt to annex, all available sources of power and prestige, however unlikely. This voracious appetite for esteem of all kinds explains the persistence of ceremonies which seem otherwise obscure.

Touching for scrofula: background and preparations

The tale of the royal touch for scrofula reveals how the failure of royal officials to engage with the local parties most concerned with that ceremony made no difference to its success. The enactment of this rite in 1775 has been interpreted as proof of the young king's outmoded attachment to neglected rituals. But, as we shall see, Louis XVI did not 'demand to carry out … a rite which had not been current for forty years';[6] on the contrary, preparations for the ritual were made regardless of the absence of instructions to do so. Popular enthusiasm for the ceremony dominates this story. Scrofula was the old name for an infection of the lymph nodes of the neck which caused unsightly swelling. Unlike smallpox, discussed in Chapter 1 above, it was a chronic rather than acute illness and generally not fatal though, since the disfiguring swellings would continue to grow if untreated – and the sufferer could also experience fever, weight loss, open wounds and subsequent infection – it was feared in its own right. Its prevalence in eighteenth-century France is reflected in the numbers of claims to cure it.

The touch should also be seen in terms of belief in miraculous healing. The royal touch was not an isolated instance. Rather, in 1775, it arose in a context of wider appetite for wondrous cures which were explained with both religious and non-religious terminology. Orthodox Catholicism endorsed the intercession of saints as a pathway to the preservation and restoration of health while, more sensationally, the Jansenist *convulsionnaires* had proclaimed cures in the heart of Paris in the 1730s, and continued their gatherings into the nineteenth century in spite of harsh police measures against them. With less religious content and a higher social profile, the animal magnetism of Anton Mesmer was enthusiastically embraced from the late 1770s.[7] Mesmer's theories were to provide some of the seed material for flourishing spiritist movements in the nineteenth century as well as, more remarkably, inspiration for revolutionary thinkers including Marat and Brissot. Againt this backdrop, the royal touch appears staid, almost mainstream. What do these wilder reaches of politics and spirituality have to do with a ceremony performed at the last coronation of the *ancien régime*? This chapter will describe the royal touch as an instance of 'marvellous royalty', as will be discussed below, capturing its charm and resonance for contemporaries, arguing that the ceremony made sense in fundamental ways mirrored by wider concerns and, thus, demonstrating that the rite was of great significance to the population.

The historiography of the ceremony of the royal touch in France is sparse and sporadic.[8] Marc Bloch's groundbreaking and still unmatched study of the ritual of royal touching to heal scrofula was considered by the author to be a study of the supernatural character attributed to royalty.[9] His term '*royauté merveilleuse*' presages our concern with the irrational as a motivating force in ceremony. Irrationality is, of course, a judgement imposed on these proceedings from our modern standpoint: we should not assume that all French people in 1775 viewed either ceremonial or healing by touch as irrational pursuits though some, a small minority even among intellectuals, voiced such opinions. Given the state of medical knowhow in dealing with scrofula, availing of a freely offered miraculous cure could well have seemed a highly rational decision. The lines between religion, magic and the sciences remained rather blurred.[10] This chapter will describe the preparations and performance of the royal touch in June 1775 and reveal the surprising fact that this ritual was organised almost entirely by Reimois, echoing Bloch's assertion that without roots in the collective consciousness a ritual cannot be imposed on a people from above.[11] Bloch noted the peculiar difficulty of writing the history of the later eighteenth-century ritual and, although he suspected that the touch was exercised throughout the reign of Louis XVI and probably to 1789, could confirm with certainty only that it took place at the coronation. While Louis XVI's personal attachment to *bienfaisance* seems to point towards that monarch's enthusiastic embrace of the possibilities of the royal touch, it does seem strange, if the ceremony were taking place regularly, that contemporary satires do not refer to it.[12] We cannot currently say with confidence whether Louis XVI touched only in 1775 or throughout his reign. However, thanks to archival work in Reims, we will here shed new light on this specific instance of 'marvellous royalty', drawing on a memoir of the event which has not, to our knowledge, been brought to historians' attention previously. In 1775, people were aware that the touch was part of the coronation ceremonies: it exerted a pull on sufferers who made their way to Reims in the hope of being touched by the king.

The origins of this rite in idea of the supernatural nature of the king, and of kingship, endured through the ages, adapting to new practices but maintaining always the core mystical belief in the special power of the monarch.[13] Bloch's study has little to say about the royal touch in the eighteenth century, beyond noting the long hiatus under Louis XV and the lack of documentary evidence for the rite under Louis XVI.[14] This is not a gap that has yet been filled by historians of France. Recent publications on the royal touch are rare and tend to conform to the old Weberian mould, predicting a waning of the practice, and of belief in the practice, as part of a pattern of increasing rationalism, paired with disenchantment with the monarchy and the coming of modernity.[15] More recent scholarship has tended to emphasise the slow pace of change in belief structures and concommitant continuities in belief over time.[16]

While a veneer of Enlightenment learning was, by the 1770s, part and parcel of the common culture of the French élite, the tools of rational debate usually associated with a sceptical Enlightenment characterised by deism were adopted in the 1770s and 1780s by Catholic apologists to argue for the validity of their faith: thus, reason, much like sentiment, was common currency in the 1770s.[17]

In an influential interpretation linking the royal touch to sermons preached around the time of the coronation, Hermann Weber has argued that Louis XVI's touching of scrofula victims in 1775 proved his intention to use his reign to 'restore morals'. While it is entirely understandable that sermonisers would expound on the theme of the new reign as a chance to change the tone of the court – or indeed the country – through the promotion of a religious reform, the performance of the touch is entirely explicable without resorting to such an overtly politico-religious agenda, given the king's personal piety, respect for tradition and inclination towards beneficence.[18] While exciting research has emerged on the prevalence of the royal touch in England in the late seventeenth and early eighteenth centuries,[19] it is not the purpose of this chapter to wholly re-evaluate scholarship on the French side. Such a project would necessitate highly focused, exhaustive archival research, beyond the scope of this current more wide-ranging endeavour, in order to reconstruct patterns of touching in the eighteenth century.[20] If popular demand was an engine for the performance of such a ceremony, belief in and attraction to the marvellous powers of the monarch must have remained strong in at least some sectors of society. Other elements of society may have experienced a 'growing mood of scepticism [which] demanded the abolition of the 'royal touch'[21] but they were not in evidence in Reims on 14 June.

The royal healing touch for scrofula was exercised by kings of France and England throughout their reigns. In France, kings did not touch for scrofula until after their coronation. Having come to the throne in 1715, Louis XV exercised the touch for the first time at his coronation in 1722 but, since he abstained from receiving the eucharist from the end of the 1730s, he did not perform the rite for most of the middle century.[22] Whether this is evidence of self-absorption, lack of political nous, or religious abnegation, is a matter of interpretation. Louis XV himself linked his non-performance to the impossibility of attaining the necessary state of grace, thus adding weight to the religious explanation. In July 1769, he wrote in resigned tones to his grandson, Ferdinand, duke of Parma, '[i]t is true, my dear grandson, that at my coronation I acquired the gift of being the instrument of God's grace in dispensing the cure for scrofula, but to do it, I must be there [in a state of grace] myself, and it is some time since that has occurred. We do have remedies here which cure this sickness. If you wish, I will send them to you with instructions.'[23] A memorandum written by the marquis de Sourches, *grand prévôt de l'hôtel* with responsiblity for aspects of organisation of the royal touch, dated 18 April 1767, offers a tantalising possibility. The note takes the form of an aide-mémoire: the marquis is noting for future use what he recalls of the usual form of the ceremony at Versailles, not seen for thirty years. He does not mention his motive for this notation: was it thought possible that a chastened Louis XV, bereaved of his son and daughter-in-law, could start to touch again at this late juncture in his reign?[24]

Even in the heyday of the royal touch, and much like the *lit de* justice,[25] there had always been periods when no touch was offered, or when it was offered with less regularity. Indeed, much of our knowledge of the periodicity of the touch in France remains conjectural in the absence a rigorous chronology of these ceremonies. In the early modern period, we know that due to the minorities of Louis XIV and Louis XV there was no royal touch available between 1643–54 and 1715–22. The parlous state of the monarchy following the assassination of Henri IV in 1610 is well attested by the rapidity with which the coronation of Louis XIII followed: Henri died in May and Louis was crowned in October. His doctor Héodard's journal bears witness to the prompt and frequent deployment of the young king's miraculous powers to bind together a shaky polity.[26] Writing about Charles II's return to England in the Restoration, Marc Bloch notes that the idea of 'marvellous royalty' and the possibility of cure remained vigorously alive throughout that king's absence.[27] There is no reason why this was not also the case in France during periods when no touch was provided, including in the mid eighteenth century.[28] It was certainly the case, for example, that individuals convicted of certain crimes waited twenty years, or longer, to travel from outside France to seek the king's grace in person on the occasion of the coronation in 1775: this, despite the availability of other easier and less hazardous channels and despite the elapse of over fifty years since the previous coronation.[29] The powers of royalty had their own special, enduring attraction.

Louis XVI's coronation provided sufferers with the first opportunity to avail of the miraculous cure in a generation. It was a well-established tradition that the newly crowned king would perform the ceremony of the royal touch for the first time in his reign. Louis XIII, Louis XIV and Louis XV touched hundreds of sufferers in Reims in the days following their coronations. Henri IV was crowned at Chartres, not Reims, and is not recorded as touching scrofula sufferers on the occasion of his *sacre*, though he regularly exercised this kingly power from Easter 1594, shortly after his entry into Paris and his first Easter communion as a king and a Catholic.[30] The Easter communion is of course more germane to the performance of the rite than the entry into Paris, though the city and the time provided an excellent opportunity for crowd-pleasing show of uniquely royal benevolence.[31]

While the ceremony of the touch was strongly associated with the coronation, the French king's ability to cure scrofula did not derive from it alone but from a combination of elements, some of which were interdependent – dynastic pedigree, consecration, achievement of a state of grace through absolution, and prayer to Saint Marcoul.[32] Correct lineage and coronation were mutually reinforcing confirmations of entitlement to rule, of which the gift of the cure was a further proof. The exercise of the gift was always more important than the number of miracles procured, mirroring the key noble concepts of liberality and open-handed generosity, in that the readiness to dispense the cure mattered more than the outcome. Coronation immediately preceded only one performance of the touch: its effect, of rendering one man a fit instrument of God's grace, was taken to endure throughout his reign though absolution and prayer were required before every iteration of the touch. Precisely what enabled the king to cure scrofula – unction or intercession of the saint – was a matter for disagreement and debate; not only, as one would expect, between the canons of Reims cathedral who presided over the coronation and the monks who guarded the relics of Saint Marcoul at Corbeny, but also between theorists of monarchy. Those with absolutist tendencies ignored or rejected the notion of blessed intervention and insisted that the miracle flowed solely from the consecrated hands of the king.[33] The emphasis shifted in line with local or national political requirements. In one version of events, the cure was the saint's thanks to the kings of France for providing a safe resting place at Corbeny for his earthly remains; in another, the ability was due solely to the coronation unction and correct title of succession with no mention of the saint.[34] André du Laurens completely overlooked the role of the saint in order to emphasise the sacred powers of coronation and the importance of lineage: given that he was first doctor to the formerly Protestant Henri IV who had acceded to the throne through correct but distant lines of descent, one can see why.[35]

While it seems very likely, it is not known whether kings always prayed to Saint Marcoul before, and after, touching:[36] it is certain that they did

18 Henri IV performing the healing touch for scrofula. The simplicity of the ritual is clear.

not always have the relics to hand when the rite was practised by the king on occasions other than the coronation – as it mostly was – wherever he was in residence on high feast days such as Easter, Pentecost, All Saints and Christmas, though the touch might be administered on other favourable occasions.[37] Even without the relics, spiritual preparation for the touch was ample: the king attended Vespers the night before, heard at least one mass and made a confession on the day of the touch. The intercession of saints had of course been rejected by Protestants so that the inclusion and rising importance of a saint in the French rite could be interpreted as a deliberate mark of Catholicism, particularly when counterposed with the New Testament readings which distinguished the English iteration of the rite. Saint Marcoul *was* a late addition to French coronation traditions: kings began to include a stop to honour his relics at Corbeny, a well known pilgrimage site roughly 30 kilometres to the north west of Reims, on their return journey from Reims, probably from the fourteenth century.[38] Even then the kings did not handle the relics and then touch the sick; this came later. The numbers of sufferers coming to Corbeny to be touched by the king grew significantly from a low base at the end of the fifteenth century: a mere six sufferers gathered around Charles VIII at the shrine of Saint Marcoul in 1484, while thousands assembled in the time of the Bourbons.[39] The numbers seeking the king's touch therefore seem to have increased, rather than decreased, over time, perhaps as the procedure became more regular and organised, nonetheless effectively undermining the standard hypothesis of movement away from belief in the supernatural and towards more scientific understandings. Part of the purpose of the king's journey to Corbeny was to commence a novena, a series of nine days of prayer, devoted to the saint which was then continued on his behalf by a monk. Attendance on the relics signalled more than a punctual encounter; it was a longer relationship than that. This veneration of the saint, though a comparatively late addition to traditions around the touch, was – by 1775 – as much a part of the royal touch as the coronation, and an act with great local resonance.

By 1775, the practice had arisen of the relics being brought to Reims rather than the royal entourage making its way to Corbeny. The coronation of Louis XIV was the first occasion on which the relics were brought to the king rather than the king going to the relics. Previous practice had been for the king to pass through Corbeny on his return from Reims, to hold Saint Marcoul's skull in his hands and then to touch for scrofula. Bringing the relics to Reims highlights the king and subordinates the role of the saint: the ceremony is now less about the saint and more about the king. This could be construed as a victory for those who wished to emphasise the king's power to cure without saintly assistance, though the scale of the celebrations welcoming the relics into Reims was impressive and certainly underlined their healing mission. This starring role for a local saint goes some way to explaining the resonance of this aspect of coronation ceremonies for the people of Reims, in spite of ecclesiastical proclamations on the primacy of unction and the late emergence of a legend associating the first act of touching for scrofula with the first French king to be anointed, Clovis. There is no reason to choose between these glosses on the ceremony of the royal touch since it, like so many other ceremonies, was the subject of a process of layering of meanings and acts. By 1775, it was firmly associated with both the coronation and prayer to Saint Marcoul.[40]

Such was the strength of this link in the Champagne region that when a refuge for scrofula sufferers was established in Reims, it was named in honour of the local saint. Founded in 1645, following the decision of the Hôtel-Dieu to exclude scrofula patients due to concerns about contagion, the Hôpital des Incurables de Saint-Marcoul was recognised by letters patent issued in May 1683.[41] The establishment had the full support of the municipal authorities.[42] Though one initial impulse behind its foundation was the isolation of those struck by the contagious and apparently incurable disease, by the 1770s, the usual population of the hospital consisted of ten lay sisters who, under the medical direction of a surgeon and a doctor, cared for about eighty patients and were credited with frequent cures by medical means.[43] Scrofula was the meeting point of medicine and miracles for centuries. André du Laurens, first doctor to Henri IV, in his 1613 treatise on scrofula, combines a description of the miraculous touch with a detailed medical discussion on the cures possible through 'medical art and industry'.[44] Du Laurens, a dedicated expert medical practitioner and teacher, in his role as first doctor to the king, had responsibility for the organisation of ordinary sessions of the royal touch and attested that more than five hundred out of a thousand people touched were cured within days.[45] It will be countered that he wrote at the beginning of the seventeenth century and that medicine had changed radically by 1775: there is evidently truth in this assertion.[46] Over this span of years, there certainly were significant advances in *savant* medical circles, though the field remained remarkably open. In April 1782, for example, Pierre Jean Claude Mauduyt de la Varenne received the approval of the Royal Society of Medicine – which, around the same time, strenuously rejected the teachings of Mesmer – to pursue his use of electricity in the treatment many ailments, including scrofula.[47] Popular medicine continued to draw on the wondrous to effect cures for many ailments: but the qualitative difference between remedies employed by professional and popular medicine was not always easy to discern.

One treatment for scrofula in the mid-to-late eighteenth century was the *remède de Rotrou*, a complete system of purgatives and medicines for cold humours which included dosing the patient over a period of weeks with an exotic mix of ground Indian pinenuts combined with Virginia snake-root.[48] Anatomist and doctor-regent of the University of Paris, Pierre Lalouette, published the most thorough study of scrofula in the second half of the eighteenth century based on his special study of the disease, complete with close and continued observation of patients over a number of years. He concluded that scrofula was an affliction particularly of the lower orders and bemoaned that they were abandoned to the hands of empirics, that is, non-professional medics.[49] The undoubted expense of the imported Rotrou treatment, and the likelihood that a doctor would be required to attend several times a day to administer it, points to an absence of treatment options for the people he said were most likely to be afflicted. Inevitably, street healers, empirics and charlatans often claimed the ability to cure scrofula.[50] Pierre Dionis, anatomist and surgeon to Louis XIV, recommended that the gentle possibilities of the miraculous touch should be assayed before attempting medical intervention: his view was echoed by Marc Bloch who noted the utility of the miracle in tempting sufferers away from potentially damaging, if not actually dangerous, remedies.[51] Apart from the litany of noxious or fortuitously benign substances to be ingested prescribed by doctors and quacks alike, surgical interventions were also practised in the eighteenth-century treatment of scrofula. Procedures for the extirpation of tumours and abscesses and the piercing of affected bones were all invasive, painful and potentially lethal in their own right. The hope of a cure by simple touch was seductive indeed.[52]

In June 1775, as Reims prepared to receive the king, the hospital of Saint Marcoul saw an influx of scrofula sufferers from outside Reims. A detailed record of the hospital sisters' experiences has survived in the form of a handwritten memoir by Soeur Jeanne Marie Madeleine Jeunehomme, a member of the community which cared for the scrofula sufferers.[53] From the scant details we have on the sisters of Saint Marcoul, it is likely that Soeur Jeanne was a native of Reims or the surrounding region and from a lower economic stratum. Her ability to write a lengthy and coherent document, however, raises interesting questions about her personal history; questions we are sadly unlikely to be able to answer. Characteristically, more details have survived about the male administrators of the house than about the female carers.[54] Soeur Jeanne was well placed to describe the preparations and conduct of the ceremony and had no polemical purpose in her writing, which appears to have been intended as an internal record for the community, since she began by lamenting the absence of such a record from the previous coronation.

Appropriately enough, her account begins with tidings of the transport of the relics of Saint Marcoul to Reims for the coronation. The procession, which took the relics from Corbeny to the monastery of Saint-Rémi in Reims on Tuesday 6 June, was organised on the back of a royal request to the religious of Saint Rémi.[55] While the account of Louis XIV's coronation emphasises that the king 'knew' these relics should be at Corbeny but were in Saint Rémi 'where they have been carried during the wars',[56] the idea in the royal letter of 1775 that the provincial intendant had requested the king not to attempt the pilgrimage to Corbeny because 'the roads were impassible' is probably a polite fiction, given that the coronation took place in summer time. The procession set out from Corbeny at three in the morning and had covered the 28 kilometres to Reims by five in the afternoon, the golden reliquary carried by six citizens of Corbeny. The procession was large, with banners and crosses waving aloft. It included many religious groups but also mounted guards from the *maréchaussée* and a great crowd of local people. It was met at the gate into Reims by a second procession which joined with it, winding through the streets to the sound of psalm-singing. It stopped outside the Hôpital de Saint Marcoul where the sisters had erected an altar decked in borrowed crimson velvet. The chaplain censed the reliquary and prayers followed while the reliquary rested on the temporary altar, a welcome respite for those who had carried it from Corbeny. As the procession recommenced, the patients from the hospital and their carers joined it, segregated from the rest of the participants. On arrival at Saint-Rémi, the sisters and their charges were conducted to a place of honour in the choir. Separated by sex, men on one side and women on the other, the scrofula sufferers lined up beside the reliquary to hear the *Te Deum* given in thanks for the safe arrival of the relics at the Abbey. Afterwards they were permitted to walk under the reliquary, an honour which they repeated the following day on the occasion of a solemn mass in honour of Saint Marcoul. By then, their numbers were already augmented with newcomers arriving for the touch ceremony. On the night of 6 June, sisters and patients began a novena, a nine-day series of prayers, to their patron saint for his intercession in favour of the king, carefully timed to conclude on the day of the royal touch ceremony, 14 June. Though experienced and successful in the medical management of the disease of scrofula, the sisters approached the possibility of miraculous cures through the person of the king with great seriousness. This mingling of religion, medicine and the marvellous is borne out in the case of the comte Maxime de Puységur, an army officer and pupil of Mesmer, who, in 1784, was granted a room for his para-medical practice in the Augustinian seminary in Bayonne in gratitude for his magnetic cure of one of the members of that order.[57]

These were the first ceremonies connected with the coronation and scrofula. Although prompted by a royal request for the removal of the relics to Reims, it should be noted that this request went to the Abbey of Saint-Rémi and that the attendant ritual forms were generated locally. The sisters of the hospital learned of the plans through rumour and had to visit the religious of Saint-Rémi to confirm arrangements. Strangely, for an institution so centrally concerned with scrofula, the hospital 'has received neither formal letters nor orders from the Court to receive scrofula sufferers …'.[58] On 3 June, posters advertising the event began to appear at crossroads and announcements were made in all the parishes of Reims. Issued by the marquis de Sourches, *grand prévôt de France*, on behalf of the king, it simply stated:

> [l]et it be known that the king will touch those afflicted with scrofula on the 14 June 1775 in the park of the Abbey of Saint Remy in the town of Reims. Those who wish to be touched by His Majesty should arrive early in the morning of the day indicated.[59]

This bland instruction to appear at the Abbey glossed over significant administrative preparations at the scrofula hospital. Without official instructions or financial support, the sisters had to improvise a system to manage, lodge and feed the large numbers of scrofula sufferers who began to appear at their door. Given the high level of demand, the sisters determined only to grant lodgings to those who had travelled some distance – some had already arrived from 80 kilometres or more away – and to send local people home. By 7 June, 560 additional people, who must have begun their journeys prior to the rather tardy prevotal advertisement, were registered with the hospital.[60] Not only is this evidence of the agency of sufferers in seeking to alleviate their illness,[61] it is also a telling testament of faith and attachment to royal ritual. Marc Bloch tells the story of a man called Guilhelm who, in 1307, travelled from the Hautes-Pyrénées to Nemours seeking the royal touch and comments 'all that literature tells us about royalty, about its prestige, its sacred role, is it as eloquent as the story of this humble believer?'[62] Other than the passage of years, what difference is there between Bloch's medieval traveller and the hundreds who went to Reims to be welcomed by Soeur Jeanne? Both cases bear eloquent testimony to the enduring prestige of royal ritual. It is lamentable, from the historian's viewpoint, that there is no record remaining of who these people were and exactly where they came from, but come they did.

On the day of the king's arrival in Reims, 9 June, La Marque (sic), first surgeon to the king, called at the hospital 'to ask for information there about the ceremony of touching scrofula sufferers'.[63] This was the first contact between the hospital and the court. Soeur Jeanne and her sisters had no knowledge of preparations being made by court officials but, since the hospital was the epicentre of practical measures, it seemed to her that the court sought information from her order and relied on local knowledge and on local structures for the arrangement of the ceremony. There is nothing in the archives or journals of the time to contradict her conclusions. The surgeon obtained the king's assistance for the hard-pressed sisters through the king's valet, de Livry. Twenty-five louis was provided that afternoon and in the following days a similar amount was forthcoming as part of the king's official programme of alms-giving.[64] The officers responsible for provisioning the royal household gave instructions to local merchants to provide for the hospital's needs. The role of the *prévôté*, though nominally charged with organisation of the ceremony, was minimal, seemingly limited to issuing the poster advertising the event and providing a guard of honour for the king at the ceremony.[65] There is little sense of royal officials taking charge: their supportive role began only with their arrival in Reims and was limited to meeting needs expressed by the sisters for financial assistance in procuring the necessary supplies to feed the hundreds of sick people arriving at their door.

The apparent absence of promotion of the ceremony from the royal side seems curious in itself. However, before we are tempted to conclude that the court had lost interest in the thaumaturgic powers of the monarch, we do well to remember that we currently have scant knowledge of the usual approaches to publicising the touch and therefore no sound basis on which to judge the events of 1775. Interestingly, the most prolific dispensers of the royal touch in England, the Stuarts, seem to have expended more effort in attempting to regulate crowds of sufferers than in encouraging them.[66] The various notices published in the English press aimed to control the flow of sufferers towards the king rather than to entice them. The royal touch for healing attracted expectant crowds who drew on their own knowledge of patterns of touching, or simply their hopes, and did not rely on formal summons. The healing ceremony was driven by demand: a demand that was constant enough over time to permit reliance on the appearance of sufferers even with minimal advance notice. Since, unlike in England, sufferers seeking to be touched by the French king were not required to procure certificates from their ministers prior to presenting themselves to court physicians, the less rigid French rite lent itself to self-determination and spontaneity by the ill.[67] Subjects expected this boon of their king, as a demonstration of Christian charity, noble liberality and the unique relationship between subject and monarch. Given the firm association of the healing touch with the coronation in France, it may well have been that there was little established practice of exciting an interest which was evident to contemporaries. The announcement of the *prévôté* formally confirmed the king's intention to touch, though many had already acted on their assumption that the touch would follow the coronation as was traditional.

On Monday and Tuesday, 12 and 13 June, the days after the coronation, a team of ten of the king's medical staff conducted inspections of those who had been registered at the hospital. On the first day, there were well over a thousand sufferers lodged in all the rooms of the hospital and in the courtyard.[68] Overcrowding was such that guards were introduced to keep order. The sisters had given up trying to accommodate the new arrivals in beds and were grateful to receive gifts of cart-loads of straw for bedding. The danger of fire was so acute that pipesmoking was forbidden. Every registered patient was issued with a card bearing an official royal stamp: two thousand were not sufficient for the numbers present.[69]

A small group of cancer patients was discovered among the new arrivals. The king's surgeons' insistence that they could not be touched by the king gave way before their lamentations, in a move which compromised any notion of strict segregation of medical conditions.[70] Though Henri IV's first doctor, André du Laurens, claimed to have operated just such a selective system, the idea that medical staff always acted as gatekeepers on the exclusivity of the ceremony seems questionable in view of the evidence of practice.[71] Reports of segregation generally come from the pens of medics who are naturally concerned, by establishing diagnostic parameters, to stamp their authority on proceedings; and, of course, it is possible that the rigour with which segregation was imposed varied with the personalities involved. Whether the kings complied by restricting their touch is an entirely different question. Here again there is a contrast between the controlled English rite in which sufferers were pre-screened by doctors and clergy and then brought before the monarch who remained seated indoors, and the French rite, in which the king moved about in the open air and was the active principle in the ritual, the leader as well as the centre of attention. In 1775, the evidence of strict obedience to diagnostic categorisation is not convincing. The cancer patients did not receive official cards validating them as participants in the ceremony, but they were allowed into the grounds of Saint-Rémi to witness the ceremony and, while the standard amount of alms was three livres, received four times that amount, twelve livres each. Thus they were generously compensated for not receiving the king's touch. This contradicts theories that the medical inspection was performed to prevent those unaffected by scrofula from participating and receiving alms under false pretences.[72] This inclusivity appears to have been a normal part of the rite. An account of a healing ceremony conducted by Louis XIV in 1686 describes the king smiling at some of the candidates and asking: 'Are you sick too?' The observer, an Italian traveller Gemelli Careri, was sure they had come only to obtain alms, but even so they were not excluded from the king's bounty, another echo of the noble ethos of liberality.[73]

'This coarse and repugnant ceremony'[74]

Early in the morning of 14 June, 'consecrated to religion, to humanity and to magnificence',[75] the sisters served bread and meat to the non-resident scrofula sufferers and conducted them to Saint-Rémi to await the king. The residents of the hospital of Saint Marcoul remained there to watch the king pass in a magnificent cavalcade, escorted by the military companies of his household and accompanied by his brothers and the princes of the blood.[76] All were magnificently dressed in white hose and golden cloaks, displaying the *cordons bleus* of the Order of the Holy Spirit. Their mounts were equally splendid,[77] and impressively ornamented.[78] Immediately the parade had passed, the party from the hospital made their way to the grounds of Saint-Rémi escorted by the grenadiers whose fixed bayonets ensured them a passage through the crowds. The hospital chaplain went with them, carrying the holy oils for last rites 'en cas d'accident'.

On entering the church of Saint-Rémi, the king went to the sacristy to don the cloak and uniform of the Order of the Holy Spirit, as required by the statutes of the order.[79] Since that order was founded only in 1578, this is another example of adding layers of meaning to ceremonies. He heard two masses, prayed at the relics of Saint Marcoul and received communion before heading out into the grounds of Saint-Rémi where the sick waited, kneeling in rows. The smaller group of hospital residents and sisters stood apart from those who had travelled, who were in the vast majority in the crowd of over two thousand people.[80] The sisters applied bandages to those whose ailments were judged particularly unsightly. It was around midday when an unidentified gentleman of the royal household urged the scrofula sufferers to pray: 'my children unite your prayers with those of His Majesty, he has taken communion for your intentions, he will touch you fasting'. Prayer here was undertaken on a personal basis rather than any orchestrated recitation of a liturgy. The ceremony in France was a much less-developed liturgical form than had been practised in England. In France, the king repeated a short formula of non-liturgical words with each touch. Formal prayer anticipated the act of touching and any subsequent devotions were of a personal nature.

Wearing the beplumed hat typical of the Order of the Holy Spirit, the king emerged from the Abbey of Saint-Rémi accompanied by a sizeable entourage comprising the guards of the *prévôté*, royal bodyguards, his brothers and princes of the blood, as well as four doctors and four surgeons of the royal household and by the bishop of Senlis, who had responsibility for distributing alms. This official group was followed by a number of curious aristocrats, including the duc de Croÿ. The touch followed the same pattern for each individual. One of the medical staff placed their hand on the head of the patient, the captain of the bodyguard held their hands together in a prayer position and the king then touched the patient saying 'May God heal you, the king touches you'.[81] The king 'really did touch each sufferer twice, with his fingers and open hand, on the cheeks, and then, in the other direction, from forehead to chin', thus tracing the sign of the cross on the sufferer's face.[82] The ceremony of the royal touch as practised in France was supremely simple. The need for repetition and circulation among large crowds dictated simplicity of word and gesture, and mobility on the part of the king.

This was a model of gestural efficiency, in contrast to the usual English practice where the monarch was seated indoors and sufferers were conducted to kneel before him or her. The English rite was a slower process than the French: the English ceremonial space was religious with ecclesiastics reading Bible verses and prayers; the French ceremonial space, where the king was officiant in an outdoors ceremony, markedly less so. The only religious official in the French ceremony followed behind the king distributing alms. Under Charles II, the English ceremony included the reading of a verse from the gospel on presentation of each sufferer with the surgeons and sufferers executing bows before kneeling in homage to allow the touch to be performed on each individual. The gospel verses used in the ceremony as performed by the Stuarts explicity associated the act of touching to heal with bearing witness to the New Testament and with true belief. The recipients of the touch were led away and then presented a second time to permit the king to distribute touch pieces, again accompanied by a reading from the gospel. The ceremony concluded with ensemble recitation of more prayers, including the Lord's Prayer.[83] The ceremony as revived and reformed by Anne disposed of the repeated gospel readings with touch pieces dispensed immediately after touching, thus accelerating the process. The touch continued to be performed by the seated monarch indoors upon a kneeling sufferer until Anne's death in 1714, when the royal healing touch for scrofula ceased in England. The Stuarts in exile continued to practise their kingly prerogative of healing.

Charles Edward Stuart is known to have touched a child in Edinburgh during the rebellion of 1745, the French influence evident in his words 'I touch, but God heals!'[84]

The elaborate liturgy of the English ritual, in particular the seating of the monarch and the performance of the ceremony in indoors,[85] shows the English ritual to be more controlled, more dignified and more managed. The French ritual was more personal and far more dependent on the human, rather than sacred, person and choices of the king.[86] This is well illustrated by the following details from June 1775.

Having touched the scrofula sufferers, Louis XVI asked if there were any more patients waiting. The first surgeon informed him that 'there was another waiting area; but those sufferers were hideous'. 'I will touch them on the bandages' replied the king. This last action was judged particularly praiseworthy, according to Soeur Jeanne,

> Louis XVI is the first of the kings of France who performed this ceremony on cancer sufferers: without appearing moved or disgusted by their disfiguring illness, he went of his own accord and acquitted himself with the graciousness of a truly royal heart.[87]

The king's contravention of the strict limits of the ceremony was construed as an unexpected act of charity towards a group whose afflictions were thought specially hideous, in tune with the king's widely recognised penchant for *bienfaisance.* His attitude gives the lie to the idea of an increasing distaste on the part of fastidious kings for the performance of this ritual which had challenging physical aspects, as experienced by the duc de Croÿ:

> because of the heat, it really stank and was markedly disgusting, so that it took real courage and strength for the king to perform this ceremony, which I would not have believed, if I had not seen it myself, so crude and so repugnant.[88]

The king, in touching cancer sufferers, violated ritual strictures which would limit his supposed powers, though it is not unlikely that his predecessors transgressed in the same manner, being less concerned about strict categorisation than their medical officers. In this spontaneous act, he endorsed the beliefs of those who had optimistically presented themselves to him in spite of the widespread knowledge that the royal touch was dispensed for scrofula. His touching of the religious sisters, who, since they were dedicated to the care of the sick, must be assumed to have been in good health, indicates a far wider receptivity to the benefits of being touched by the king.[89] The king's touch here strongly resembles the dispensation of general benediction, as by a Catholic priest or bishop moving through a crowd. Though the royal touch was a sovereign remedy for scrofula, its benefits were clearly generally appreciated.

It would be difficult to show that the practice of healing touch was ever the sole province of kings in France.[90] While there were numerous saints whose intercession could be sought for scrofula sufferers, there were also individuals and families with enduring reputations for healing by touch as well as individuals.[91] In 1773, a faith healer (*toucheur*) known as prophet Elias was working in Paris. He operated simply by touching the site of the ailment – saying 'go, you are healed' – and claimed cures for various ailments before he was asked to leave Paris by the police.[92] People flocked to him and said that he cured 'just like Jesus Christ, he received his powers from him'.[93] Pierre Jean Baptiste Nogaret, in his *Tableau mouvant de Paris*, drew comparison between this lowly healer and the worldly success of Doctor Mesmer from his arrival in Paris in 1778.[94] Initiates into Mesmer's methodology were gravely instructed 'go, touch, heal'.[95] Healing by touch was a common enough practice: whereas English kings may have attempted to suppress competition with what they saw as their unique prerogative of healing scrofula by touch, the French – consistent with the less elaborate and liturgical form of their healing ceremony – were much less concerned.[96] As recently as 1963, there were over 40,000 faith healers of this kind in France, more than medical doctors, indicating that faith in the wondrous healing touch endured.[97] The royal touch, for whatever affliction, should therefore be seen as a ritualised instance of a more widespread, popular practice; another example of monarchy laying claim to diverse sources of power, harnessing the marvellous to bolster the monarchy.

Conclusion

The king remained in Reims until 16 June, taking part in the walking procession in honour of the feast of Corpus Christi on the morning of 15 June. The duc de Croÿ reported large crowds along the route and cries of joy and, often, frustration as people struggled to get a good view of the monarch.[98] The coronation came close to recapturing the effervescence of the early days of Louis XVI's accession.[99] Later that summer, songs to celebrate the royal nameday compared the young king to his well-loved ancestor Henri IV and looked forward to days of plenty with a chicken in every pot:

Once Henry IV
Humanity's friend
Tiring of wars
Wished in the end
Each Frenchman could put
A chicken in his pot
Thanks to our master
We will soon have it.[100]

The grand choreographed ceremonies we described in the previous chapter were matched by the less grandiose, though equally remarkable, ceremony of this chapter. Sufferers from scrofula dedicated time and energy to the cause of their participation in coronation ceremonies and in the name of coming closer to their king. The king himself was an active participant and took an interest in their public presentation. In July 1775, he reviewed and heavily annotated the official account of the coronation ceremonies for publication.[101]

The coronation of Louis XVI saw religion neither triumphant nor defeated but one of a panoply of resources used by the monarchy and the people to express and frame the diverse strands of their reciprocal relationship. These ceremonies drew on deep wells of tradition, on chivalric rites and memory. Royal public ceremonies in this period were neither stale nor failed, they were complex, colourful, layered, material events; ceremonies bearing witness to the great potential for emotional engagement of the people with the monarchy. These events fostered and enhanced the bond between the king and the people, creating space for the king to give intangible yet valued gifts directly to his subjects.

Notes

1 *Description du bouquet présenté au roi, lors de son sacre par les Poissardes de Reims, en 1775, de leurs compliments*, Bibliothèque Municipale de Reims (BMR) MS 1511 (3).
2 Including the duc de Choiseul. See *Journal Inédit Du Duc De Croÿ, 1718–1784. Publié D'après Le Manuscrit Autographe Conservé à La Bibliothèque De l'Institut, Avec Introduction, Notes Et Index, Par Le Vte De Grouchy Et P. Cottin*, volume 3, 196 *passim*.
3 Pierre Jean Baptiste Nogaret, *Anecdotes du règne de Louis XVI, 1774–1776* (Paris, 1776), 87. See Chapter 4 for discussion of *bienfaisance*.
4 See Chapter 3 above.
5 Hermann Weber, 'Das *Sacre* Ludwigs XVI vom 11 Juni 1775 und die Krise des Ancien Régime', in *Vom Ancien Régime zur französischen Revolution:*

Forschungen und Perspecktiven, Erich Hinrichs, Erberhardt Schmidt and Rudolf Vierhaus (editors) (Göttingen, 1978), 553.

6 Chantal Grell, 'The *sacre* of Louis XVI: the end of a myth', in *Monarchy and Religion: The transformation of royal culture in eighteenth century Europe*, Michael Schaich (editor) (Oxford, 2007), 351.

7 Hipploÿte Blanc, *Le Merveilleux dans le jansénisme, le magnétisme, le méthodisme et le baptisme américains, l'épidémie de Morzine, le spiritisme. Recherches nouvelles* (Paris, 1865), 22 *passim*, 32. Robert Kreiser, *Miracles, Convulsions, and Ecclesiastical politics in Eighteenth-century Paris* (Princeton, 1978); Brian E. Strayer, *Suffering Saints: Jansenists and* convulsionnaires *in France 1640–1799* (Brighton, 2008); Robert Darnton, *Mesmerism and the End of the Enlightenment in France* (Cambridge, Mass, 1968).

8 Louis XVI's modern biographers pass over this ritual. The most detailed treatment is given in Jean-Christophe Petitfils, *Louis XVI* (Paris, 2005), 211. See also Évelyne Lever, *Louis XVI* (Paris, 2005), 136.

9 Marc Bloch, *Les Rois thaumaturges: étude sur le caractère surnaturel attribué à la puissance royale particulièrement en France et en Angleterre* (Paris, 1983), first published 1924.

10 Paul Kléber Monod, *Solomon's Secret Arts: The occult in the age of enlightenment* (New Haven and London, 2013), 9.

11 Bloch, *Les Rois thaumaturges*, 86.

12 Ibid., 399, 401. The royal touch does not appear in Petit de Bachaumont's *Marie Antoinette, Louis XVI, et la famille royale. Journal anecdotique tiré des Mémoires Secrets pour servir à l'histoire de la république des lettres Mars 1763 – Février 1782* (Paris, 1886), for example. Further research is required, as Bloch noted in 1924.

13 Bloch, *Les Rois thaumaturges*, 185.

14 Ibid., 385.

15 Georges Livet, 'Le toucher royale au siècle des lumières', in *Le Sacre des rois: actes du colloque international d'histoire sur les sacres et couronnements royaux (Reims 1975)* (Paris, 1983), 157–81; Stanis Perez, 'Le toucher des écrouelles: médecine, thaumaturgie et corps du roi au grand siècle', *Revue d'histoire moderne et contemporaine*, 53:2 (2005), 92–111; but see Roy Porter, 'The patient's view: doing medical history from below', *Theory and Society*, 14:2 (March, 1985), 175, and Judith Devlin, *The Superstitious Mind: French peasants and the supernatural in the nineteenth century* (New Haven and London, 1987), 63, 216 *passim*, and the Introduction above.

16 See Introduction above, and William Doyle, 'Desacralising desacralisation', in *France and the Age of Revolution: Regimes old and new from Louis XIV to Napoleon Bonaparte* (London and New York, 2013), 103–11; Alexandra Walsham, 'The Reformation and the disenchantment of the world', *The Historical Journal*, 51:2 (2008), 497–528.

17 Darrin McMahon, *Enemies of the Enlightenment: The French Counter-Enlightenment and the making of modernity* (Oxford, 2001).
18 Hermann Weber, 'Le sacre de Louis XVI', in *Le Sacre des rois*, Hinrichs et al. (editors), 266.
19 Stephen Brogan, *The Royal Touch in Early Modern England: Politics, medicine and sin* (Woodbridge, 2015).
20 Bloch notes that his search of newspaper entries for the period revealed scant information, *Les Rois thaumaturges*, 399.
21 Schaich, 'Introduction', *Monarchy and Religion*, 27.
22 John McManners, 'Authority in church and state: reflections on the coronation of Louis XVI', *Christian Authority: Essays in honour of Henry Chadwick* (Oxford, 1988), 286.
23 *Lettres de Louis XV à son petit-fils l'Infant Ferdinand de Parme, Introduction et notes par Philippe Amiguet* (Paris, 1938), 135. Philip I (r 1060–1108) was reputed to have lost his ability to cure by touch following his double adultery with Bertrade de Montfort, for which he was excommunicated. However, this allegation was never made about Louis XIV's equally scandalous liaison with Madame de Montespan. Louis XIV continued to exercise the touch throughout his reign, to my knowledge. Bloch, *Les Rois thaumaturges*, 31.
24 See 'Instructions pour la touche des écrouelles', in Le duc des Cars et l'abbé Ledru, *Le Château de Sourches et ses seigneurs* (Paris, 1887), 369.
25 See Chapter 3 above.
26 Jehan Héroard, *Journal du Roy Louis XIII*, in *Archives curieueses de l'histoire de France*, volume 4 (Paris, 1838).
27 Bloch, *Les Rois thaumaturges*, 379.
28 Unlike the Stuarts in exile, the Bourbons do not appear to have exercised the touch in their period outside France, although they clung to other proofs of royalty. This is most likely because of a difference in tradition: French kings touched only after they were crowned, and not merely by virtue of blood.
29 See AN O1 242, *Procès verbal des grâces accordées par Sa Majesté à l'occasion de son Sacre.*
30 He made his final conversion to Catholicism in July 1593.
31 For Bloch, this example demonstrates the power of unction, as opposed to the intercession of the saint. He overlooks the question of absolution and grace. Bloch, *Les Rois thaumaturges*, 357.
32 Ibid., 82. On Saint Marcoul, whose feast day fell on 1 May, see Louis De Broc De Segange, *Les Saints patrons des corporations et protecteurs spécialement invoqués dans les maladies et dans les circonstances de la vie* (Paris, 1887) volume 1, 319.
33 Bloch, *Les Rois thaumaturges*, 284–89.
34 De Broc de Segange, *Les Saints patrons*, 320.
35 André Du Laurens, *Discours des écrouelles*, in Théophile Gelée, *Oeuvres de Monsieur André du Laurens* (Rouen, 1661), 91.

36 Bloch, *Les Rois thaumaturges*, 286. Du Laurens refers to a special prayer said by the king, *Discours des écrouelles*, 89.

37 Du Laurens, *Discours des écrouelles*, 89. Francis I touched in Italy and while in captivity in Spain: the political implications of the act are clear. We can say with certainty that he did not have the relics of Saint Marcoul with him. Bloch, *Les Rois thaumaturges*, 313.

38 Bloch, *Les Rois thaumaturges*, 281, 282.

39 Ibid., 283.

40 Alfred Franklin, *La Vie privée d'autrefois: Les médecins*, volume 11 (Paris, 1892), 222, suggests there were fifteen saints associated with curing scrofula. Eight are listed on 229.

41 Henri Jadart, *L'Hôpital Saint-Marcoul de Reims (1645–1900)* (Reims, 1902), 4.

42 Ibid., 15.

43 Ibid., 43.

44 Du Laurens, *Discours des écrouelles*, book two.

45 Du Laurens, *Discours des écrouelles*, 90.

46 Michael Ramsay, *Professional and Popular Medicine in France, 1770–1830* (Cambridge, 1988); Lawrence Brockliss and Colin Jones, *The Medical World of Early Modern France* (Oxford, 1997); Alexandre Lunel, *La Maison médicale du roi XVIe-XVIIIe siècles: le pouvoir royal et les professions de santé* (Paris, 2008).

47 Louis Petit Bachaumont et al., *Mémoires secrets pour servir l'histoire de le république des lettres* (London, 1782), volume 17, 197–98.

48 Pierre Lalouette, *Traité des scrophules, vulgairement appellées écrouelles ou humeurs froides* (Paris, 1785), Second Edition, volume 1, x. Antoine Baumé, *Eléments de pharmacie, théorique et pratique* (Paris, 1773), Third Edition, 847 *passim*. Indian pinenuts are the seeds of the jatropha plant, now known to be highly toxic. Virigina snake-root was widely used in medicines including for the treatment of snakebite, see article 'Serpentaire de Virginie' in *Encyclopédie: ou dictionnaire raisonné des sciences, des arts et des métiers* (Neufchastel, 1765), volume 15, 111.

49 Lalouette, *Traité des scrophules*, 3.

50 See the sample of handbills in Ramsay, *Professional and Popular Medicine*, 136 *passim*.

51 Dionis quoted in Louis Landouzy, *Le Toucher des écrouelles, l'hôpital Saint Marcoul, le mal du Roi* (Paris, 1907), 29; Bloch, *Les Rois thaumaturges*, 429.

52 See also Brogan, *The Royal Touch*, 92, on the pragmatism of Quakers, Puritans and one senior parliamentarian who sought the king's healing touch during the captivity of Charles I. His last healing touch took place eleven days before his execution (93).

53 *Mémoire de ce s'est passé au Sacre de Sa Majesté Louis XVI concernant l'hopital de St Marcoul et les Malades des Ecrouelles*, BMR MS 1508, f 123

passim. A copy appears in BMR MS 1512 (3) attributed to M Desperthes, avocat, who notes that he has copied it from the documents produced by Soeur Jeanne.

54 Jadart, *L'Hôpital de Saint-Marcoul*, 10.

55 *Lettre du Roi (mai 1775) relativement à la visite de l'hôpital de Saint Marcoul*, BMR MS 1508, f 51.

56 Jean Rousset de Missey, *Supplément au Corps Universel diplomatiqe du droit des gens* (Amsterdam/The Hague, 1739), 220.

57 Ernest d'Hauterive, *Le Merveilleux au XVIIIe siècle* (Paris, 1902, reprinted Geneva, 1973), 212.

58 *Mémoire de ce s'est passé* … , 3.

59 *Avis relatif aux écrouelles*, BMR MS 1511 (2).

60 *Mémoire de ce s'est passé* … , 5.

61 See Porter 'The patient's view', 175.

62 Bloch, *Les Rois thaumaturges*, 107.

63 *Mémoire de ce s'est passé* … , 5. Soeur Jeanne here mistakes the surname of Germain Pichault de la Martinière, who continued as first surgeon to the new king just as he had for Louis XV.

64 Ibid., 10.

65 See 'Fonction des gardes de la Prévôté de l'hôtel, pendant le séjour du Roi à Reims en 1775, à l'occasion du Sacre de Sa Majesté', in, Le duc des Cars et l'abbé Ledru, *Le Château de Sourches*, 371.

66 Brogan, *The Royal Touch*, 67.

67 It is not certain that this requirement was always fulfilled in England. See Brogan, *The Royal Touch*, 124.

68 *Mémoire de ce s'est passé* … , 6.

69 Ibid.

70 Ibid.

71 Du Laurens, *Discours sur les écrouelles*, 89.

72 Perez, 'Le toucher des écrouelles', 94.

73 Quoted in Raymond Crawfurd, *The King's Evil* (Oxford, 1911), 131. Similarly, James I and VI is known to have touched the Turkish ambassador's son, although he was not a Christian, according to Brogan, *The Royal Touch*, 76.

74 Croÿ, *Journal*, volume 3, 204.

75 Louis Jean Lévesque de Pouilly, 'Précis historique de ce qui s'est passé depuis l'arrivée du roi à Rheims, jusqu'au jour de son départ', in *Journal Encyclopédie*, volume 5, part 3, August 1775 (Bouillon, 1775), 521.

76 An innovation: neither Louis XIV nor Louis XV went to the touch ceremony in cavalcade, Rousset de Missey, *Supplément*, 220, 233.

77 *Frais des equipages des chevaux*, AN K 1714 no 21 (38).

78 *Relation du voyage à Reims d'Antoine-Nicolas Duchesne, à l'occasion du Sacre de Louis XVI (5–21 juin 1775), publié sur le manuscrit de l'auteur avec*

un préambule et des notes par Henri Jadart, bibliothécaire de la ville de Reims (Reims, 1902), 73; Croÿ, *Journal*, volume 3, 201.

79 The king had been inducted as grand master of the Order on the previous day.

80 The hospital had around ninety residents. All accounts of this ceremony agree that the king touched 2,400 people. Hence, even allowing for exaggeration, non-Reimois substantially outnumbered the regular patients.

81 Du Laurens reports that Henri IV said 'le roi te touche, dieu te guerit', a simpler phrase in the indicative case and present tense. Du Laurens, *Discours des écrouelles*, 89.

82 Croÿ, *Journal*, volume 3, 204; *Mémoire de ce s'est passé.*

83 Crawfurd, *The King's Evil*, frontispiece; Brogan, *The Royal Touch*, 139 *passim.*

84 Crawfurd, *The King's Evil*, 157–58.

85 Though Queen Anne held some sessions outdoors at St James's Palace, this was seen as exceptional. Brogan, *The Royal Touch*, 200.

86 *Pace* Crawfurd, *The King's Evil*, 81.

87 *Mémoire de ce s'est passé …* , 6. Bloch, *Les Rois thaumaturges*, 95.

88 Croÿ, *Journal*, volume 3, 204. See also Perez, 'Le toucher des écrouelles', 101.

89 On the original breadth of the remit for touching, see Bloch, *Les Rois thaumaturges*, 38–39.

90 Livet, 'Le toucher royal', 177. Bloch, *Les Rois thaumaturges*, p 383–4.

91 See, Franklin, *Les Médecins*, volume 11, 259; Constant Leber, *Des Cérémonies du sacre* (Reims, 1825), 460; Pierre Lalouette, *Traité des scrophules, vulgairement appelées écrouelles* (Paris, 1785), Second Edition, 152–54.

92 It is not clear whether he claimed to heal scrofula. Hauterive, *Le Merveilleux*, 69–70. Pierre Jean Baptiste Nogaret, *Tableau mouvant de Paris, ou Variétés Amusantes* (London, 1787), volume 2, 238.

93 Louis-Sebastien Mercier, *Tableau de Paris*, volume 8 (Amsterdam, 1783), 271.

94 Nogaret, *Tableau mouvant*, 235 *passim*. Nogaret claims Mesmer also *killed* by touch: asked to relieve one man's suffering, he unexpectedly and, he said, purposely, hastened what he said was his inevitable death. Ibid., 245.

95 Darnton, *Mesmerism*, 76.

96 Bloch, *Les Rois thaumaturges*, 371.

97 Devlin, *The Superstitious Mind*, 43.

98 Croÿ, *Journal*, volume 3, 207.

99 Ibid., 206.

100 *Chanson pour la fête de Sa Majesté Louis XVI, faite & chantée par les Habitants du Marché-aux-Draps, de la Ville de Reims, le 25 Août 1775, sur l'air: Malgré la Bataille*, BMR MS 1492, f 459. 'Du grand, du bon Henri, renaissait les beau jours'. *La Religion des français*, BMR MS 1492, f 464.

101 He sent it on to Vergennes for recopying to hide his amendments. Letter from Louis XVI to Vergennes, 14 July 1775. Cited in Paul and Pierette Girault de Coursac, *Louis XVI a la parole: lettres, discours, écrits politiques*, Second Edition (Paris, 1997), 47.

Conclusion

This book has concentrated very closely on the events of the years 1774–75. It has examined a series of interrelated rituals, developing a rich social and political context for them, examining the immediate prompts and longer term roots of these events. While it has looked back from that point in time to incorporate the influences that shaped them, and historians' revisions of our readings of these influences, it has not looked ahead to 1789. The reason for this is clear. More than any other period in French history, our understanding of the reigns of Louis XV and Louis XVI has developed stunted by the overweening shadows of the colossal mythologies of Louis XIV and of the Revolution.

Neither the funeral of Louis XV nor the coronation of Louis XVI presents the entrails of the French constitution, and we are not soothsayers to pick them over in order to discern the future. As set out in Chapter 2 above, an interpretation of subsequent events built on one man's misrepresentation of Louis XV's funeral rituals is bound to be flawed. Even if Louis XV's corpse had been bundled away hastily from Versailles (which it was not), that assertion remains an unreliable basis for an analysis of his reign. Likewise, no one in Reims in June 1775 knew that the young king they saw crowned would one day go to the guillotine. This book is above all an effort to reappraise these events on their own terms, as they occurred and were seen at the time, and without a distorting overlay of hindsight.

There are inevitably some readers who will feel that any work on this period must centrally address the coming of the Revolution, but to do so is to deny precisely the aims of the project. Questions about what this account might mean, given that the Revolution *did* come some fifteen years later, have been left to last to avoid the kind of foreshadowing which has often dictated the interpretation of these events. As the work of William Doyle, Timothy Tackett and Marisa Linton among others eloquently attests, the most fruitful location for the development of revolutionary thinking about the king was in the course of the Revolution itself.[1] Timothy Tackett's work on the deputies of the French National Assembly emphasises their process of 'becoming' revolutionaries. He cites repeated instances where the deputies revealed their attachment to the king. Indeed, Tackett's account captures well the high intensity of relations, or, to be more accurate, the intensity with which the deputies experienced their reactions to the king – the ebb and flow of emotion. From the incident on 15 July 1789, the day after the fall of the Bastille, when one deputy was said to have 'died for joy' when the king addressed the deputies at Versailles; to February 1790, when the 'citizen' king's speech was felt as 'the most wonderful moment of my life' and greeted with effusions of (joyful) tears.[2] Certainly, there was an element of the resolution of political tension in this moment. The king's intervention, scripted by his ministers, was thought to have vindicated various parties. The fact remains that it was the king who could perform this act: a minister making the same speech would not have had the same effect. The king was a focal point with deep political and emotional resonance as he had been in different ways in French politics for hundreds of years.

Very few came to the Revolution prepared to reject outright the role of monarchy in their society. It was the experience of politics and the intervention of circumstance, in the shape of real and imagined internal and external threats, that led some people, first, to seek to abolish the monarchy and, eventually, to regicide.[3] As Professor Tackett puts it, '[t]he ideological choices that emerged most dominant in the course of the Revolution developed, above all, as a function of specific political contingencies and social interactions'.[4] This approach is lent further weight by Marisa Linton's absorbing forensic examination of the period which shows the evolving mindset and emotional lexicon conditioning the journey of revolutionary leaders through crisis after crisis, ultimately leading them to choose terror.[5] Both Tackett and Linton demonstrate that premeditation was not the order of the day. If one's concern in reading the current work is to learn more about the Revolution, it will assist mostly by striking long-incubated mass hatred for the king off the list of possible causes. The French monarchy, suggests Michel Antoine, was experienced by most early moderns as a natural order, a pyramid of communities and privileges, traditions and symbols, with the king at its head.[6]

On the other hand, it is important to highlight that this book is not meant to suggest some edenic state of royalist bliss in the 1770s, or at any other time. The work of Arlette Farge, among others, demonstrates just how hard life was for many in eighteenth-century France.[7] Then, as now, people were free in apportioning blame to those whose lives were materially easier, including, on occasion, the king. In 1774–75, ritual provided a vehicle for people to express their approval and disapproval of royal policy and conduct, as well as optimism and attachment to the new king, attachment which was later demonstrated by the deputies of the National Assembly who sealed their Tennis Court Oath with cries of 'Long live the king!'[8] The point here is not that there was, at any time, a simple, or simple-minded, and unshakeable devotion to the royal person, but that love for the king was one of a repertoire of emotional states that bound the French people to each other and to familiar institutions. Even if Louis XV, over his long reign and due to his private and public actions, had lost public esteem, Louis XVI came to the throne on a wave of goodwill and was at times popular and unpopular as events unfolded during his reign. What this current work seeks to show is that attachment to the king was one of a range of options available and that neither love nor hate for the king were static states.

The truly salient point is the extent to which the rituals of 1774–75 reflected the impact of the Enlightenment on political thinking in the 1770s. Had the Enlightenment fatally undermined the monarchy in ways that presaged the coming disturbances? The multiple nature of the Enlightenment at this juncture is rapidly apparent. Pigeon-holing individuals, as *philosophe* or not, seems particularly unhelpful since attachment to the Enlightenment in its most readily identifiable forms is not a reliable predictor of political stance. Complexity ruled. The grand old man of the Enlightenment, Voltaire, wrote in favour of the Maupeou coup, reviled by others as 'despotic'. Anne-Robert Turgot, a dyed-in-the-wool man of the Enlightenment, reformer and royal minister, has been shown here not to have opposed the coronation in any real sense. His close friend, the radical marquis de Condorcet, had nothing but scorn for that occasion, while agreeing with Voltaire about the disbanding of the parlement. The 1775 coronation cannot be portrayed as a victory of conservatism over progress: it was simply an accepted fact of politics. The related question of the desacralisation of the monarchy has been addressed and dismissed in the Introduction. As the body of this book has shown, the French monarchy was not primarily sacral, or religious, but an adventitious amalgam of claimed and imputed attributes. With the advent of a *bienfaisant* and sexually continent king, the Catholic Enlightenment made a fair bid for significant political influence, though without any overtly supportive response from the monarch himself. The very emphasis on *bienfaisance*, as discussed in Chapter 4, reflects the ease with which supposedly 'regressive' forces adopted 'progressive' Enlightenment vocabulary. We do well to remember that those actively campaigning under such banners were always a tiny minority. The overwhelming majority of deputies to the National Assembly in 1789 had no discernible connection to either institutions or thinkers associated with the Enlightenment. As well-educated men of their time, they would have had familiarity with elements of what we consider classic Enlightenment discourse. However, they came to Versailles in 1789 making no link between those ideas and the concrete difficulties of contemporary politics.[9] The same, only more so, can be said of the general population France in 1789 – and in 1774.

For most people, most of the time, a day out with new things to see was satisfaction and distraction enough. Though there were, of course, ups and downs; it would be wrong to characterise the situation in the 1770s and for most of the 1780s as one of the government struggling to hold down the lid on a hot and increasingly ebullient pot of political stew. In the mid 1780s, as perspicacious an observer as Louis-Sebastien Mercier could confidently write that '[t]he prospect of a riot degenerating into sedition has become morally impossible'.[10] These comfortable certainties would not be tenable for long. A concerned contemporary, the expert legal and political commentator Lamoignon de Malesherbes, noted that '[t]he situation of France in 1787 bears no relationship even to France in 1786'.[11] The situation changed suddenly in the late 1780s with the growing stress of several complex crises unfolding in and around France. The political and social context in France of 1774–75 was related, but entirely different, to that of 1787.

At the time they were performed, in 1774–75, the rituals discussed here, of funeral, *lit de justice* and coronation, performed two main political functions: the enactment and binding together of the dynastic Bourbon group; and the binding of the wider polity to that group. The binding of the wider polity was performed purposively through the invited participation of certain social groupings, from dukes-and-peers to parlementaires, municipal officials and religious leaders, down to and including the fishwives of Les Halles and Reims, scrofula victims and, although they are not dealt with in a detailed manner here, those who sought the king's pardon. The binding of the wider polity also occurred incidentally as rituals provided employment, distraction, gossip and prompted street festivities. As we have seen, political expression on the street did not start in 1789, and it was certainly not a one-way process. In commenting with ritual and festival on current events, which they followed with interest, people sent their own political messages.

These royal rituals were not empty antiquated enactments but had real impact on the social and political world. The most evidently and immediately politically effective ritual was the *lit de justice* for the recall of the old parlement in November 1774. The 1771 dismissal had confirmed the parlement's weakness relative to a ruthless and united ministry: the effects of their exile demonstrated that the monarch was not free to make and unmake the constituent elements of the monarchy at will. Innovation was not the friend of a composite collaborative entity grounded in precedent like the French monarchy. Disrupting the status quo, and for what could be construed as merely personal reasons – the honour of the duc d'Aiguillon – sat ill with the grace of kingship and was ceaselessly contested. The recalled parlement was, from 1774, dutiful without being quiescent: its priority was its work. The parlement was perhaps the least-changed institution on the French political landscape by 1788, and the least flexible. While the ministry had evolved significantly since the early seventeenth century, and the role of the king with it, the parlement was little changed since 1614. Memories of the drama of their exile, and the repetition of the experience in 1787, lent the parlement's political position in the late 1780s a certain colour that did not match their mindset. Miscast as liberal heroes, their decision that the Estates General should vote separately and by order was a massive disappointment to those who immediately, and wrongly, accused them of betrayal. Exile had not made them liberals or revolutionaries: it had confirmed them in their dual loyalty to the king and to the fundamental laws of France, a point from which the parlement rarely swerved. Any criticism of the king by the parlement was always based on legal grounds. They appealed to him based on what they understood as their mutual respect and shared loyalty to justice, and saw him as the first among equals, a sophisticated fellow magistrate.[12] Their reiteration of an established precedent was as predictable as it was politically unacceptable. The parlement had not changed; the times had.

Rituals of royalty were triggered by events concerning the person of the king: if the king entered a new town, celebrations were in order;

if the king reached his majority, got married or became a father, this event was also worthy of commemoration; if the king were gravely ill, this was a matter of political concern. To say that these events were triggered by the king's doings does not mean that these events were entirely dictated by the king and his staff. None of the rituals related in this book was commanded in the last detail from Versailles: to imagine that they could be is to attribute super-human powers of control, not to mention inhuman capacity for work, to the king and his servants. In every new place, in each new iteration, royal rituals were remoulded and used as vessels for local messages. Louis XVI's celebratory entry into Reims for his coronation, discussed in Chapter 4, is a case in point. Rituals were not limited in form to stage-managed occasions of adulation but were used as opportunities to express opinions on many topical matters; and, it seems clear, that organised ritual also provided focal points, or acted as prompts, for actions beyond the scope of the official event. The passivity of the spectator should not be overstated.

Though Louis XVI's coronation was not the last grand public ceremony of his reign, crucially, there were no more occasions of royal public ceremonies involving the king outside Paris and Versailles since, by this time, the great public ceremonies were events related to the royal life cycle. The same held true of the previous two reigns, though the events, in these cases, occurred at longer intervals due to the simple fact of the age of the kings in question on accession and the extraordinary length of their reigns. While Louis XVI came to the throne in 1774, was crowned one year later and celebrated the births of his first two children four and seven years later, Louis XIV was crowned nine years after his accession to the throne and celebrated his majority, his wedding and the birth not only of his son but grandsons and great-grandsons while king. The pattern for Louis XV resembles that of Louis XIV. When seized with enthusiasm, the king might put himself at the head of his armies: both Louis XIV and Louis XV saw the northern part of the kingdom in this manner. But there were few other stimuli to royal travel and, in both cases, as the years went by, the king formally showed himself to his people more rarely.

There was no European land war to draw Louis XVI from the Île-de-France in the 1770s and 1780s but, in June 1786, he set out to view naval improvements at Cherbourg. The king was received rapturously with one woman hugging his knees and saying 'I see a good king, I desire nothing more in this world.'[13] The king, as at his coronation Reims, mingled freely with the crowd who he addressed, to great acclaim, as his children.[14] The trip was a great success, showing the sort of connection that might have been sustained between the king and his people by the simple expedient of travelling around the kingdom. As he travelled without the queen, the king was free to indulge his taste for simplicity, stopping at a tavern for an impromptu meal, calling the sailors he encountered by name and inspecting the works at Cherbourg in a uniform stained with tar. The pressing urgency of government business inevitably put paid to any further expeditions, and the king's next major journey through France was the ill-fated flight that ended abruptly at Varennes. To this extent, Norbert Elias was right. Versailles was a gilded cage, but it was one that served to imprison the king more than the nobility, as we can see from the sharp decline in monarchical travel over the preceding two centuries and in the bizarre preparations – the building of a bespoke carriage 'fit for a king' – for the royal family's attempted escape. Having created a universe of luxury, it proved inescapable since the sheer expense of recreating that environment was prohibitive.

The extent to which this was a real problem for the monarchy is a fascinating question. Subsequent experiences might be taken to suggest that a more tangible royal presence in various parts of the kingdom could have served a valuable purpose in bolstering popular sentiment towards the king. Indeed, Letellier's account of the visit to Normandy in 1786 bears as an epigraph advice given by Louis XIV to his grandson, Philip V of Spain. 'The people ardently wish to see their sovereign,' he wrote, 'listen to their complaints, give them justice, communicate graciously with them; you will soon see the usefulness of your visit and the good effect your presence produces.'[15] While Louis XIV did not model this behaviour himself, his expertise in kingcraft makes this advice worthy of notice. The idea was taken up again in the concluding paragraphs. Letellier, the former mayor of the Norman town of Harfleur, hoped that Louis XVI would be inspired to journey to other parts of his kingdom, saying that good intentions alone are not enough because it is *only* through knowing the people and the country in person that the king can truly be their benefactor.[16] The intention to travel again, to return to Normandy but also to visit other provinces, was definitely imputed to the king at the time.[17] Thus the sentimentalist trope of personal interaction was politicised as a call for contact with the king and for the king, if he truly wished to do good, to go out among the people. In the midst of a bread crisis,[18] when the hungry people of Paris brought the royal family to live in their city in October 1789, they called them the baker, the baker's wife and the baker's boy, as though a king who lived among them had some magical power to ensure that vital staple: their daily bread. Sociological approaches to ritual offer support to this line of thinking: some theorists suggest that the absence of ritual interaction can deplete the store of symbolic capital and emotional investment, affecting current feeling and undermining the success of future rituals.[19] Already in July 1786, it was feared that intrigues had begun to prevent the king developing a first-hand knowledge of his realm.[20] The pressure of events was certainly enough to demand the king's presence in Versailles, the centre of government as well as the royal court. The death of Louis's most trusted minister, Vergennes, in February 1787 coincided with the first meeting of the Assembly of Notables and the first powerful stirrings of the multiple crises that would, eventually, lead Louis to the guillotine.

The king was stopped at Varennes because he was recognised: to be known is not always to be loved. Nonetheless, the people of Cherbourg received the king with rapture in 1786; the deputies of the Third Estate swore the Tennis Court Oath and then cried 'long live the king!' in 1789; the people of the Vendée rose in the king's name. Clearly, their loyalty was not inspired only by the physical presence of the king, or by fear of the consequences if they failed to acknowledge the monarch. They held their own ideas about the world and did not need the king's touch in order to act on them. The king provided a convenient shorthand for their own ideas about social order.

While the events described in this book are unusual – one clearly cannot argue that the death or accession of a monarch was a regular occurrence – the underlying argument is that politics and ceremony were always closely allied in early modern France, since both are mainly about power. The magpie aspect of early modern monarchy, the will to co-opt whatever enhanced prestige and ensured the prolongation of the dynasty's hold on power, suggests that the nature of monarchical influence shifted over time. The kingship of Louis XVI could not be identical to the kingship of Louis XIV. This implies change, rather than decline. Royal power in early modern France was multi-faceted and contingent, not merely projected from the centre but also growing up from deeper roots and older ideas in wider society. Only through a more sophisticated understanding of what knitted the polity together, can we hope to penetrate the reasons for its unravelling.

Notes

1 See in particular William Doyle, 'The French Revolution: possible because thinkable or thinkable because possible?' in *Proceedings of the Western Society for the Study of French History: Selected papers of the 2002 Annual Meeting* (2004), volume 30, 178–83, and Keith Michael Baker's response in the same volume.

2 Timothy Tackett, *Becoming a Revolutionary: The deputies of the French National Assembly and the emergence of a revolutionary culture (1789–1790)* (Princeton, 1996), 164, 275. See also Barry M. Shapiro, *Traumatic Politics: The deputies and the king in the early French Revolution* (Pennsylvania, 2009).

3 On the importance of ideas of threat and conspiracy, see Marisa Linton, *Choosing Terror: Virtue, friendship and authenticity in the French Revolution* (Oxford, 2013); Peter R. Campbell, Thomas E. Kaiser and Marisa Linton, *Conspiracy in the French Revolution* (Manchester, 2010); Barry Coward and Julian Swann (editors) *Conspiracy and Conspiracy Theories in Early Modern Europe* (Aldershot, 2004).

4 Tackett, *Becoming a Revolutionary*, 76.

5 Linton, *Choosing Terror*, 24.

6 Michel Antoine, *Louis XV* (Paris, 1989), 173.

7 Arlette Farge, *Fragile Lives: Violence, power, and solidarity in eighteenth century Paris*, translated by Carol Shelton (Cambridge, 1993).

8 Tackett, *Becoming a Revolutionary*, 152.

9 Ibid., 54, 65.

10 Louis-Sebastien Mercier, *Tableau de Paris* (Amsterdam, 1783) volume 6, 16.

11 Malesherbes, quoted by John Hardman in 'The view from above', in *The Oxford Handbook of the French Revolution*, David Andress (editor) (Oxford, 2015), 132.

12 See my '"We disobey by serving you well": the paradox of the *lit de justice* in eighteenth century France' in *Rituals of Power*, Anna Kalinowska (editor) (forthcoming).

13 Jeanne Marie Gaudillot, *Le Voyage de Louis XVI en Normandie, 21–29 juin 1786* (Caen, 1967), 35.

14 Letellier, *Voyage de Louis XVI dans sa province de Normandie* ('Philadelphie', 1786), 13, 21. See also my forthcoming article '"Vive mon peuple!" royal ritual, travel and emotion in eighteenth century France'.

15 Letellier, *Voyage*, 1.

16 Ibid., 89

17 *Correspondance secrète inédite sur Louis XVI, Marie-Antoinette, la cour et la ville de 1777 à 1792*, volume 2, 52.

18 From early September 1789, bakeries in Paris were under armed guard. See David Andress, *The French Revolution and the People* (London, 2004), 120 *passim*.

19 See Erika Summers-Effler, 'Ritual theory', in *Handbook of the Sociology of Emotions*, Jan E. Stets and Jonathan H. Turner (editors) (New York, 2006), 135–54.

20 *Correspondance secrète inédite ...* , volume 2, 54.

Bibliography

Primary sources

Manuscripts

Archives Nationales, Paris

Series K: Cartons des rois: *princes du sang, cérémonial.*

K 138, no 12 (3).

K 1714 no 16 (1), *Cérémonies du sacre de Louis XIV à Reims, le 7 juin 1654.*

K 1714 no 21 (3).

K 1714 no 21 (38), *Frais des equipages des chevaux.*

K 1717 no 10 (1).

K 1716 no 2 (7), *Mémoire touchant la reception des corps des Roys Reines Princesses de la Maison Royale par les Religieux de l'abbaye royalle de St Denis en France.*

Series O^1: Maison du roi sous l'ancien régime: papiers du grand maître des cérémonies, papiers du grand écuyer, menus plaisirs.

O^1 242, *Procès verbal des grâces accordées par Sa Majesté à l'occasion de son Sacre.*

O^1 1042 (133), *Lettres expédiés à l'occasion de la mort de Mme Infant.*

O^1 1043 (67), *Pompe funèbre de Monseigneur le Dauphin, 1711.*

O^1 3250, *État des effets employés au Sacre de Louis XVI.*

O^1 3262, *Décoration du choeur de St Denis pour la pompe funèbre de Monseigneur le dauphin et madame la dauphine, 1712.*

Archives privés

144 AP 120, *Journal du President d'Ormesson de Noiseau.*

Bibliothèque Mazarine

MS 2346, *Pompe funèbre de Louis XIIII, mort à Versailles le premier septembre 1715, par Desgranges.*

MS 2397–99, *Nouvelles à la main de Penthièvre.*

Bibliothèque Municipale de Versailles

MS 120 G, *Recueil des arrêtés, arrêts, etc., enregistrements d'édits, déclarations, et lettres patents du parlement de Paris, concernant les affaires publiques, ou les particuliers de distinction, des différens événemens qui y ont donné lieu, avec la description des différents prestations de serment, réceptions et installations; des cérémonies publiques, et des séances du Roy, princes du sang et ducs au Parlement 1765–1788, par Regnault huissier au Parlement.*

Bibliothèque Municipale de Reims

MS 1508, folio 123 *passim*, *Mémoire de ce s'est passé au Sacre de Sa Majesté Louis XVI concernant l'hopital de St Marcoul et les Malades des Ecrouelles.*

MS 1508, folio 51, *Lettre du Roi (mai 1775) relativement à la visite de l'hôpital de Saint Marcoul.*

MS 1510, folio 5–11, *Mémoire sur l'assistance des habitants de Chesne-le-Populeux pour le sacre des Rois de France.*

MS 1510, folio 17 *passim*, *Requeste presentée à Sa Majesté Louis XVI par les habitans du Chesne le Populeux, pour assister à la Cérémonie de son sacre.*

MS 1511 (2), *Avis relatif aux écrouelles.*

MS 1511 (3), *Description du bouquet présenté au roi, lors de son sacre par les Poissardes de Reims, en 1775, de leurs compliments.*

MS 1510, folio 40, *Procès verbal du 8 June 1775.*

MS 1510, folio 150, *Procès-verbal du transport de la Sainte Ampoule pour le Sacre de Louis XVI, extrait des minutes du greffe des baillage et mairie de l'abbaye et bans de Saint-Rémi.*

Bibliothèque Nationale de France (BNF), Paris

Manuscrits Français 6681, Samuel Prosper Hardy, *Mes Loisirs, ou journal des événements tels qu'ils viennent à ma connoissance.*

National Archives, London

State Papers Foreign, SP 78/286–295, *letters from Viscount Stormont to the Earl of Rochford.*

Cérémonies qui doivent avoir lieu au sacre de Charles X d'après la relation de celles qui ont été observées au sacre de Louis XVI, par F.G. (Paris, 1825).

Chanson pour la fête de Sa Majesté Louis XVI, faite & chantée par les Habitants du Marché-aux-Draps, de la Ville de Reims, le 25 Août 1775, sur l'air: Malgré la Bataille (Reims, 1775).

Correspondance Inédite de Condorcet et de Turgot, 1770–1779. Publiée avec des notes et une introduction … Par M. Charles Henry (Paris, 1883).

Correspondance secrète, politique et littéraire ou Mémoires pour servir à l'histoire des cours, des sociétés et de la littérature de France, depuis la mort de Louis XV (London, 1787).

'Dernière maladie de Louis XV: mort et funérailles', *Revue des documents historiques* (Paris, 1873–74).

Description du mausolée érigée dans l'Abbaye Royale de St Denis pour les obsèques, qui se feront dans cette église, le 27 juillet 1774, de très-grand, très-haut, très-puissant et très-excellent prince Louis XV le Bien-Aimé, roi de France et de Navarre (Paris, 1774).

Encyclopédie, ou dictionnaire raisonné des sciences, des arts et des métiers ('Neufchâtel', 1765).

*Explications des emblèmes heroiques inventées par M le Chevalier D*** pour la décoration des Arcs de Triomphe érigez aux Portes de Reims lors de la Cérémonie du Sacre de Louis XV* (Reims, 1722).

Explication des emblêmes inventés et mis en vers par M Bergeat, vidame de Reims, & M l'abbé Deloche, tous deux Chanoines de l'Église Métropolitaine, pour la décoration des Édifices, Arc de Triomphe & autres monumens érigés par les soins Messieurs du Conseil de la Ville, lors du cérémonie du Sacre de Sa Majesté (Reims, 1775).

Extrait des registres de Parlement de samedi douze novembre mil cent soixante-quatorze, du matin (Paris, 1774).

Gazette de France.

Gazette de Leyde.

'Je ne crois pas me tromper, Monsieur ...' (Paris, 1771).

Journal Encyclopédique Dédié à Altesse Sérénissime Mgr le Duc de Bouillion, Grand Chambellan de France, &c &c &c (Bouillon, 1774–75).

Journal historique du rétablissement de la Magistrature: pour servir de suite à celui de la révolution opérée dans la Constitution de la Monarchie Françoise, par M de Maupeou, Chancelier de France (London, 1775).

Le Comte Louis-Philippe de Ségur, Souvenirs et anecdotes sur le règne de Louis XVI, avec une préface de M le marquis de Ségur (Paris, n.d.).

Les Efforts du patriotisme ou recueil complet des écrits publiés pendant le règne du Chancelier Maupeou, pour démontrer l'absurdité du despotisme qu'il vouloit établir, & pour maintenir dans toute sa splendeur la Monarchie Française... avec l'approbation unanime des bons & fidèles sujets de Sa Majesté Louis XV (Paris, 1775).

Lettres de Louis XV à son petit-fils l'Infant Ferdinand de Parme, Introduction et notes par Philippe Amiguet (Paris, 1938).

'Lettres De M. R** à M. M** Concernant Ce Qui S'est Passé D'intéressant à La Cour Depuis La Maladie Et La Mort De Louis XV. Jusqu'au Rétablissement Du Parlement De Paris', in *Mélanges publiés par la Société des Bibliophiles Français* (Paris, 1826).

Mercure de France.

Mémoires de Louis XIV pour servir à l'instruction du dauphin (Paris, 1860), 2 volumes.

Memoirs of the Princess Daschkaw, Lady of Honour to Catherine II (London, 1840).

Ordonnance de M l'Intendant de Champagne concernant les frais du sacre de Louis XVI du 15 août 1778 (Reims, 1778).

Procès-verbal de ce qui s'est passé au lit de justice tenu par le Roi, le 12 novembre 1774. (Paris, 1774).

Procès-verbal du transport de la Sainte Ampoule pour le Sacre de Louis XV (Reims, 1722).

Récit de ce qui a précédé et suivi le lit de justice (Paris, 1774).

Récit exact de ce qui s'est passé au sujet du retour de M le prince de Condé à la cour (Paris, 1772).

Relation de la cérémonie du sacre et couronnement du roi faite en l'église métropolitan de Rheims le dimanche 11e jour de juin 1775 (Paris, 1775).

Relation de la marche et des cérémonies qui ont été observées au sacre et couronnement de Sa Majesté Louis XVI (Paris, 1775).

Relation du voyage à Reims d'Antoine-Nicolas Duchesne, à l'occasion du Sacre de Louis XVI (5–21 juin 1775), publié sur le manuscrit de l'auteur avec un préambule et des notes par Henri Jadart, bibliothécaire de la ville de Reims (Reims, 1902).

Richesses Tirées du Trésor de l'abbaye de St Denis, du gardemeuble de la couronne et de différens artistes de Paris pour servir au sacre de l'auguste monarque de France le roi Louis XVI (Paris, 1775).

Printed primary sources

Allonville, Armand François de, *Mémoires secrétes de 1770 à 1830* (Paris, 1838–45), 6 volumes.

Arneth, Alfred von, and Mathieu Auguste Geoffroy, *Correspondance secrète entre Marie-Thérèese et le Comte de Mercy-Argenteau, avec les lettres de Marie-Therese et de Marie-Antoinette* (Paris, 1874), 2 volumes.

Augeard, Jacques Mathieu, *Mémoires secrets de J-M Augeard, secrétaire des commandements de la reine Marie-Antoinette (1760 à 1800)*, Évariste Bavoux (editor) (Paris, 1866).

Bachaumont, Louis Petit de, *Marie Antoinette, Louis XVI, et la famille royale. Journal anecdotique tiré des Mémoires Secrets pour servir à l'histoire de la république des lettres Mars 1763 – Février 1782* (Paris, 1886).

Barbier, Edmond, *Journal historique et anecdotique du règne de Louis XV* (Paris, 1847–56), 4 volumes.

Besenval, Pierre Joseph Victor de, *Mémoires de M le baron de Bésenval … Écrits par lui-même, imprimés sur son manuscrit original et publiés par son exécuteur testamentaire [A. J. P. de Ségur]* (Paris, 1805), 3 volumes.

Broc De Segange, Louis De, *Les Saints patrons des corporations et protecteurs spécialement invoqués dans les maladies et dans les circonstances de la vie* (Paris, 1887).

Campan, Jeanne Louise Henriette de, *Mémoires sur la vie privée de Marie-Antoinette, Reine de France et de Navarre, suivis de souvenirs et anecdotes historiques sur les règnes de Louis XIV, de Louis XV et de Louis XVI* (Paris, 1822), 3 volumes.

Cars, le duc des, et l'abbé Ledru, *Le Château de Sourches et ses seigneurs* (Paris, 1887).

Creutz, Gustav Philip, comte de, *La Suède et les lumières: lettres de France d'un ambassadeur à son Roi (1771–1783)* (Paris, 2006).

Croÿ, Emmanuel de, *Journal Inédit Du Duc De Croÿ, 1718–1784. Publié d'après le manuscrit autographe conservé à la bibliothèque de l'Institut, avec introduction, notes et index, par le vicomte de Grouchy et P. Cottin* (Paris, 1906), 4 volumes.

Flammermont, Jules, *Le Chancelier Maupeou et les parlements* (Paris, 1883).

___ *Remontrances du parlement de Paris au XVIIIe siècle* (Paris, 1898), 3 volumes.

Gallier, Anatole de, 'Laurent Aymon de Franquières, le sacre de Louis XVI à Rheims', *Revue de Champagne et de Brie* (1880), VIII, 97–102.

Genlis, Stephanie Félicite de, *Les Souvenirs de Félicie L**** (Paris, 1808), 2 volumes.

Godefroy, Denis, *Le Cérémonial François* (Paris, 1649).

Godefroy, Théodore, *Le Cérémonial de France, ou déscription des Cérémonies ... observées aux couronnemens, entrées, et enterremens des roys et roynes de France et autres actes et assemblées solemnelles. Recueilly des mémoires de plusieurs sécrétaires du Roy, Hérauts d'Armes, et autres* (Paris, 1619).

Héroard, Jehan, *Journal du Roy Louis XIII*, in *Archives curieueses de l'histoire de France*, volume 4 (Paris, 1838).

Lalouette, Pierre, *Traité des scrophules, vulgairement appelées écrouelles* (Paris, 1785).

Lantenay, Antoine (Antoine Louis Bertrand), 'L'Abbé Maudoux: confesseur de Louis XV', *Mélanges de biographie et d'histoire* (Bordeaux, 1885), 485–87.

Laurens, André du, *Discours des écrouelles*, in Théophile Gelée, *Oeuvres de Monsieur André du Laurens* (Rouen, 1661).

Letellier, *Voyage de Louis XVI dans sa province de Normandie* ('Philadelphie', 1786).

Loyseau, Charles, *Traité des ordres et des dignitez* (Paris, 1610).

Luynes, Charles Philippe d'Albert, duc de, *Mémoires du duc de Luynes sur la cour de Louis XV*, 17 volumes (Paris, 1860–65).

Marmontel, Jean-François, *Correspondance, Tome I (1744–1780)*, Texte établi, annoté et présenté, par John Renwick (Clermont-Ferrand, 1974).

___ *Lettre de M Marmontel à M *** sur la cérémonie du sacre de Louis XVI* (Paris, 1775).

Moreau, Jacob-Nicolas Moreau, *Mes Souvenirs* (Paris, 1898, 1901), 2 volumes.

Nogaret, Pierre Jean Baptiste, *Anecdotes du règne de Louis XVI, 1774–1776* (Paris, 1776).

___ *Tableau mouvant de Paris, ou Variétés Amusantes* (London, 1787).

Oberkirch, Henriette Louise baronne d', *Mémoires de la baronne d'Oberkirch sur la cour de Louis XVI et la société française avant 1789* (Paris, 1989).

Papillon de la Ferté, Denis Pierre Jean, *L'Administration des menus plaisirs, Journal de Papillon De La Ferté, intendant et contrôleur de l'argenterie, menusplaisirs et affaires de la chambre du roi, 1756–1780. Publié avec une introduction et des notes par E. Boysse* (Paris, 1887).

Pichon, Thomas Jean, *Sacre et Couronnement de Louis XVI* (Paris, 1775).

Pidansat de Mairobert, Mathieu-François, *L'Espion anglois, ou correspondance secrète entre milord All'Eye et milord Alle'Ar* (1779).

___ *Mémoires secrets pour servir à l'histoire de la république des lettres en France, depuis MDCCLXII jusqu'à nos jours* (London, 1780–89), 36 volumes.

Pissot, Noël Laurent, *Le Cérémonial de la cour de France* (Paris, 1816).

Pouilly, Louis Jean Lévesque de, 'Précis historique de ce qui s'est passé depuis l'arrivée du roi à Rheims, jusqu'au jour de son départ', in *Journal Encyclopédie*, volume 5, part 3, August 1775 (Bouillon, 1775).

Raunié, Émile, *Chansonnier historique du dix-huitième siècle* (Paris, 1883), volume 8.

Rochefoucauld, Frédéric Gaëtan, comte de la, *Vie du duc de la Rochefoucauld-Liancourt* (Paris, 1827).

Rochefoucauld-Liancourt, François Alexandre Frédéric de la, 'Relation inédite de la dernière maladie de Louis XV', in Charles Augustin Sainte-Beuve, *Portraits Littéraires* (Paris, 1862–64), volume 3, 512–40.

Rousset de Missy, Jean, *Supplément au Corps Universel diplomatiqe du droit des gens, tome quatrième, Le Cérémonial diplomatique des cours de l'Europe ou Collection des actes, memoires et relations concernant les Dignitez, Titulaires, Honneurs & Prééminences; les Fonctions publiques des Souverains, leurs Sacres, Couronnemens, Mariages, Batêmes, & Enterrements; les Investitures des grands Fiefs; les Entrées publiques, Audiences, Fonctions, Immunitez & Franchises des Ambassadeurs & autres Ministres publics; leurs Disputes & Démêlez de Préséance; et en général tout ce qui a rapport au Cérémonial & à l'Étiquette. Recueilli en partie par Mr Du Mont. Mis en ordre et considérablement augmenté par Mr Rousset, membre des Académies des Sciences de St Petersbourg & de Berlin. Tome Premier* (Amsterdam/The Hague, 1739).

Soulavie, Jean Louis Giraud de, *Mémoires historiques et politiques sur le règne de Louis XVI* (Paris, 1801), 2 volumes.

Véri, Joseph Alphonse, abbé de, *Journal de l'Abbé Véri* (Paris, 1928), 2 volumes.

Secondary sources

Adamson, John, 'The making of the ancien régime court, 1500–1700', in *The Princely Courts of Europe 1500–1700* (London, 2000), first published 1999, 7–42.

Andress, David, *The French Revolution and the People* (London, 2004).

Anglo, Sydney, *Images of Tudor Kingship* (Guildford, 1992).

Antoine, Michel, *Louis XV* (Paris, 1995).

Ardascheff, Paul, *Les Intendants de province sous Louis XVI* (Paris, 1909).

Asch, Ronald G., *Nobilities in Transition, 1550–1700: Courtiers and rebels in Britain and Europe* (London, 2003).

___ *Sacral Kingship between Disenchantment and Re-enchantment: The French and English monarchies, 1597–1688* (New York and London, 2014).

Aston, Nigel, *Religion and Revolution: 1780–1794* (Basingstoke, 2000).

Bailey, Merridee L., and Katie Barclay (editors), *Emotion, Ritual and Power in Europe, 1200–1920: Family, state and church* (Cham, Switzerland, 2017).

Barber, Gilles, '"Il fallut même réveiller les Suisses": Aspects of private religious practice in a public setting in eighteenth-century Versailles', in *Religious Change in Europe 1650–1914: Essays for John McManners*, Nigel Aston (editor) (Oxford, 1997), 75–101.

Barker, Emma, *Greuze and the Painting of Sentiment* (Cambridge, 2005).

___ 'From charity to *bienfaisance*: picturing good deeds in late eighteenth-century France', *Journal for Eighteenth Century Studies*, 33:3 (September 2010), 285–311.

Barlow, Frank, 'The king's evil', *English Historical Review*, 95:374 (January 1980), 3–27.

Bastard d'Estang, Henri, *Les Parlements de la France: essai historique, sur leurs usages, leur organisation et leur autorité* (Paris, 1857), 2 volumes.

Beik, William, *Absolutism and Society in Seventeenth-Century France: State power and provincial aristocracy in Languedoc* (Cambridge, 1985).

___ 'The absolutism of Louis XIV as social collaboration: *Louis XIV and the parlements: the assertion of royal authority* by John J Hurt', *Past and Present*, 188:1 (August 2005), 195–224.

Bell, Catherine, *Ritual Theory, Ritual Practice* (Oxford, 2009).

Bell, David A., 'The "public sphere", the state and the world of law in eighteeenth cenury France', *French Historical Studies*, 17:4 (Autumn 1992), 912–34.

___ *Lawyers and Citizens: The making of a political elite in old regime France* (Oxford, 1994).

Bély, Lucien, 'Les Cours européennes', in *Fastes de cour et cérémonies royales: le costume de cour en Europe, 1650–1800, sous la direction scientifique de Pierre Arizzoli-Clémentel et Pascale Gorguet Balesteros* (Paris, 2009).

Biondi, Carmelina, 'Il "variolico veleno" alla corte di Parma', in *Un viaggio infinito ... salute, malattia e morte percorsi di lettura tra Belgio, Francia e Italia in ricordo di Paola Vecchi*, Carmelina Imbroscio (editor) (Bologna, 2001), 69–89.

Blanc, Hipployte, *Le Merveilleux dans le jansénisme, le magnétisme, le méthodisme et le baptisme américains, l'épidémie de Morzine, le spiritisme. Recherches nouvelles* (Paris, 1865).

Blanning, Tim, *The Pursuit of Glory: Europe 1648–1815* (London, 2008).

Bloch, Marc, *Les Rois thaumaturges: étude sur le caractère surnaturel attribué à la puissance royale particulièrement en France et en Angleterre* (Paris, 1983), first published 1924.

Bluche, François, *La Vie quotidienne de la noblesse française au XVIIIe siècle* (Paris, 1973).

___ *Les Magistrats du parlement de Paris* (Paris, 1986).

___ *Louis XV* (Paris, 2000).

Bonney, Richard, *L'Absolutisme* (Paris, 1989).

Bourdieu, Pierre, 'Epreuve scolaire et consecration sociale: Les classes préparatoires aux grandes écoles', *Actes de la recherche en scienes sociales*, 39 (Septembre 1981), 3–70.

___ *La Noblesse d'état: grandes écoles et esprit de corps* (Paris, 1989).

Boureau, Alain, 'Ritualité politique et modernité monarchique', in *L'État ou le roi: les fondations de la modernité monarchique en France (XIVe–XVIIe siècles) textes réunis par Neithard Bulst, Robert Descimon et Alain Guerreau* (Paris, 1996).

___ *Le Simple corps du roi: l'impossible sacralité des souverains français – XVe–XVIIIe siècle* (Paris, 1988/2000).

Bouton, Cynthia A., *The Flour War: Gender, class, and community in late ancien régime French society* (Ithaca, 1993).

Broglie, Gabriel de, 'La mort de Louis XV d'après des lettres inédites du duc d'Orléans', *Nouvelle revue des deux mondes* (mars 1974), 559–75.

Brown, E.A.R. and Richard C. Famiglietti, *The Lit de Justice: Semantics, ceremonial, and the parlement of Paris, 1300–1600* (Sigmaringen, 1994).

Braddick, Michael J, 'Introduction: the politics of gesture', *The Politics of Gesture: Historical perspectives, Past and Present: supplement 4* (2009), 9–35.

Bremond, Henri, *Histoire littéraire du sentiment religieux en France: Tome 9: la vie chrétienne sous l'Ancien Régime* (Paris, 1968).

Brockliss, Lawrence, and Colin Jones, *The Medical World of Early Modern France* (Oxford, 1997).

Brogan, Stephen, *The Royal Touch in Early Modern England: Politics, medicine and sin* (Woodbridge, 2015).

Bryant, Lawrence M., *The King and the City in the Parisian Royal Entry Ceremony: Politics, ritual and art in the Renaissance* (Geneva, 1986).

Buc, Philippe, *The Dangers of Ritual: Between early medieveal texts and social scientific theory* (Princeton, 2001).

Burguière, André, 'Processus de civilisation et processus national chez Norbert Elias', in *Norbert Elias: la politique et l'histoire*, sous la direction de Alain Garrigou et Bernard Lacroix (Paris, 1997), 145–65.

Burke, Peter, *The Historical Anthropology of Early Modern Italy* (Cambridge, 1987).

___ *The Fabrication of Louis XIV* (New Haven and London, 1992).

___ *History and Historians in the Twentieth Century* (Oxford, 2002).

Byrne, Anne, 'The deathbed of Louis XV', *French History*, 19:4 (December 2015), 491–509.

___ '"We disobey by serving you well" the paradox of the *lit de justice* in eight-

eenth century France', in *Rituals of Power*, Anna Kalinowska (editor) (forthcoming).
___ '"Vive mon peuple!" royal ritual, travel and emotion in eighteenth century France' (forthcoming).
Caiani, Ambrogio A., *Louis XVI and the French Revolution* (Cambridge, 2012).
Campardon, Émile, *Madame de Pompadour et la cour de Louis XV* (Paris, 1867).
Campbell, Peter R., Thomas E. Kaiser, and Marisa Linton, *Conspiracy in the French Revolution* (Manchester, 2010).
Cannadine, David, *Rituals of Royalty: Power and ceremonial in traditional societies* (Cambridge, 1987).
Carcassone, Élie, *Montesquieu et le problème de la constitution française* (Paris, 1926), 2 volumes.
Carroll, Stuart, 'The peace in the feud in sixteenth and seventeenth century France', *Past and Present*, 178 (February 2003), 74–115.
Chaline, Olivier, 'Combien des royaumes nous ignorent: la cour dans l'historiographie française', *Annali di Storia moderna e contemporanea*, 2 (1996), 384–92.
___ *Godart de Belbeuf: Le parlement, le roi et les normands* (Paris, 1996).
___ 'The Valois and Bourbon Courts c. 1515–1750', in *The Princely Courts of Europe 1500–1750*, John Adamson (editor) (London, 2000), 67–94.
Chartier, Roger, *Cultural History: Between practices and representations* (Cambridge, 1988).
Chastel-Rousseau, Charlotte (editor), *Reading the Royal Monument in Eighteenth Century Europe* (Farnham, 2011).
Chaunu, Pierre, *La Mort à Paris: XVIe, XVIIe, XVIIIe siècles* (Paris, 1978).
Chaussinand-Nogaret, Guy, *The French Nobility in the Eighteenth Century*, translated by William Doyle (Cambridge, 1985).
___ *Louis XVI* (Paris, 2006).
Chrościcki, Juliusz A., Mark Hengerer and Gérard Sabatier (editors), *Les Funérailles princières en Europe, XVIe-XVIIIe siècle*, 3 volumes (Rennes, 2012–15).
Clarke, Joseph, *Commemorating the Dead in Revolutionary France* (Cambridge, 2007).
Cobban, Alfred, *A History of Modern France, Volume I, Old Régime and Revolution, 1715–1799* (London, 1957).
Collins, James B, *The State in Early Modern France* (Cambridge, 1995, 2009).
Corp, Edward, *A Court in Exile: The Stuarts in France 1689–1718* (Cambridge, 2004), 219.
Cosandey, Fanny, *La Reine de France: symbole et pouvoir, XVe–XVIIIe siècles* (Paris, 2000).
___ *Dire et vivre l'ordre sociale en France sous l'ancien régime* (Paris, 2005).
Cosandey, Fanny, and Robert Descimon, *L'Absolutisme en France: histoire et historiographie* (Paris, 2002).

Coulomb, Clarisse, *Les Pères de la patrie: la société parlementaire en Dauphiné au temps des Lumières* (Grenoble, 2006).

Coward, Barry, and Julian Swann (editors), *Conspiracy and Conspiracy Theories in Early Modern Europe* (Aldershot, 2004).

Crawfurd, Raymond, *The King's Evil* (Oxford, 1911).

Darmon, Pierre, *La Variole, les nobles et les princes: la petite vérole mortelle de Louis XV* (Paris, 1989).

Darnton, Robert, *Mesmerism and the End of the Enlightenment in France* (Cambridge, Mass, 1968).

___ *The Literary Underground of the Old Regime* (Cambridge and London, 1982).

David, Marcel, *Le Serment du sacre du IXe au XVe siècle* (Strasbourg, 1951).

Denby, David J., *Sentimental Narrative and the Social Order in France, 1760–1820* (Cambridge, 1994).

Devlin, Judith, *The Superstitious Mind: French peasants and the supernatural in the nineteenth century* (New Haven and London, 1987).

De Waele, Michel, *Reconcilier les Français: Henri IV et la fin des troubles réligieux, 1589–1598* (Paris, 2010).

Dion, Marie-Pierre, *Emmanuel de Croÿ, 1718–1784: itinéraire intellectuel et réussite nobiliaire au siècle des lumières* (Brussels, 1987).

Douglas, Mary, 'The contempt of ritual', in *In The Active Voice* (London, 1982). First published 1966, 34–38.

Doyle, William, 'The parlements of France and the break-down of the Old Regime, 1774–1788', *French Historical Studies*, 6:4 (Fall 1970), 415–58.

___ *The Parlement of Bordeaux and the End of the Old Regime* (London, 1974).

___ 'The French Revolution: possible because thinkable or thinkable because possible?' *Proceedings of the Western Society for the Study of French History: selected papers of the 2002 Annual Meeting* (2004), volume 30, 178–83.

___ *Aristocracy and its Enemies in the Age of Revolution* (Oxford, 2009).

___ 'Desacralising desacralisation', in *France and the age of Revolution: Regimes old and new from Louis XIV to Napoleon Bonaparte* (London and New York, 2013).

Duindam, Jeroen, *Myths of Power: Norbert Elias and the Early Modern court* (Amsterdam, 1995).

___ 'Ceremony at court: Reflections on an elusive subject', *Francia: Forschungen zur westeuropäischen Geschichte*, 26:2 (1999), 131–40.

___ *Vienna and Versailles: The courts of Europe's dynastic rivals, 1550–1780* (Cambridge, 2003).

Duprat, Catherine, *"Pour l'Amour de l'humanité" Le temps des philanthropes: La philanthropie parisienne des Lumières à la monarchie de Juillet* (Paris, 1993).

Echeverria, Durand, *The Maupeou Revolution: A study in the history of libertarianism, France 1770–1774* (Baton Rouge, 1985).

Egret, Jean, 'L'aristocratie parlementaire française à la fin de l'ancien régime', *Revue historique* (1952), 1–14.

___ *Louis XV et l'opposition parlementaire* (Paris, 1970).
Elias, Norbert, *The Court Society*, translated by Edmund Jephcott, The Collected Works of Norbert Elias, volume 2, edited by Stephen Mennell (Dublin, 2006).
Engels, Jens Ivo, 'Beyond sacral monarchy: a new look at the image of the early modern French monarchy', *French History*, 15:2 (2001), 139–58.
Enright, Michael J., *Iona, Tara and Soissons: The origin of the royal anointing ritual* (Berlin, 1985).
Everdell, William, 'The rosières movement, 1766–1789: a clerical precursor of the revolutionary cults', *French Historical Studies*, 9:1 (Spring 1975), 23–36.
Fantoni, Marcello, 'The future of court studies: the evolution, present success and prospects of a discipline', *The Court Historian*, 16:2 (June 2011), 1–6.
Farge, Arlette, *Fragile Lives: Violence, power, and solidarity in eighteenth century Paris*, translated by Carol Shelton (Cambridge, 1993).
Félix, Joël, *Les Magistrats du Parlement de Paris (1771–1790), dictionnaire biographique et généalogique* (Paris, 1990).
___ *Louis XVI et Marie-Antoinette: un couple en politique* (Paris, 2005).
___ 'Monarchy', in *The Oxford Handbook of the French Revolution*, David Andress (editor) (Oxford, 2015).
Fogel, Michèle, *Les Cérémonies de l'information dans la France du XVIe siècle au XVIIIe siècle* (Paris, 1989).
Ford, Franklin L., *Robe and Sword: The regrouping of French aristocracy after Louis XIV* (Cambridge, Mass, 1953).
Franklin, Alfred, *La Vie privée d'autrefois* (Paris, 1887–1902), 22 volumes.
Furet, François, 'Le catéchisme révolutionnaire', *Annales: Economies, Sociétés, Civilisations*, 2 (mars–avril 1971), 255–89.
___ *Penser la révolution française* (Paris, 1978).
Garrioch, David, *Neighbourhood and Community in Paris, 1740–1790* (Cambridge, 1986).
Gaudillot, Jeanne Marie, *Le Voyage de Louis XVI en Normandie, 21–29 juin 1786* (Caen, 1967).
Geertz, Clifford, 'Thick description: towards an interpretative theory of culture', in *The Interpretation of Cultures: Selected essays* (London, 1993), first published 1973, 3–30.
Giesey, Ralph E., *The Royal Funeral Ceremony in Renaissance France* (Geneva, 1960).
___ *Cérémonial et puissance souveraine, France XVe–XVIIe siecles* (Paris, 1987).
___ '*Inaugural Aspects of French Royal Ceremonials*', in *Coronations: Medieval and Early Modern monarchic ritual*, Janos M. Bak (editor) (Berkeley, 1990), 35–45.
___ *Rulership in France, 15th–17th Centuries* (Aldershot, 2004).
Girault de Coursac, Paul and Pierette, *Louis XVI a la parole: lettres, discours, écrits politiques*, Séconde Édition (Paris, 1997).

Goldstein, Claire, *Vaux and Versailles: The appropriations, erasures and accidents that made modern France* (Philadelphia, 2007).

Gooch, George Peabody, *Louis XV: The monarchy in decline* (London, 1956).

Goodman, Dena, *The Republic of Letters: A cultural history of the French enlightenment* (Ithaca, 1996).

Grant, Sarah, *Toiles de Jouy: French printed cottons 1760–1830* (London, 2014).

Grell, Chantal, 'The sacre of Louis XVI: the end of a myth', in *Monarchy and Religion: The transformation of royal culture in eighteeenth century Europe*, Michael Schaich (editor) (Oxford, 2007), 345–66.

Grellet-Dumazeau, André, *L'Affaire du bonnet et les mémoires de Saint-Simon* (Paris, 1913).

Gruber, Alain, *Les Grandes fêtes et leur décorations à l'époque de Louis XVI* (Geneva, 1972).

Habermas, Jürgen, *The Structural Transformation of the Bourgeois Public Sphere: An inquiry into a category of bourgeois society*, translated by Thomas Burger with the assistance of Frederick Lawrence (Cambridge, 1989).

Hamscher, Albert, *The Parlement of Paris after the Fronde, 1653–1673* (London, 1976).

Hanley, Sarah, *The* Lit de Justice *of the Kings of France: Constitutional ideology in legend, ritual and discourse* (Princeton, 1983).

Harding, Vanessa, 'Whose body? A study of attitudes towards the dead body in early modern Paris', in *The Place of the Dead: Death and remembrance in late medieval and early modern Europe*, Bruce Gordon, (editor) (Cambridge, 2000), 170–87.

___ *The Dead and the Living in Paris and London* (Cambridge, 2002).

Hardman, John, *French Politics 1774–1789: From the accession of Louis XVI to the fall of the Bastille* (London, 1995).

___ 'The view from above', in *The Oxford Handbook of the French Revolution*, David Andress (editor) (Oxford, 2015).

___ *The Life of Louis XVI* (Yale, 2016).

Hardman, John and Munro Price, *Louis XVI and the Comte de Vergennes: Correspondence 1774–1787* (Oxford, 1998).

Hauterive, Ernest d', *Le Merveilleux au XVIIIe siècle* (Paris, 1902, reprinted Geneva 1973).

Henshall, Nicholas, *The Myth of Absolutism: Change and continuity in early modern European monarchy* (London, 1992).

Holt, Mack P, 'The king in parlement: the problem of the *lit de justice* in sixteenth-century France', *The Historical Journal*, 21 (1988), 507–23.

Horowski, Leonhard, '"Such a great advantage for my son": office-holding and career mechanisms at the court of France, 1661–1789', *The Court Historian*, 8:2 (December 2003), 125–71.

___ *Die Belagerung Des Thrones: Machtstrukturen und Karrieremechanismen am Hof von Frankreich, 1661–1789* (Ostfildern, 2012).

Hours, Bernard, *Louis XV et sa cour: le roi, l'étiquette et le courtisan* (Paris, 2002).
___ *Louis XV: un portrait* (Toulouse, 2009).
Hunt, Lynn, *Politics, Culture, and Class in the French Revolution* (Berkeley, 1984).
___ *The Family Romance of the French Revolution* (Berkeley, 1993).
Hurt, John J, *Louis XIV and the Parlements: The assertion of royal authority* (Manchester, 2002).
Isambert, Decrusy, Taillandier, *Recueil des anciennes lois françaises* (Paris, 1830), 29 volumes.
Jackson, Richard A., 'The sleeping king', *Bibliothèque d'Humanisme et de la Renaissance*, 31:3 (1969), 525–51.
___ 'Peers of France and princes of the blood', *French Historical Studies*, 7:1 (Spring 1971), 27–46.
___ *Vive le Roi! A history of the French coronation from Charles V to Charles X* (Chapel Hill, 1984).
___ *Ordines coronationis Franciae* (Philadelphia, 2002), 2 volumes.
Jadart, Henri, *L'Hôpital Saint-Marcoul de Reims (1645–1900)* (Reims, 1902).
Johnson, James H., *Listening in Paris: A cultural history* (Berkeley and London, 1995).
Jouanna, Arlette, *Le Pouvoir absolu: naissance de l'imaginaire politique de la royauté* (Paris, 2013).
Jullien, Adolphe, *Un Potentat Musical: Papillon de la Ferté son règne à l'Opéra de 1780 à 1790* (Paris, 1876).
Kantorowicz, Ernst, *The King's Two Bodies: A study in medieval political theology* (Princeton, 1957).
Knecht, R.J., 'Francis I and the "Lit de Justice": a "legend" defended', *French History*, 7 (1993), 53–83.
Koziol, Geoffrey, 'The dangers of polemic: is ritual still an interesting topic of historical study?', *Early Medieval Europe*, 11:4 (December 2002), 367–88.
Kreiser, Robert, *Miracles, Convulsions, and Ecclesiastical Politics in Eighteenth-century Paris* (Princeton, 1978),
Kwass, Michael, 'Big hair: a wig history of consumption in eighteenth century France', *The American Historical Review*, 111:3 (June 2006), 631–59.
Landes, Joan B., *Women and the Public Sphere in the Age of the French Revolution* (Ithaca, 1988).
Leber, Constant, *Des Cérémonies du sacre* (Reims, 1825).
Le Moël, Michel, *Le Sacre des rois de France* (Paris, 1983).
Leroy Ladurie, Emmanuel, 'Système de la cour', *L'arc*, 65 (1976), 21–35.
___ 'Système de la cour', in *Le Terroire de l'historien* (Paris, 1978), volume 2, 275–99.
Leroy Ladurie, Emmanuel, in collaboration with Jean-François Fitou, *Saint-Simon ou le système de la cour* (Paris, 1997).
Lever, Évelyne, *Madame de Pompadour* (Paris, 2000).
___ *Les Dernières Noces de la monarchie: Louis XVI* (Paris, 2005).

Lewis, Ann, *Sensibility, Reading and Illustration: Spectacles and signs in Graffigny, Marivaux and Rousseau* (London, 2009).

Lilti, Antoine, *Le Monde des salons: sociabilitié et mondanité à Paris au XVIIIe siècle* (Paris, 2007).

Linton, Marisa, *The Politics of Virtue in Enlightenment France* (Basingstoke, 2001).

___ *Choosing Terror: Virtue, friendship and authenticity in the French Revolution* (Oxford, 2013).

Lough, John, *Paris Theatre Audiences in the Seventeenth and Eighteenth Centuries* (London, 1957/1965),

Lucas, Colin, 'Nobles, bourgeois, and the origins of the French Revolution', *Past and Present*, 60 (August 1973).

Lunel, Alexandre, *La Maison médicale du roi XVIe-XVIIIe siècles: le pouvoir royal et les professions de santé* (Paris, 2008).

McMahon, Darin M., *Enemies of the Enlightenment: The French counter-enlightenment and the making of modernity* (Oxford, 2001).

McManners, John, 'Death and the French historians', in *Mirrors of Mortality: Studies in the social history of death*, Joachim Whaley (editor) (London, 1981).

___ *Death and the Enlightenment: Changing attitudes to death in eighteenth century France* (Oxford, 1983).

___ 'The religious observances of Versailles under Louis XV', in *Enlightenment Essays in memory of Robert Shackleton*, Gilles Barber and C.P. Courtney (editors) (Oxford, 1988), 175–88.

___ 'Authority in church and state: reflections on the coronation of Louis XVI', in *Christian Authority: Essays in honour of Henry Chadwick* (Oxford, 1988), 278–95.

Mansel, Philip, 'Uniform and the rise of the *frac* 1760–1830', *Past and Present*, 92 (August 1986), 103–32.

___ *The Court of France, 1789–1830* (Cambridge, 1988).

___ *Dressed to Rule: Royal and court costume from Louis XIV to Elizabeth II* (London, 2005)

Margolf, Diane Claire, *Religion and Royal Justice in Early Modern France* (Missouri, 2003).

Maza, Sarah, 'The Rose-Girl of Salency: Pre-revolutionary representations of virtue', *Eighteenth Century Studies*, 22:3 (Spring 1989), 395–412.

___ *Private Lives and Public Affairs: The causes célèbres of Prerevolutionary France* (Berkeley, 1993).

___ *The Myth of the French Bourgeoisie: An essay on social imaginary 1750–1850* (Cambridge, Mass. and London, 2003).

Medlam, Sarah, 'Callet's portrait of Louis XVI: a picture frame as diplomatic tool', *Furniture History*, 43 (2007), 143–54.

Mennell, Stephen, *Norbert Elias: Civilisation and the human self-image* (Oxford, 1989).

Merrick, Jeffrey, 'The coronation of Louis XVI: the waning of royal ritual', *Proceedings of the Eighth Annual Meeting of the Western Society for French History* (1981), 191–204.

___ *The Desacralization of the French Monarchy in the Eighteenth Century* (Baton Rouge, 1990).

___ 'Le suicide de Pidansat de Mairobert', *Dix-huitième siècle*, 35 (2003), 331–40.

___ 'Louis XV's deathbed apology', *European History Quarterly*, 38 (2008), 205–26.

Mettam, Roger, *Power and Faction in Louis XIV's France* (Oxford, 1988).

Mitford, Nancy, *Madame de Pompadour* (London, 1976).

Monod, Paul Kléber, *The Power of Kings: Monarchy and religion in Europe 1589–1715* (London, 1999).

___ *Solomon's Secret Arts: The occult in the age of enlightenment* (New Haven and London, 2013).

Mousnier, Roland, *Les Institutions de la France sous la monarchie absolue*, volume 1 (Paris, 1974).

Muir, Edward, *Ritual in Early Modern Europe*, Second Edition (Cambridge, 2002).

Nora, Pierre, 'Introduction', in *Realms of Memory: The construction of the French past, Volume II: Traditions*, under the direction of Pierre Nora, translated by Arthur Goldhammer (New York, 1997), ix–xii. First published as *Lieux de Mémoire* (Paris, 1992).

Ozouf, Mona, *Festivals and the French Revolution*, translated by Alan Sheridan (Cambridge, Mass, 1988).

Perez, Stanis, 'Le toucher des écrouelles: médecine, thaumaturgie et corps du roi au grand siècle', *Revue d'histoire moderne et contemporaine*, 53:2 (2005), 92–111.

Perreau, Stéphan, *Hyacinthe Rigaud, 1659–1743: Le peintre des rois* (Montpellier, 2004).

Petitfils, Jean-Christian, *Louis XVI* (Paris, 2005).

Pissot, Noël Laurent, *Le Cérémonial de la cour de France* (Paris, 1816).

Porter, Roy, 'The patient's view: doing medical history from below', *Theory and Society*, 14:2 (March 1985), 175–98.

Price, Munro, *Preserving the Monarchy: the Comte de Vergennes, 1774–1787* (Cambridge, 1995).

___ 'Politics: Louis XVI', in *The Short Oxford History of France: Old Regime France* (Oxford, 2002).

___ *The Fall of the French Monarchy: Louis XVI, Marie Antoinette and the baron de Breteuil* (London, 2003).

Ramsay, Michael, *Professional and Popular Medicine in France, 1770–1830* (Cambridge, 1988).

Reddy, William, *The Navigation of Feeling: Framework for a history of emotions* (Cambridge, 2001).

Revel, Jacques, 'The court', in *Realms of Memory: The construction of the French past, Volume II: Traditions*, under the direction of Pierre Nora, translated by Arthur Goldhammer (New York, 1997), 71–122. First published as *Lieux de Mémoire* (Paris, 1992).

Ribeiro, Aileen, *Dress in Eighteenth Century Europe, 1715–1781* (London, 1984).

Ritchey Newton, William, *L'Espace du roi: la cour de France au château de Versailles, 1682–1789* (Paris, 2000).

Roche, Daniel, *La Culture des apparences* (Paris, 1989).

Rogister, John, *Louis XV and the parlement of Paris, 1737–1755* (Cambridge, 1995).

Rondel, Auguste, *Fêtes de Cour et cérémonies publiques* (Florence, 1927).

Rosenwein, Barbara H., *Emotional Communities in the Early Middle Ages* (Ithaca, 2006).

___ 'Modernity: a problematic category in the history of emotions', *History and Theory*, 53 (February 2014), 69–78.

Rowlands, Guy, *The Dynastic State and the Army under Louis XIV: Royal service and private interest, 1661–1701* (Oxford, 2002).

Sabatier, Gérard, 'Beneath the ceilings of Versailles: towards and archaeology and anthropology of the use of the king's 'signs' during the absolute monarchy', in *Iconography, Propaganda and Legitimation*, Allan Ellenius (editor) (Oxford, 1998), 217–42.

Saler, Michael, 'Modernity and enchantment: a historiographic review', *American Historical Review*, 111:3 (June 2006), 692–716.

Schaich, Michael (editor), *Monarchy and Religion: The transformation of royal culture in eighteenth century Europe* (Oxford, 2007).

Scheff, Thomas, 'The distancing of emotion in ritual', *Current Anthropology* (September 1977).

Schelle, Gustave, *Oeuvres de Turgot et documents le concernant* (Paris, 1922), 4 volumes.

Seth, Caitriona, *Les Rois aussi en mouraient: les lumières en lutte contre la petite vérole* (Paris, 2008).

Ségur, Pierre de, *La Dernière des Condés* (Paris, 1899).

Shapiro, Barry M., *Traumatic Politics: The deputies and the king in the early French Revolution* (Pennsylvania, 2009).

Shennan, J.H., *The Parlement of Paris*, Second Edition (Stroud, 1998).

Shils, Edward, 'The meaning of coronation', in *Center and Periphery: Essays in macrosociology* (Chicago, 1975).

Smith, Jay M., '"Our Sovereign's Gaze": kings, nobles and state formation in seventeenth century France', *French Historical Studies*, 18:2 (Autumn 1993), 396–415.

Solnon, Jean-François, *La Cour de France* (Paris, 1987).

Sorkin, David, *The Religious Enlightenment: Protestants, Jews, and Catholics from London to Vienna* (Princeton, 2008).

Sternberg, Giora, 'Epistolary ceremonial: corresponding status at the time of Louis XIV', *Past and Present*, 204 (August 2009), 33–88.

___ *Status Interaction during the Reign of Louis XIV* (Oxford, 2014).

Stone, Bailey, *The Parlement of Paris, 1774–1789* (Chapel Hill, 1981).

___ *The French Parlements and the Crisis of the Old Regime* (Chapel Hill, 1986).

Strayer, Brian E., *Suffering Saints: Jansenists and* convulsionnaires *in France 1640–1799* (Brighton, 2008).

Strong, Roy, *Coronation: From the eighth to the twenty-first century* (London, 2006).

Summers-Effler, Erika, 'Ritual theory', in *Handbook of the Sociology of Emotions*, Jan E. Stets and Jonathan H. Turner (editors) (New York, 2006), 135–54.

Swann, Julian, 'Parlement, politics and the *parti janséniste*: the *grand conseil* affair, 1755–56', *French History*, 6:4 (1992), 435–61.

___ 'Parlements and political crisis in France under Louis XV: the Besançon affair, 1757–1761', *The Historical Journal*, 37:4 (1994), 803–28.

___ *Politics and the Parlement of Paris under Louis XV: 1748–1774* (Cambridge, 1995).

___ 'Robe, sword and aristocratic reaction revisited: the French nobility and political crisis (1748–1789)', in *Der europäische Adel in Ancien Régime: von der Krise der ständische Monarchien bis zur Revolution (1600–1789)*, Roland Asch (editor) (Cologne, 2001), 151–78.

___ *Provincial Power and Absolute Monarchy: The estates general of Burgundy, 1661–1790* (Cambridge, 2003).

___ 'Disgrace without dishonour: the internal exile of French magistrates in the eighteenth century', *Past and Present*, 195 (May 2007), 87–126.

___ 'Repenser les parlements aux XVIIIe siècle: du concept de "l'opposition parlementaire" à celui de "culture juridique des conflits politiques"', in *Le Monde parlementaire au XVIIIe siècle: l'invention d'un discours politiques*, Alain J. Lemaître (editor) (Rennes, 2010).

Tackett, Timothy, *Becoming a Revolutionary: The deputies of the French National Assembly and the emergence of a revolutionary culture (1789–1790)* (Princeton, 1996).

Valensise, Marina, 'Le sacre du roi: stratégie symbolique et doctrine politique de la monarchie française', *Annales ESC* (mai–juin 1986), 543–77.

Van Horn Melton, James, *The Rise of the Public in Enlightenment Europe* (Cambridge, 2001).

Van Kley, Dale, *The Damiens Affair and the Unravelling of the Ancien Régime, 1750–1770* (Princeton, 1984).

Viguerie, Jean de, 'Les serments du sacre des rois de France à l'époque moderne, et plus spécialement le "serment du royaume"', in *Le Sacre des rois: actes du colloque international d'histoire sur les sacres et couronnements royaux (Reims 1975)* (Paris, 1983).

___ *Histoire et dictionnaire du temps des lumières, 1715–1789* (Paris, 1995).

Vila, Anne C., *Enlightenment and Pathology: Sensibility in literature and medicine in Enlightenment France* (Baltimore and London, 1998).

Vincent-Buffault, Anne, *The History of Tears: Sensibility and sentimentality in France* (Basingstoke, 1991).

Vovelle, Michel, *Piété baroque et déchristianisation en Provence au XVIIIe siècle: les attitudes devant la mort d'après les clauses des testaments* (Paris, 1973).

___ *Mourir autrefois: attitudes collectives devant la mort aux XVIIe et XVIIIe siècles* (Paris, 1974).

___ *La Mort et l'Occident de 1300 à nos jours* (Paris, 1983).

Walsham, Alexandra, 'The dangers of ritual', *Past and Present*, 180:1 (2003), 277–87.

___ 'The Reformation and the "disenchantment of the world" reassessed', *The Historical Journal*, 51:2 (June 2008), 497–528.

Weber, Hermann, 'Das *Sacre* Ludwigs XVI vom 11 Juni 1775 und die Krise des Ancien Régime', in *Vom Ancien Régime zur französischen Revolution: Forschungen und Perspecktiven*, Erich Hinrichs, Erberhardt Schmidt and Rudolf Vierhaus (editors) (Göttingen, 1978).

Wintroub, Michael, *A Savage Mirror: Power, identity, and knowledge in early modern France* (Stanford, 2006).

Wittman, Richard, *Architecture, Print Culture, and the Public Sphere in Eighteenth Century France* (London, 2007).

Woodbridge, John D., *Revolt in Pre-revolutionary France: The prince de Conti's conspiracy against Louis XV, 1755–57* (Baltimore, 1995).

Woodward, Jennifer, *The Theatre of Death: The ritual management of royal funerals in Renaissance England, 1570–1625* (Woodbridge, 1997).

Wunder, Richard P., 'Charles Michel-Ange Challe: a study of his life and work', *Apollo* (January 1968), 22–39.

Unpublished theses

Burley, Peter, 'Louis XVI and a new monarchy: an institutional and political study 1768–1778', unpublished PhD thesis (University of London, 1981).

Nguyen, Marie-Lan, *Les Grands Maîtres des cérémonies et le services des cérémonies à l'époque moderne, 1585–1792*, Mémoire de maîtrise sous la direction de M. le Professeur Lucien Bély (Paris, 1998–99).

Index

Lightning Source UK Ltd.
Milton Keynes UK
UKHW021334090622
404183UK00013B/53

9 781526 160768

Studies in Modern French and Francophone History

Edited by
Máire Cross, David Hopkin and Jennifer Sessions

This series is published in collaboration with the Society for the Study of French History (UK) and the French Colonial Historical Society. It aims to showcase innovative monographs and edited collections on the history of France, its colonies and imperial undertakings, and the francophone world more generally since *c.* 1750. Authors demonstrate how sources and interpretations are being opened to historical investigation in new and interesting ways, and how unfamiliar subjects have the capacity to tell us more about France and the French colonial empire, their relationships in the world, and their legacies in the present. The series is particularly receptive to studies that break down traditional boundaries and conventional disciplinary divisions.

Recently published in this series

Emile and Isaac Pereire: Bankers, Socialists and Sephardic Jews in nineteenth-century France Helen Davies

From empire to exile: History and memory within the pied-noir and harki communities, 1962–2012 Claire Eldridge

The stadium century: Sport, spectatorship and mass society in modern France Robert W. Lewis

Nobility and patrimony in modern France Elizabeth C. Macknight

The republican line: Caricature and French republican identity, 1830-52 Laura O'Brien

In pursuit of politics: Education and revolution in eighteenth-century France Adrian O'Connor

Mutinous memories: A subjective history of French military protest in 1919 Matt Perry

Terror and terroir: The winegrowers of the Languedoc and modern France Andrew W. M. Smith

Robespierre and the Festival of the Supreme Being: The search for a republican morality Jonathan Smyth

The Society for the Study of French History

FCHS SHCF
FRENCH COLONIAL HISTORICAL SOCIETY
SOCIÉTÉ D'HISTOIRE COLONIALE FRANÇAISE

Studies in
Modern French and
Francophone History

Death and the crown

MANCHESTER
1824
Manchester University Press

Death and the crown

Ritual and politics in France before the Revolution

ANNE BYRNE

Manchester University Press

Published by Manchester University Press
Oxford Road, Manchester M13 9PL

www.manchesteruniversitypress.co.uk

British Library Cataloguing-in-Publication Data
A catalogue record for this book is available from the British Library

ISBN 978 1 5261 4330 3 hardback
ISBN 978 1 5261 6076 8 paperback

First published 2020

Typeset by
Servis Filmsetting Ltd, Stockport, Cheshire